ONLY
A VOICE

ONLY A VOICE

Essays

George Scialabba

VERSO
London • New York

First published by Verso 2023

1 3 5 7 9 10 8 6 4 2

Verso
UK: 6 Meard Street, London W1F 0EG
US: 388 Atlantic Avenue, Brooklyn, NY 11217
versobooks.com

Verso is the imprint of New Left Books

ISBN-13: 978-1-80429-200-6
ISBN-13: 978-1-80429-204-4 (US EBK)
ISBN-13: 978-1-80429-203-7 (UK EBK)

British Library Cataloguing in Publication Data
A catalogue record for this book is available from the British Library

Library of Congress Cataloging-in-Publication Data

Names: Scialabba, George, author.
Title: Only a voice : essays / by George Scialabba.
Description: London ; New York : Verso, 2022.
Identifiers: LCCN 2022048772 (print) | LCCN 2022048773 (ebook) | ISBN
9781804292006 (hardback) | ISBN 9781804292044 (ebk)
Subjects: LCSH: Civilization, Modern—21st century. | Civilization,
Modern—20th century. | Civilization, Modern—Historiography. |
Intellectuals—Western countries. | Western countries—Intellectual
life.
Classification: LCC CB428 .S417 2022 (print) | LCC CB428 (ebook) | DDC
909.82—dc23/eng/20230214
LC record available at https://lccn.loc.gov/2022048772
LC ebook record available at https://lccn.loc.gov/2022048773

Typeset in Fournier by Biblichor Ltd, Scotland
Printed and bound by CPI Group (UK) Ltd, Croydon CR0 4YY

To Chomsky and Nader
for decades of inspiration

All I have is a voice
To undo the folded lie,
The romantic lie in the brain
Of the sensual man-in-the-street
And the lie of Authority
Whose buildings grope the sky:
There is no such thing as the State
And no one exists alone;
Hunger allows no choice
To the citizen or the police;
We must love one another or die.

Defenceless under the night
Our world in stupor lies;
Yet, dotted everywhere,
Ironic points of light
Flash out wherever the Just
Exchange their messages:
May I, composed like them
Of Eros and of dust,
Beleaguered by the same
Negation and despair,
Show an affirming flame.

—W. H. Auden, "September 1, 1939"

Contents

Introduction:

What Are Intellectuals Good For?

Do intellectuals matter? In this age and country, there's room for doubt. Certainly we haven't diffused general enlightenment, which is our job. Among the countless examples of American un-enlightenment I've seen reported in recent years: 50 percent of Americans told pollsters that the earth has been visited by UFOs, and nearly all of them also believed that the US government has covered up this fact. Forty percent did not know whom the United States fought in World War II. Six percent reported reading one or more books a year.

Majorities of Americans believed that Saddam Hussein helped al-Qaeda carry out the atrocities of 9/11 and that weapons of mass destruction were found in Iraq after the US invasion. In a recent NPR poll, a majority of Americans either agreed or were not sure whether "a group of Satan-worshiping elites who run a child sex ring are trying to control our politics and media." The pandemic spawned its own delusions: early in 2020 approximately one-third of Americans believed that scientists had created and disseminated the coronavirus; a few months later, another third believed that the virus was sent by God to teach humanity a lesson. On the day of the Capitol Hill riot, 39 percent of Americans believed the 2020 election had been stolen, for no better reason than that President Trump said so. To all such people, the American intelligentsia has been of very little use. We may as well have been publishing our books, essays, and op-eds on Mars.

In another sense, however, we matter too much. A loathing for intellectuals was almost a defining characteristic of Trump's base. At one point in the 2016 campaign, Trump told a crowd gleefully: "I love poorly educated people!" He didn't love them enough, apparently, to offer them more than a few crumbs in his huge, one-percent-friendly tax cut the following year. But did intellectuals succeed in pointing out that hypocrisy to the poorly educated? Did we try?

It's not entirely our fault, perhaps. If we had tried, we would have encountered a profound mistrust of intellectuals, skillfully cultivated by generations of Republican political strategists. "Eggheads," "pointy-heads," "New Class," "silent majority," "real Americans," "feminazis," "baby-killers," "sushi-eating," "latte-drinking"—with these and many other tropes, Republican politicians and their operatives and media surrogates, from Paul Weyrich to Lee Atwater to Frank Luntz to Karl Rove to Rush Limbaugh and Sean Hannity have planted in less-educated voters not a healthy and discriminating skepticism toward experts but a belligerent and preemptive rejection of all complexity, leaving them vulnerable in turn to Republicans' kindergarten-level ideas about supply-side economics, abortion, immigration, race, evolution, and climate change.

What's more, we wily intellectuals allegedly have designs on everything our stalwart countrymen hold dear. In concert with power-hungry liberal politicians, we are planning to introduce radical innovations in every sphere of social life: child care, schooling, zoning and city planning, law enforcement, marriage, and religious liberties, trampling on long-settled customs and traditional understandings, until ordinary Americans no longer recognize their country. As a sales campaign, this has been fantastically successful. And as always with successful propaganda, there's a grain of truth in it. Intellectuals and liberal politicians have rarely taken seriously enough their democratic obligation to persuade people before legislating for them. (Of course, this may partly be because politicians now have no time to talk to voters: they must spend 50 percent of every day raising money, an entirely predictable result of *Citizens United* and other Supreme Court decisions that have enshrined money as the arbiter of American politics.)

Whatever blend of liberal arrogance and conservative chicanery is to blame, the gulf between intellectuals and our fellow citizens is very wide. What's more, political propaganda and campaign finance laws are not even the most important obstacles to a democratic culture. They are, so to speak, contingent obstacles; there are other, more fundamental ones that arise from the very structure of ownership in this society. Marx observed: "In every age, the ideas of the rulers are the ruling ideas." He did not mean, of course (it is generally necessary in the United States, when discussing Marx, to begin by explaining that he did not mean what he is usually taken to mean), that capitalists go into the marketplace to buy young intellectuals, like young slaves or young peasant girls, whom they then train up to service; nor that intellectuals, once established, offer themselves in the marketplace to the highest bidder; and certainly not that the ideas of the rulers are usually the best and most persuasive ones. He meant that, since the rich get the social and economic arrangements they want in virtually every society, and since legitimation is an essential part of accomplishing this, and since intellectuals are the primary agents of legitimation, the rich will take care that intellectuals and the institutions in which they operate—most of them, anyway; uniformity looks bad, so a certain amount of dissent is tolerated—foster the right ideas. Mencken agreed with Marx, about this if nothing else: "Freedom of the press is limited to those who own one." Mencken and Marx are pointing out the obvious: who pays the piper calls the tune. To the extent we believe this, we are historical materialists. To the extent we disbelieve it, we are naïve indeed.

Many intellectuals and journalists nonetheless do disbelieve it, insisting that "no one tells me what to write." Very true; ideological control is much subtler in capitalist societies than it was in communist ones. Usually, in fact, it is not overt control at all; that is, not one person or group laying down the law for another. It is, rather, circumstantial or structural control, a matter of the constraints imposed simply by living in a minimally regulated market society.

Imagine a society in which intellectuals are free to write anything they want but it is forbidden to sell magazines or books. Under these peculiar circumstances, intellectuals would technically be free, but their freedom wouldn't be worth much. Now imagine a society in which intellectuals are still free but the overwhelming majority of the society's members—their intended readers, who desperately need the truths the intellectuals have to offer—are tired and stressed, have very little spare money for books or free time to read, are continually distracted by gaudy and often sexualized advertisements in every medium, did not receive a high-quality education, and have internalized the society's dominant ethic of competitive individualism rather than cooperative solidarity. These are not, unfortunately, peculiar circumstances but pretty much the way things are in the United States and have been for the last forty years. Under these circumstances the freedom of intellectuals is, again, not worth much.

How did things get this way? The rise of the New Right, funded by corporations, foundations, and wealthy individuals, guided by political consultants and neoconservative intellectuals, and channeled by the Republican Party, is a familiar story. Highlights include: the destruction of labor unions (accomplished by appointing antilabor lawyers and business executives to the National Labor Relations Board, where they ignored labor-law violations or delayed addressing them for so long that the organizing drive in question simply died); the sabotage of Hillarycare, the attempted sabotage of Obamacare, and other unflagging Republican efforts to prevent tens of millions of Americans from having health insurance; NAFTA and financial deregulation (bipartisan efforts, the Democratic Party having turned sharply rightward); a massive shift of the tax burden away from the rich and toward the non-rich (accomplished by three large and lopsided tax cuts, in the Reagan, Bush II, and Trump presidencies, as well as by policy directives to the IRS to audit more taxpayers from the bottom half of the income distribution and fewer from the top 1 percent); and an all-out Republican assault on government, including constant efforts to privatize education, prisons, war-fighting, Medicare, the Post Office, and Social Security. This is how one produces an insecure, atomized, and resentful populace with a short attention span.

Along with these obstacles on the receiving end, intellectuals face difficulties on the delivery end. Newspapers and even television once functioned more or less as public utilities. No longer. Media are big business. Concentration and centralization are the rule in a capitalist economy, as companies pursue tax advantages, market power, and organizational synergies. With expansion comes debt, and with debt comes pressure to cut costs and stabilize revenues. This has regularly meant, as *New York Times* editor Max Frankel once wrote in frustration, "more sex, sports, violence, and comedy," while "slighting, if not altogether ignoring, news of [serious subjects]." And conglomeration often means eliminating family ownership, which has at least occasionally allowed non-commercial values some scope within media organizations.

The new owners may have conservative opinions, as moneyed people often do, but whatever their opinions (if any), they are powerless to impose them on an institution that ultimately answers to the market. The institution will adopt a point of view—usually the conventional wisdom—least likely to upset the average reader/viewer and most likely to put him/her in a receptive frame of mind toward the upcoming commercials, which, for the newspaper or magazine or station, are what really matter.

The conventional wisdom is sometimes right and sometimes wrong. But it is always—by definition—easier to state than a critique of the conventional wisdom. It is simply what everyone knows: for example, that raising the minimum wage increases unemployment; that governments, like households, must balance their budgets; that the private sector is always more efficient than the public sector; that the United States promotes freedom and democracy throughout the world; that the truth generally lies between the "extremes" of left and right. The sources of conventional wisdom, in any society, are those in authority: state agencies or administrators, business managers or their spokesmen, and accredited experts—the latter are those who have undergone professional or academic socialization and have not forfeited their credibility by too pronounced an opposition to the conventional wisdom.

In most situations, editors, publishers, and producers will default to the conventional wisdom, for two main reasons. First, it is very much cheaper to source. Government and business both run colossal propaganda operations, which helpfully supply reports, research summaries, informational films, and other materials presenting their point of view, often even before they're asked. Those willing to accept the official perspective (either public or corporate) find their work already done for them. Those who aren't willing must do a lot of extra work, often involving extra expense.

Another, probably more important, reason for hewing to the conventional wisdom is that the penalties for departing from it can be severe. Those same friendly government and business propaganda outfits stand ready to contest every fact and interpretation in a critical story, and sometimes to sue, even on frivolous grounds. Media executives don't want this kind of grief, as they make very clear to editors and producers. For all these reasons, wide-ranging, properly antagonistic investigative reporting, which public intellectuals cannot do without, is an endangered species in America.

All this pressure toward conformity, notice, has been produced without anyone telling anyone else what to write. That does happen, to be sure: *New York Times* executive editor A. M. Rosenthal tilted the paper's coverage of Central America and the Middle East rightward during the 1970s and 1980s, in accordance with his own neoconservative views; and William Sarnoff, chairman of Warner Books, personally intervened to suppress publication of the first monograph edition of Noam Chomsky and Edward Herman's *The Political Economy of Human Rights*. But for the most part, neither censorship nor any other kind of coercion is necessary. The ideas of the rulers are transmuted into the ruling ideas smoothly and frictionlessly, by a series of buffers, barriers, and pre-settings, shepherding us toward safe opinions or, if we persist in inconveniently radical opinions, shunting us toward the cul-de-sac of publication at the margins of public conversation, isolated with like-minded eccentrics.

Why write, then, if failure and frustration are virtually inevitable? Underneath the usual reasons—vanity, righteous indignation, a simple pleasure in fashioning sentences—I believe there's usually gratitude. From admired writers—in my case, most of those discussed in this collection—we've received a gift that we're eager to pass on. They model probity, fearlessness, tact; they make the intellectual virtues irresistible and their exercise compelling. To impart to even a few readers my intense and complicated affection for Serge and Orwell and Pasolini, Trilling and Illich and I. F. Stone, seems a duty both to them and to those readers. To help install figures like these in our culture's permanent memory is one responsibility of us lesser intellectuals. (And to let a little air out of the reputations of William F. Buckley and Irving Kristol is also worthwhile, and very satisfying.)

T. S. Eliot observed that "Dante and Shakespeare divide the world between them; there is no third." If I had to choose the exemplary public intellectual of my generation (or spanning my generation), I would say Noam Chomsky, and I might very well add: "There is no second." Certainly no one else approaches his preternatural rigor or dialectical virtuosity. One critic described Chomsky as "a logic machine with a well-developed moral imagination." That's good, but it leaves out the astonishing abundance of detail that makes his books an encyclopedic history of

American depredations in Southeast Asia, Central America, and the Middle East over the last sixty years, as well as the (barely) restrained sarcasm, unshowy but lethal, that makes of his indignation a high style.

If there is one theme that unifies Chomsky's vast corpus, it is moral universalism: the insistence that we apply to ourselves and our government the same moral standards we apply to others. This directly contradicts American exceptionalism: the belief, usually assumed rather than argued, that the United States is unique in contemporary, perhaps even world, history in acting abroad for selfless purposes, often at considerable sacrifice, in order to bestow or defend freedom, democracy, and prosperity. American exceptionalism is so commonplace that it is unusual to read a whole issue of the *New York Times*, the *Washington Post*, *Time*, *Foreign Affairs*, the *Atlantic*, the *New York Review*, or even the *New Yorker* without encountering some version of it. American policy always gets the benefit of the doubt, even when there is no doubt. The US was "containing Soviet expansionism" after World War II, even though the left-wing movements in Greece, Italy, Guatemala, or Iran were indigenous and by no means Soviet creations, while in each of those countries the US brought to power right-wing governments, all of them unpopular, and most of them harshly repressive. The US was "defending South Vietnam," though it knew perfectly well (and admitted in internal documents) that the insurgency it was bombing so unrestrainedly had the support of South Vietnam's population. The US invaded Iraq in order to "liberate" the country from the tyrant Saddam, although it had warmly supported the tyrant Saddam for a dozen very brutal years, until his fealty was no longer assured. Right through the Obama administration, much of the press and academic scholarship maintained their habits of deference to the conventional wisdom. Chomsky's powerful criticisms and extraordinary public reach have provided a small but important skeptical counterweight.

Undoubtedly Eliot had third and fourth great authors up his sleeve, and I have many other keenly admired public intellectuals up mine: Ralph Nader (who in addition to founding and strategizing for dozens of citizens' groups, lobbying tirelessly on Capitol Hill, and exhorting students at practically every law school in America to do something useful with their lives, has written two dozen books and countless newspaper columns), Barbara Ehrenreich, Thomas Frank, Thomas Geoghegan, and plenty of others, many of them celebrated in the essays that follow: Serge, Silone, Orwell, Pasolini, Bourne, Stone, Macdonald, Howe, Rorty, Lasch. What they have in common with Chomsky, and with one another, is a combination of discrimination and democratic passion. Their discrimination—moral intelligence, really—allowed them to make relevant distinctions and get difficult decisions right. Mostly right, anyway: they made mistakes, like Macdonald's pacifism in World War II and Howe's harsh and ungenerous response to the New Left of the 1960s, and more consequentially, Nader's failure to overlook the Democratic Party's outrageous treatment of him throughout the 2000 presidential campaign and magnanimously bow out of the contested states. Howe and Macdonald did, though, get another, very important distinction right. The majority of their contemporaries went from uncritical support of the Soviet Union to uncritical support of the United States, unable to orient themselves in the political world without wholehearted partisanship. It is a very common disability, which is why the example of Macdonald and Howe, who kept their critical antennas pointed in all directions, was so useful. Nader's immense usefulness was a result not so much of judgment as of energy and persistence. That our air and water are not even dirtier than they are, the atmosphere not more full of poisons and particulates, our product labels more misleading, and our regulatory agencies more beholden to the industries they're supposed to regulate, is Nader's doing more than anyone else's.

By democratic passion I mean the constant remembrance that democracy entails not merely that the people should be governed well but also that the people should govern. For the last century, since the defeat of Populism—the most significant working-class movement in American history—there have been two broad factions in American politics: the business party and the Progressives. Unlike the former, the latter at least had an idea of the general welfare and acknowledged the need for some regulation of business. But they envisioned no role for most citizens except to vote every two or four years. Government should be left to experts, who would duly take note of the public's biennial or quadrennial bleating.

Randolph Bourne, one of my subjects (and heroes), smartly rebuked the Progressives for their misconceived support of American entry into the First World War. I. F. Stone, another subject (and hero), rebuked them by example, with countless demonstrations over the years of government incompetence and mendacity. I've tried to do my bit here with an essay on the *New Republic*, where Progressivism was born and where it lasted through the Peretz era, for better and worse.

Most of my American subjects were New York intellectuals at one time or another. For many generations, New York City had an enlarging and enriching effect on the imagination of writers living there. But that was when writers could afford to live there. It's possible that the doughty little cohort of writers in contemporary Brooklyn will pick up the torch and continue the tradition. One hopes so.

Most of these essays are about politics as usually understood: justice, equality, power. But a number are about culture. The main issue here, as it has been for a couple of centuries, is modernity, pro and con. Since the Romantic era, a host of questions have swirled around rationalism, individualism, secularism, technology, and the other legacies of the Enlightenment. Are there other ways of knowing—imaginative, intuitive, or metaphysical—to which logic must sometimes give way or risk superficiality? Are the (sometimes) transcendent joys of belonging to a family, community, religion, or other beloved group available only to those who are willing to surrender their individuality? Is too insistent an emphasis on individual rights corrosive of institutions—the family, for example—that we all recognize are imperfect but don't see how to repair and are unwilling to do without? And is faster/easier/more—the promise of technology—addictive, leaving us unable to recognize when harder and slower and less would actually be more satisfying?

Confusingly, there is no longer a one-to-one correspondence between embracing science and progress, on the one hand, and humane, democratic values on the other. The antimodernist left that includes Pasolini, Lasch, Illich, Berry, and many others would once have been an oxymoron. Royal absolutism and clerical authoritarianism once seemed the only alternatives to the militant skepticism and individualism of the Enlightenment. But modernity has not turned out as planned. In our brand of capitalist modernity, capitalism has pretty much swallowed modernity. The generous imagination and spiritual heroism of nineteenth- and early twentieth-century utopians—of Bellamy and Morris,

Wells and Wilde, Le Guin and Callenbach—have dwindled to commercial trickery: high-speed trading, private equity financing, data mining, automated customer service, and incessantly, in every medium, every waking minute, ads. If these damnable inventions are the true avatars of modernity, then the anti-modernists have won the argument.

These and other anxieties about modernity have structured my intellectual life and figure in all my previous essay collections. In this volume I've lined up D. H. Lawrence, T. S. Eliot, Pier Paolo Pasolini, Christopher Lasch, Ivan Illich, and Wendell Berry for the prosecution; Vivian Gornick, Ellen Willis, and Richard Rorty (and in some cases, me) for the defense.

Contemporary intellectuals—intellectuals in every age—need plenty of discrimination. Here are some discriminations that seem to me worth making now, though others may feel they are too obvious to need stating. Although Yeats sympathized with Irish fascists, he was nevertheless the best English-language poet of the twentieth century. Although Eliot disdained working-class politics and made several anti-Semitic remarks, he was the next best. Although Lawrence briefly despaired of democracy and flirted with authoritarianism, he was a great novelist and a great spirit. Although Flannery O'Connor used the N-word and declared herself a "segregationist by taste," she also declared herself (well in advance of most other Southerners) an "integrationist in principle" and, more important, wrote powerful fiction in which Blacks were fully imagined. Although Saul Bellow and Philip Roth were unpleasant to the women in their lives and their novels, they were master stylists and storytellers.

Cancel culture also calls for discrimination. Leon Wieseltier was a much-admired (for good reasons and bad) literary editor

of the *New Republic* who behaved badly to his female subordinates. Certainly any future female subordinates should be
protected from him (as all female subordinates everywhere
should be protected). But that an ambitious and exciting new
magazine he had organized should be disbanded and its first
issue pulped when his transgressions were revealed—this panicky overreaction was a sin against culture. (Fortunately, he
found a braver patron and returned with an even more successful magazine.) In my hometown (Cambridge, Massachusetts), a
school committeewoman with a strongly progressive record
was taking part in a public discussion of a proposed high school
course on racist language in American history. At one point,
referring to some material that used the N-word in full, she
used the N-word in full, clearly referring to the word as part of
the course material and not to any person, present or past. It
could not have been a more obvious case of mention rather than
use. Nevertheless, three days later, under pressure, she resigned
from the school committee. Surely cancellation should be
reserved for unrepentant mass murderers: Henry Kissinger,
Dick Cheney, and Donald Rumsfeld, for example, all of whom
went on to live serene and prosperous post-criminal lives.

Intellectuals should also be discriminating about where their
energies go. Symbolic politics has its claims, but it has occupied
a disproportionate share of left/liberal attention for some time.
Increased minority and female representation in elite professions
does not trickle down, after all, any more than tax cuts for the
rich do. In the eastern United States, Black neighborhoods have
on average 66 percent more air pollution than white ones. If leftists and liberals had paid as much attention to this disparity as
they lavished on, say, the case of Rachel Dolezal, who believed
that because she grew up with four Black siblings, married a

Black man, taught Black history, and got herself elected president of her local NAACP chapter, she was entitled to call herself Black, the EPA might not have found it quite so easy last year to ignore pleas from scientists and community activists to lower permissible pollution levels. Which would have saved a lot of Black lives.

According to the Urban Institute, the median net worth of African American families is around $17,000 (the median for white families is several times higher). The 50 percent of Black households below the median could probably not meet a medical emergency or invest in their children's education or buy a house without taking on crippling debt. Recently thousands of theater professionals signed a manifesto demanding that more than half of Broadway theaters be named after people of color and that more than half of all actors, writers, directors, and designers employed by theater companies be people of color. The National Book Critics Circle publicly apologized last year because only 30 percent of its annual book awards went to people of color and only 25 percent of its board are people of color, while the fact that Blacks make up only 5 percent of the publishing industry's work force was considered clear evidence of "institutionalized racism." Is it possible that economically vulnerable Blacks would prefer to have more Black and white allies in their desperately unequal struggle for economic fairness than more Broadway theaters named for Blacks and more Black actors, directors, and book reviewers? Perhaps we should we ask them.

One more example: several million girls (and roughly the same number of boys) in the developing world die each year from malnutrition, pneumonia, diarrhea, malaria, and other easily preventable diseases. A hundred thousand adult women suffer obstetric fistulas each year: easily repaired by a simple surgery but devastating if not repaired, and often not repaired for lack of facilities. Aren't these horrors worth many orders of magnitude more Twitterstorms than, say, J. K. Rowling's views on transgender rights—which, right or wrong, can hardly produce as much suffering as an obstetric fistula?

The responsibility of intellectuals has been a live topic since intellectuals came into existence in the eighteenth century. Clearly our responsibility is to *écraser l'infâme*, or, put more modestly, to lessen the monstrous injustice in the world at least a little. In the eighteenth century, *l'infâme* was superstition and the clerical power that imposed it. In the second half of the twentieth century it was, for American intellectuals, American power, which instigated or supported more than a dozen right-wing coups, resulting in the murder, torture, and imprisonment of millions and the economic exploitation of scores of millions. Since the comprehensive failure of American policy in Afghanistan, Iraq, Syria, and Libya, both elites and the public are wary of further interventions, which the US cannot afford in any case. America's grotesque economic inequality would seem like a natural candidate for the twenty-first century's *infâme*, other things being equal. Unfortunately, other things are not equal—far from it.

For intellectuals and everyone else, one responsibility, I would say, now trumps all others. It's not justice. The near-demented zeal of today's Republican Party for further enriching the already rich is novel in degree, but plutocracy has been the rule in America since John Jay admonished his fellow Founding Fathers that "those who own the country ought to govern it." Those of us who reject that ignoble creed have the memory of the New Deal and European social democracy to pit against it; and what is the current popularity of "socialism" among the young but a revulsion against the obscene inequality that disfigures twenty-first-century America? Of course we must defeat plutocracy. But it may have to wait.

I don't mean nuclear disarmament, either. In the Nuclear Non-Proliferation Treaty of 1968—like the UN Charter, the most solemnly binding of legal instruments, however routinely disregarded by the Great Powers—the United States promised to gradually reduce its stockpile of nuclear weapons to zero. It has not done so, of course, and neither has any other signatory. The deadly, delusional logic of deterrence still prevails, despite many accidents and (at least) one false alarm that brought the Soviets to within minutes of a full response and the world to within minutes of unthinkable calamity. It is insane to expect that no accidental or deliberate use of nuclear weapons will ever occur—that our luck will hold forever. Activism to keep the danger in public view will always be necessary. But seventy-five years without an actual apocalypse has induced an almost insuperable mental inertia among Americans, intellectuals and ordinary citizens alike. Practically no one believes that nuclear catastrophe is really possible—or at any rate, likely enough to make it worthwhile to try to resurrect the international antinuclear movement of the 1980s.

It is likely that the human race would survive a full-scale nuclear war, in some form. We would probably also survive the results of burning fossil fuels at present rates indefinitely. The casualty level in both cases would probably be similar—in the hundreds of millions—though more drawn out in the case of global warming. The difference is that the earth is already burning. Earth's average temperature has already increased by nearly 1.2° Celsius (roughly 2.5° Fahrenheit) since 1800. An increase of 6°C (approximately 11°F) would be, insofar as one can compare unimaginable things, equivalent to an all-out nuclear exchange.

But while the aftermath of nuclear war would see countless deaths from radiation and starvation, it is possible to imagine a gradual return to normalcy over several decades, with the debris clouds dispersed and much of the remaining population conscripted to scrub all affected surfaces of radiation. On the other hand, if we reach 6°C—which we could very well do sometime in the next century by burning every reachable drop of oil, gas, and coal still in the ground, as the energy industry would like to do and most Republicans would be happy to let them do—there will be no return to normalcy. It will have taken an inconceivable amount of energy to have reached 6°—to have melted the ice caps and the permafrost, supercharged hurricanes and typhoons, created large dead zones too hot for human or animal habitation, killed off millions of species, and raised sea levels dozens or hundreds of feet, drowning coastal cities where hundreds of millions of people now live. There will be no reversing these changes, even if geoengineering is more successful than it currently looks to be. We will have added two trillion metric tons or more of carbon dioxide to the atmosphere, and there will be little or no ice or snow left to reflect sunlight back into space. If we reach 6° hotter, the earth will probably stay at least that hot for a thousand years.

Cato the Elder ended his every speech to the Roman Senate with the exhortation: "Carthage must be destroyed!" The exigencies of Roman imperialism, and of everything else, now seem utterly trivial compared with the exigencies of planetary survival. And so you would think that every congressperson and senator would end every speech with "Leave the oil in the ground!" or "All energy from the sun!" But Republicans are deaf, dumb, and blind on this subject (and other subjects), and Democrats are, as they always are in a good cause, faint-hearted. It is up to intellectuals (and Scandinavian teenagers, apparently) to be importunate.

Three excellent books—*Falter* by Bill McKibben, *The Uninhabitable Earth* by David Wallace-Wells, and *Our Final Warning* by Mark Lynas—will put anyone in an evangelizing mood and supply irrefutable arguments.

If only arguments moved the world. The raw greed and colossal financial power of the energy companies are impervious to argument. Still, argument is what intellectuals do, and it's not always ineffectual. Silicon Valley is not beholden to Big Energy and commands similarly vast financial resources. It is not inconceivable that, lacking any positive financial incentive to ruin the planet (rather than merely colonize our inner lives), Silicon Valley might finance a popular movement and throw its weight around in Congress. If it does, or if someone else does, that popular movement will need intellectuals, above all to neutralize the pseudo-intellectuals that Big Energy has paid for several decades now to misrepresent and obfuscate climate science.

To tilt at the state and capital or to ignore them: this has always been a choice for intellectuals. Both alternatives are morally plausible, even if those who chose the first alternative have often called those who chose the second irresponsible. Nowadays, though, that charge rings hollow: next to the irresponsibility of energy executives and Republican politicians, no one else's really counts; and the colossal conformity-producing, passivity-inducing, criticism-sidelining machinery they have constructed makes withdrawal extremely tempting and almost excusable. But as Chomsky usually replies when asked by listeners for some ground of hope: to do nothing makes the worst more likely.

All we have is a voice—and not, most of us, as penetrating a voice as Chomsky's. But if there were ever a time to lift it in defense of our lovely, perishing planet and our sometimes lovely, endangered, self-destructive species, this is it.

PART I

The Problem with Progress

1

Progress and Prejudice

I.

Nietzsche taught us that our loftiest pronouncements on the most abstract, universal subjects are just as idiosyncratic, just as much the product of our individual temperament, metabolism, and earliest influences, as our most peculiar predilections, our most eccentric crotchets. So let me declare a prejudice.

Of my great-grandfather I know only that he was recruited from rural Sicily to work on constructing the Panama Canal and died there of yellow fever. My grandfather was illiterate and worked as a laborer in a factory of the Hood Rubber Company. A few months before he was eligible to retire with a pension, he was fired for no reason; speaking no English, he had no recourse. My father had a high school education, but because his childhood was shadowed by the Great Depression, he held on to a safe, undemanding civil service job for fifty years and saved every penny, much of it under his mattress. He lived on the same street throughout his adult life and never traveled outside New England. My mother's background, opportunities, and outlook were equally restricted, in some ways more so.

In *Notes Towards the Definition of Culture*, T. S. Eliot wrote, "The primary channel of culture is the family; no man wholly escapes from the kind, or surpasses the degree, of culture which he has acquired from his early environment." As far as I know, neither of my parents ever read a novel, saw a play, or heard a concert. Nevertheless, their son has two Ivy League degrees, has written books, and has seen the world, in person and at the movies. I spend hundreds of blissful hours each year listening, on splendid but inexpensive equipment, to splendid but inexpensive recordings of the works of Bach and Mozart, among many others. Durable, inexpensive paperbacks furnish my rooms and my life. Even across one generation, this seems like progress. When I imagine my great-grandfather's great-grandfather, sunk in the immemorial poverty, ignorance, and humiliation of the Sicilian peasantry, the conclusion feels irresistible: I, at least, am the lucky beneficiary of two or three centuries of progress. And since the carbon footprint of classical music, great novels, independent film, and most of my other chief pleasures is fairly low, it seems like sustainable, universalizable progress.

Do I embody moral progress as well? That's a harder case to make, but not impossible. Some astute and astringent judgments have been passed on the traditional morality of southern Italians. In *The Golden Bowl*, Prince Amerigo implores Fanny Assingham, who has brought him together with his rich but inexperienced fiancée Maggie Verver, to "keep him straight." She replies:

"Oh, you deep old Italians!"

"There you are," he returned. . . . "That's the responsible note."

"What on earth are you talking about?"

"Of my real, honest fear of being 'off' some day, of being wrong, without knowing it. That's what I shall always trust you for—to tell me when I am. No—with you people it's a sense. We haven't got it—not as you have."

"I should be interested," she presently remarked, "to see some sense *you* don't possess."

Well, he produced one on the spot. "The moral, dear Mrs. Assingham. I mean, always, as you others consider it. I've of course something that in our poor dear backward old Rome sufficiently passes for it. But it's no more like yours than the tortuous stone staircase—half-ruined into the bargain!—in some castle of our *quattrocento* is like the 'lightning elevator' in one of Mr. Verver's fifteen-storey buildings. Your moral sense works by steam—it sends you up like a rocket. Ours is slow and steep and unlighted, with so many of the steps missing that—well, that it's as short, in almost any case, to turn around and come down again."

"Trusting," Mrs. Assingham smiled, "to get up some other way?"

"Yes—or not to have to get up at all."

Later in the twentieth century, in the sociological classic *The Moral Basis of a Backward Society*, Edward Banfield theorized the southern Italian ethos as "amoral familism." This unhappy moral culture was defined by a narrow dedication to the interests of oneself and one's immediate family and a thoroughgoing absence of intellectual or political integrity, disinterestedness, trust, solidarity, generosity, civic virtue, or professional pride, along with equal measures of cynicism about and servility toward all forms of authority. Robert Putnam also found amoral familism flourishing—if that's the word—among southern Italians in his seminal *Making Democracy Work*.

Amoral familism was certainly the prevailing ethos in my largely second-generation inner-city neighborhood. At college, ivied brick walls, timbered dining halls, and portraits of Puritan college fathers prepared me for a change; and in my sophomore year enlightenment arrived, full blast and double-barreled: *On*

Liberty and *Middlemarch*, between them a complete moral education. Mill's noble purity and Eliot's wise magnanimity had their inevitable effect. I will never be, like them, incapable of a pettiness, but I am a little less of an amoral familist than I would otherwise have been. Hardly perfection, but for one whose not very distant ancestor was very likely, in the words of another Henry James character, "a squalid, savage-looking peasant, a tattered ruffian of orthodox Italian aspect," undoubtedly progress. And again, in principle at least (notwithstanding the ivied walls), universally achievable.

This two-century trajectory, from squalor to modest comfort, from ruffian to harmless schlub, doubtless predisposes me to see the slope of history tending upward. So does another accident of biography: deliverance from *l'infâme*. I grew up devout and was recruited as a high school student into Opus Dei, a Catholic lay order of the strictest Counter-Reformation traditionalism and authoritarianism. Majoring in modern European intellectual history was awkward, since much of modern European literature and philosophy was on the Index of Forbidden Books and therefore proscribed. Unwisely, however, the Church failed to forbid everything. Even more unwisely, the order tried to teach its members the elements of Scholastic philosophy, which I found extremely unconvincing. I suppressed my doubts for a long while, out of conscience and natural timidity. I confided them to my confessor, of course, who at first urged prayer and mortification of the flesh. Eventually, after consulting his superiors, he ordered a *sacrificium intellectus*: I must leave intellectual history alone, on peril of sin and perhaps damnation. This was a serious matter: I was terrified of Hell, and moreover, my confessor very much resembled my mental image of Dostoevsky's Grand Inquisitor. But it was too late: I felt the Enlightenment at my back.

Emulating the *philosophes'* great refusal, I lodged my little one, enrolling timorously but proudly in what I had learned from Peter Gay to call the Party of Humanity—of freedom, science, and progress. Because this mini-heroic auto-emancipation has been the supreme drama—to tell the truth, the only drama—in my life, I am perhaps understandably inclined to see all of history as this drama writ large: "humankind's emergence from its self-imposed minority," as Kant defined "enlightenment." Certainly I am reluctant to consider that my tiny but arduous affirmation has no resonance beyond my own life, no part in furthering a grander scheme of liberation and collective advance. But that's just a prejudice, I know.

II.

Some part of our perplexity about human progress is surely a result of the size of our sample. If we knew the histories of even a few more intelligent species, it would be much easier to extrapolate our future. All we have are imagined histories; that is, science fiction. Some of its guesses seem truly inspired, though; none more so than *Childhood's End* by Arthur C. Clarke. The fundamental intuition underlying all visions of perfection through cosmic evolution may be summed up as "matter into mind." It is a ubiquitous trope in intellectual history, from the Middle Ages through Teilhard de Chardin, and in futuristic fiction since Wells and Stapledon, if not before. Matter is limitation, disorganization, inertia. Mind gradually, inexorably rationalizes not only our material and social relations, but eventually even our organismic form, our species being. We become gods.

In Clarke's version, the path to godhead is not exactly rationalization. A race of super-intelligent, super-powerful beings

arrives on earth to midwife humankind's passage across a
cosmic evolutionary barrier. The midwives, or Overlords, have
reached a cul-de-sac of scientific rationality. Their civilization is
immeasurably superior, but humans have something they lack:
imagination. Most races with this psychic endowment have
destroyed themselves, and sometimes others, the Overlords
explain. The few that have flourished have fused into an entity
that its servants, the Overlords, call the Overmind: a being in
which (or whom) beauty, truth, power, and love are indistinguishable and are present in a degree that is, for practical purposes,
infinite. Like the Christian God (Clarke must have known some
theology), the Overmind seeks to draw up into itself those species
capable of sharing in—participating, as Thomistic theologians
would say—its beatitude. The Overlords and other apostles are
sent to harvest them.

This is not exactly what Condorcet or Spencer or Teilhard—
or Joachim da Fiore for that matter—had in mind. Some critics
(and some characters in *Childhood's End*) find Clarke's vision
objectionable, because humankind does not decide its own fate.
Of course this objection only has force if humankind is grown-up
enough to comprehend its choices and discipline its lethal (potentially on an interstellar scale, the Overlords warn) energies.
Clarke's answer, implicit in his title and indicated, though not
fully developed, in the novel, is persuasive to me. *Childhood's
End* is at once the most extreme and the most plausible futuristic
fantasy I know of. It answers to my (admittedly crude) intuition
that fourteen billion years is enough time, and trillions of light
years enough space, for a great many things to have happened
that have so far eluded most terrestrial imaginations; and also to
my (equally crude) sense that at least a few of humankind's innumerable mystics have glimpsed something ineffable. Those are

two very disparate intuitions; I don't know of any other story
that accommodates both.

III.

Other stories or (what amounts to the same thing) historical interpretations answer to different, sometimes opposite intuitions.
"Matter into mind" is a formula for limitless transcendence. Intuitions of immanence, of the necessity and wisdom of limits, produce
visions of stasis or decline and hopes for, at best, a steady state.

The two most persuasive twentieth-century antiprogressives
I've encountered could hardly be more different: D. H. Lawrence
and Christopher Lasch. Lawrence championed matter against
mind. He despised "thin-minded" rationalists like Shaw and
Wells; he scoffed at labor-saving technology; and he believed in
natural hierarchies and charismatic leaders. Yet he was hardly a
friend of any status quo, past or present. From an unpublished
manuscript:

> I know that we could, if we would, establish little by little a true
> democracy in England: we could nationalize the land and industries
> and means of transport, and make the whole thing work infinitely
> better than at present, *if we would*. It all depends on the spirit in which
> the thing is done.
>
> I know we are on the brink of a class war.
>
> I know we had all better hang ourselves at once, than enter on a
> struggle which shall be a fight for the ownership or non-ownership
> of property, pure and simple, and nothing beyond.
>
> I know the ownership of property is a problem that may have
> to be fought out. But beyond the fight must lie a new hope, a new
> beginning . . .

> I know we must take up the responsibility for the future, now. A
> great change is coming, and must come. What we need is some glim-
> mer of a vision of a world that shall be, beyond the change. Otherwise
> we shall be in for a great debacle.

Lawrence's "glimmer of a vision" flickers throughout the two
volumes of *Phoenix: The Posthumous Papers*, especially in the
"Study of Thomas Hardy," "Reflections on the Death of a Porcu-
pine," and "Education of the People." It involves a far more direct
connection with the sun and the solar plexus, with cosmic mysteries and instinctual rhythms, than he observed in his
contemporaries. Against the prevailing rationalism, he defined
reason as "the glitter of the sun on the surface of the waters" and
conceived "man's body as a kind of flame . . . and the intellect is
just the light that is shed on the things around."

What kind of future follows from that image of humanity?
Lawrence never explained in detail. His vision found its strangest
and most lyrical expression in another unpublished fragment, a
utopian fantasy in the form (and something like the spirit) of
William Morris's *News from Nowhere*. The speaker has woken up
in his native place after sleeping a thousand years. The new
humans are "flower-like" and "comely as berries"—not at all
disembodied Mind. He watches them at sunset:

> When the ball of fire touched the tree-tops, there was a queer squeal
> of bagpipes, and the square suddenly started into life. The men were
> stamping softly, like bulls, the women were softly swaying, and softly
> clapping their hands, with a strange noise, like leaves. And under the
> vaulted porticoes, at opposite ends of the egg-shaped oval, came
> the soft booming and trilling of women and men singing against one
> another in the strangest pattern of sound.

It was all kept very soft, soft-breathing. Yet the dance swept into swifter and swifter rhythm, with the most extraordinary incalculable unison. I do not believe there was any outside control of the dance. The thing happened by instinct, like the wheeling and flashing of a shoal of fish or of a flock of birds dipping and spreading in the sky. Suddenly, in one amazing wing-movement, the arms of all the men would flash up into the air, naked and glowing, and with the soft rushing sound of pigeons alighting the men ebbed in a spiral, grey and sparkled with scarlet, bright arms slowly leaning, upon the women, who rustled all crocus-blue, rustled like an aspen, then in one movement scattered like sparks, in every direction from under the enclosing, sinking arms of the men, and suddenly formed slender rays of lilac branching out from the red and grey knot of the men.

All the time the sun was slowly sinking, shadow was falling, and the dance was moving slower, the women wheeling blue around the obliterated sun. They were dancing the sun down, and dancing as birds wheel and dance, and fishes in shoals, controlled by some strange unanimous instinct. It was at once terrifying and magnificent, I wanted to die, so as not to see it, and I wanted to rush down, to be one of them. To be a drop in that wave of life.

This was Lawrence's answer to Wells's *Men like Gods* and Shaw's *Back to Methuselah*, a vision of human perfection achieved by going not onward and upward but inward and downward. Whether it means going forward or backward depends on whether one believes—and is glad—that organic, embodied human nature has unalterable limits.

Christopher Lasch believed that and preached it eloquently in *The True and Only Heaven*, his masterpiece of social criticism and intellectual history. That book, like Lasch's entire career, is an extended quarrel with modernity, defined as the advance of an overlapping, mutually reinforcing phalanx of political central-ization, mass production, expanded consumption, automation, geographical mobility, the bureaucratization of education, med-icine, and family life, moral cosmopolitanism, and legal universalism. Against this march of abstractions, Lasch insisted on the fact of human scale. The human creature has a specific evolutionary endowment and gestational history; as a result it has a specific infantile fantasy life, which it can only outgrow grad-ually, through a range of close-up interactions, involving both authority and love, with the same caregivers over many years. The bureaucratic rationalization of work and intimate life plays havoc with this scheme of development, producing a weak self, stripped of traditional skills, tools, and autonomy, entirely dependent on large forces beyond its comprehension, much less control, and crippled by ambivalence toward remote, impersonal authority. What sustained the strong premodern self was the virtue of hope; what sustains the weak modern self is the ideology of progress.

I have learned, with some reluctance, from Lawrence and Lasch how readily things go wrong, how ingeniously progress can be faked. The division of labor, advances in industrial and information technology, the growth of medical knowledge, even the emancipation of women: every liberation can be captured and exploited. We had better stay inside our own skins—and even, perhaps, within traditional social forms—until we are sure that it's safe to discard them. And as long as modernization is involuntary—imposed within a class system, for profit or social control—it's difficult to know that.

Two other, minor masterpieces teach similar lessons about false promises. Whether or not, as some have argued, the internet makes us stupid, it undeniably makes us different, especially as readers. In *The Gutenberg Elegies*, Sven Birkerts masterfully elaborates a phenomenology of "deep reading": the heightened focus, the inner stillness, the imaginative motility, the immersion in a linguistic matrix. It is a habitus that, like the attention of a meditator, strengthens gradually, as a muscle does. It requires verticality and temporary isolation. But the capacity for such concentration must erode and eventually dissipate in a horizontal, hyperlinked, continuously connected world. The alteration in our psychic metabolism that Birkerts foresees seems to me no less probable and fateful because his is a qualitative, literary description, without benefit of neurobiology or social science.

The alteration Bill McKibben discusses in *Enough* (and, not quite so sensitively and eloquently, Francis Fukuyama in *Our Posthuman Future*) is even more radical. Not all scientists agree that germ-line genetic engineering will be feasible within the next hundred years, but most do. The elimination of genetic diseases will be a blessing, of course, but a market in "designer children," programmed for outstanding cognitive, athletic, and other abilities, may transform present economic inequalities into irreversible caste distinctions—eventually even species distinctions. Of course the free market knows best, and if it decrees that the master class should become a master race, who is wise enough to interfere? As Mrs. Thatcher instructed us: "There is no alternative." Thomas Jefferson may have thundered that "the mass of mankind has not been born with saddles on their backs, nor a favored few booted and spurred, ready to ride them legitimately, by the grace of God." But that is mere sentimental egalitarian rhetoric, obsolete in an age of efficient markets and rational choice.

IV.

Perhaps the problem of progress is a pseudo-problem. Coleridge observed that every great and original poet creates the taste by which he is judged. But tastes, criteria, perspectives can also be destroyed or wither away. Print-based civilization, for example, has not answered the earliest objections to the eclipse of oral literacy; it has merely ignored them. No doubt the inhabitants of the Electronic Hive that Birkerts foresees will miss deep reading about as much as most of us miss having vast quantities of verse committed to memory, as many educated people did in the age of oral literacy. And a populace that has exchanged its skills, tools, and independence for SUVs and consumer electronics may be perfectly happy, or at least comfortable, with saddles on their backs. To measure progress, one needs a standard; and if standards alter drastically, what are measurements worth?

George Orwell had a view of the question. Though best known for his dystopias, he did write one—characteristically skeptical and downbeat—piece about Utopia, a Christmas 1943 *Tribune* essay titled "Can Socialists Be Happy?" "All efforts to describe *permanent* happiness . . . have been failures, from earliest history onwards," he began cheerfully. Utopias "seem to be alike in postulating perfection while being unable to suggest happiness." Even *News from Nowhere* induced in him "only a sort of watery melancholy." Orwell was never a blithe spirit, and in London in December 1943 it was probably hard to conceive even temporary happiness.

Anyway, he continues, happiness is not the point.

Men use up their lives in heart-breaking political struggles, or get themselves killed in civil wars, or tortured in the secret prisons of the Gestapo, not in order to establish some central-heated, air-conditioned, strip-lighted Paradise, but because they want a world in which human beings love one another instead of swindling and murdering one another. And they want that world as a first step. Where they go from there is not so certain, and the attempt to foresee it in detail merely confuses the issue. . . .

Nearly all creators of Utopia have resembled the man who has toothache, and therefore thinks that happiness consists in not having toothache. They wanted to produce a perfect society by an endless continuation of something that had only been valuable because it was temporary. The wiser course would be to say that there are certain lines along which humanity must move, the grand strategy is mapped out, but detailed prophecy is not our business.

This seems reasonable to me, and I suspect it would have seemed reasonable to Condorcet, who ended the penultimate section of his *Progress of the Human Mind* with a passage of near-Orwellian sobriety:

The labours of recent ages have done much for the progress of the human mind, but little for the perfection of the human race; much for the honour of man, something for his liberty, but so far almost nothing for his happiness. At a few points our eyes are dazzled with a brilliant light; but thick darkness still covers an immense stretch of the horizon. There are a few circumstances from which the philosopher can take consolation; but he is still afflicted by the spectacle of the stupidity, slavery, barbarism, and extravagance of mankind; and the friend of humanity can find unmixed pleasure only in tasting the sweet delights of hope.

That sounds as much like now as 1794 (except that recent ages haven't done much for "the honour of man"). "Thick darkness"

accurately describes the American economic and political outlook; and toothache is the only possible response to either
Democratic or Republican politicians and pundits. Occupy and
Jacobin and 350.org, Krugman and Thunberg and Chomsky,
seem to me a "few points" of "brilliant light," from which I "take
consolation." Are they, along with the last three centuries or so,
enough to furnish the "sweet delights of hope"? I suppose so—
but that's just a prejudice, I know.

2

The Workingman's Friend

Adam Smith

In the "Overture" to his grandly symphonic *The Enlightenment: An Interpretation*, Peter Gay describes the "international type" of the *philosophe* as a "facile, articulate, doctrinaire, sociable, secular man of letters." On this definition, was Adam Smith a *philosophe*?

Yes and no. Unlike his French counterparts and even his bosom friend David Hume, he led a retired life, much of it in the small Scottish town where he was born, and he lived with his mother until she died at a very advanced age. He was shy, destroyed most of his letters, and did not seem to relish giving brilliant performances, either in print or in conversation. He never fell afoul of civil or religious authority, had no mistresses, and engaged in no public quarrels. (A semi-public one, though. Shortly after Hume's death, Smith met Samuel Johnson at a party. Johnson spoke slightingly of Hume, Smith defended him, and their exchanges grew increasingly heated until Johnson exclaimed, "Sir, you lie!" To which Smith retorted, "Sir, you are the son of a whore!" and stalked out.)

On the other hand, Smith was modestly sociable—he had warm relationships with Turgot, Quesnay, and Condorcet. Like most of the *philosophes*, he was prolific and versatile, publishing much-admired essays on law, literature, and the history of science as well as his masterpieces on moral philosophy and political economy. And although he was not openly irreligious like Hume and Voltaire, he had as little use for the Calvinist superstitions of Scotland as his French contemporaries had for Roman Catholic ones. Perhaps the main point of difference lies in that slightly ambiguous word "doctrinaire." Smith was a critic and reformer, and there are plenty of doctrines in his writings, some of them strikingly original. But he was detached and scholarly by temperament, rather than ardently polemical. If he was a *philosophe*, he was an exceptionally philosophical one.

Adam Smith was born in 1723 in Kirkcaldy, Scotland. His father, a lawyer and civil servant, died six months before Adam's birth. He left his family well off, and young Adam's mother devoted the rest of her life to her son, who reciprocated her devotion. The first and only adventure in Smith's life took place in his childhood, when he was snatched while at play by some strolling vagabonds but was shortly afterward rescued by his uncle and a search party. He was sent to the excellent local grammar school and then, at fourteen, to Glasgow University. After three successful years there, he won a scholarship to Oxford, which was then sunk in intellectual torpor and futile scholasticism. Smith loathed it and returned to Scotland halfway through the term of his scholarship.

The academic job market was considerably brighter then than now. The twenty-five-year-old Smith was invited to give two series of lectures, on rhetoric and jurisprudence, at Edinburgh. They were a rousing success, leading to his appointment as Professor of Logic and Metaphysics at Glasgow University in 1751 and Professor of Moral Philosophy in 1752. He remained there happily until lured away, for a princely fee, to tutor and travel with a young duke. From 1767 to 1776 he largely secluded himself in Kirkcaldy, composing *The Wealth of Nations*. He returned to Edinburgh in 1778 as Commissioner of Customs, an important and lucrative post, and died there in 1790.

As Nicholas Phillipson dryly observes at the beginning of his—unavoidably—rather dry biography: "There is a general lack of visibility in Smith's life." Smith burned his letters, notes, and unpublished manuscripts; we don't even have a likeness till he was past forty. Phillipson makes up for this by sketching—in sometimes amusing and sometimes tiresome detail—the social and cultural background of the Scottish Enlightenment, the remarkable environment in which Smith's development took place. Scotland's early eighteenth-century prosperity produced an eager audience for lecturers like the young Smith, and generous patrons for prominent public intellectuals like the mature Smith. Perhaps equally important, Phillipson suggests, the bustle of Kirkcaldy and Glasgow, growing market towns, may have first planted in Smith's mind the image of incessant activity, continually expanding needs, and harmonious haggling that lurks everywhere in the background of *Wealth of Nations*.

Most important for Smith, and central to the Scottish Enlightenment, was David Hume. Smith discovered Hume while at Oxford (he was officially reprimanded when discovered reading Hume's *Treatise on Human Nature* in his rooms in Balliol College) and became first a disciple, then a close friend. Smith's brief, eloquent memorial tribute to Hume offended the orthodox and, Smith complained, "brought upon me ten times more abuse than the very violent attack I had made [in *The Wealth of Nations*] upon the whole commercial system of Great Britain."

Hume figures prominently in Phillipson's biography. Smith's lifework, he writes, was essentially to "develop a science of man on Humean principles." Hume declined to derive claims about morality and justice from reason or from metaphysical notions about the nature of being. He looked instead to the way moral sentiments were acquired in the course of social life, to the refinement of passions by conversation and commerce, and to the growth and quickening of "sympathy" or moral imagination. Hume was an astute moral psychologist but, Phillipson writes, never went on to use those insights to formulate a theory of the social origins of morality. That was Smith's ambition.

The Theory of Moral Sentiments (1759) was Smith's "account of the processes by which we learn the principles of morality from the experience of common life." This approach—a natural history of sociability—was both a response to and a continuation of Smith's predecessors, Hutcheson, Hume, and Rousseau. But Smith added something new: he replaced the solitary voice of conscience and the collective voice of mankind with a hybrid: the "man within the breast," an imaginary, impartial spectator whose judgments are not innate but formed by experience and whose sympathy is allocated with scrupulous, almost Stoic, fairness. There is perhaps a foreshadowing of Rawls's "veil of ignorance" in Smith's conception. Even this contemporary echo, however, cannot much enliven Smith's treatise, at least for this reader. It takes the literary genius of a Hume or Rousseau to make eighteenth-century moral psychology engaging. Equally, perhaps, it takes the scholarly flair of an Albert Hirschman or Deirdre McCloskey to make the intellectual history of moral theory absorbingly interesting. Phillipson, though amiable, is a bit pedestrian.

Even more disappointing is that, although Phillipson does an admirable job of recounting what is known of Smith's life, he refrains from offering opinions about Smith's afterlife, which is, after all, far more interesting. Smith has become, along with Milton Friedman and Friedrich Hayek, one of the deities in the libertarian-conservative pantheon. I suspect Smith would have firmly declined this honor, even before his more zealous devotees, the proponents of the "efficient markets" hypothesis, nearly succeeded in wrecking the economies of the United States, Britain, and their unfortunate imitators in 2008.

The Wealth of Nations appeared in the eventful year 1776. The title page described the author as "formerly professor of Moral Philosophy in the University of Glasgow." His principal influence, François Quesnay, chief of the Physiocrats, was a distinguished physician. They were both amateurs, generalists, and reformers—*political* economists, far removed in outlook and purpose from today's "specialists without spirit." The celebrated sarcasms and exhortations in *Wealth of Nations*—"All for ourselves, and nothing for other people, seems, in every age of the world, to have been the vile maxim of the masters of mankind," for example, or "People of the same trade seldom meet together, even for merriment and diversion, but the conversation ends in a conspiracy against the public, or in some contrivance to raise prices"—are not incidental but central. The book might equally well have been titled *The Welfare of Nations*.

Everyone knows, of course, what Adam Smith stood for: free trade, the division of labor, the minimal state, the invisible hand, the illimitable growth of wants and needs. "It is not from the benevolence of the butcher, the brewer, or the baker that we expect our dinner, but from their regard to their own interest." "Every individual . . . intends only his own gain, and is in this, as in many other cases, led by an invisible hand to promote an end which was no part of his intention." "Little else is requisite to carry a state to the highest degree of opulence from the lowest barbarism, but peace, easy taxes, and a tolerable administration of justice; all the rest being brought about by the natural course of things." Case closed.

What everyone knows is seldom altogether wrong; but remarkably often it is not altogether right, either. As Emma Rothschild notes at the outset of *Economic Sentiments*, her superb study of Smith and Condorcet: "They think and write about self-interest and competition, about institutions and corporations, about the 'market' and the 'state.' But the words mean different things to them, and their connotation is of a different, and sometimes of an opposite, politics." It is far from obvious that Smith would have entertained cordial feelings toward Alan Greenspan or Margaret Thatcher.

For one thing, Smith roundly mistrusted businessmen. In addition to the sallies already quoted, he insisted that businessmen, for all they may talk of freedom and fairness, "generally have an interest to deceive and even oppress the public." Two examples out of many from *The Wealth of Nations*:

> Our merchants and master-manufacturers complain much of the bad effects of high wages in raising the price, and thereby lessening the sale of their goods both at home and abroad. They say nothing concerning the bad effects of high profits. They are silent with regard to the pernicious effects of their own gains. They complain only of those of other people.

Not infrequently merchants sought favorable changes in trade or currency policy using "sophistical" arguments.

> Such as they were, however, those arguments convinced the people to whom they were addressed. They were addressed by

merchants to parliaments, and the councils of princes, to nobles, and to country gentlemen; by those who were supposed to understand trade, to those who were conscious to themselves that they knew nothing about the matter. That foreign trade enriched the country, experience demonstrated to the nobles and country gentlemen, as well as to the merchants; but how, or in what manner, none of them well knew. The merchants knew perfectly well in what manner it enriched themselves. It was their business to know it. But to know in what manner it enriched the country, was no part of their business. The subject never came into their consideration . . .

Smith did not by any means deny or gloss over class conflict. On the contrary, he was unflinchingly clear-eyed about the unscrupulousness of employers and the connivance of governments. The US Chamber of Commerce is invited to ponder the following passage:

What are the common wages of labour, depends everywhere upon the contract usually made between those two parties, whose interests are by no means the same. The workmen desire to get as much, the masters to give as little as possible. The former are disposed to combine in order to raise, the latter in order to lower the wages of labour. It is not difficult to foresee which of the two parties must, upon all ordinary occasions, have the advantage in the dispute and force the other into a compliance with their terms. The masters, being fewer in number, can combine much more easily; and the law, besides, authorizes, or at least does not prohibit their combinations, while it prohibits those of the workmen. We have no acts of parliament against combining to lower the price of work; but many against combining to raise it. . . .

He is not finished:

> We rarely hear, it has been said, of the combinations of masters, though frequently of those of workmen. But whoever imagines, upon this account, that masters rarely combine, is as ignorant of the world as of the subject. Masters are always and everywhere in a sort of tacit, but constant and uniform combination, not to raise the wages of labour above their actual rate. . . . We seldom, indeed, hear of this combination, because it is the usual, and one may say, the natural state of things which nobody ever hears of. Masters too sometimes enter into particular combinations to sink the wages of labour even below this rate. These are always conducted with the utmost silence and secrecy, till the moment of execution, and when the workmen yield, as they sometimes do, without resistance, though severely felt by them, they are never heard of by other people. Such combinations, however, are frequently resisted by a contrary defensive combination of the workmen; who sometimes too, without any provocation of this kind, combine of their own accord to raise the price of labour. . . . But whether the workmen's combinations be offensive or defensive, they are always abundantly heard of. . . . They are desperate, and act with the folly of desperate men, who must either starve, or frighten their masters into compliance with their demands. The masters upon these occasions are just as clamorous upon the other side, and never cease to call aloud for the assistance of the civil magistrate, and the rigorous execution of those laws which have been enacted with so much severity against the combinations of servants, labourers, and journeymen.

Like Hume, Smith was firmly on the side of the workers, a robust partisan of full employment and high wages.

What improves the circumstances of the greater part can never be regarded as an inconveniency to the whole. No society can surely be flourishing and happy, of which the far greater part of the members are poor and miserable. It is but equity, besides, that they who feed, clothe, and lodge the whole body of the people, should have such a share of the produce of their own labour as to be themselves well fed, clothed, and lodged.

And another sarcasm against early capitalist apologetics, which applies equally well to later ones:

That a little more plenty than ordinary may render some workmen idle, cannot well be doubted; but that it should have that effect upon the greater part, or that men in general should work better when they are ill fed than when they are well fed, when they are disheartened than when they are in good spirits, when they are frequently sick than when they are in good health, seems not very probable.

Smith strongly supported progressive taxation:

The subjects of every state ought to contribute towards the support of the government, as nearly as possible, in proportion to their respective abilities; that is, in proportion to the revenue which they respectively enjoy under the protection of the state.

Nor was Smith a proponent of the minimal state. Government has the duty of "erecting and maintaining those public institutions and those public works which may be in the highest degree advantageous to a great society," but which "are of such a nature that the profit could never repay the expense to any individual or small number of individuals." Smith was, in short, a friend of the workingman. He would definitely not feel at home in the American Enterprise Institute, the Heritage Foundation, or the University of Chicago economics department.

But although Smith's heart was in the right place, he was wrong about two important matters. The first was his advocacy of free trade, based on the theory of comparative advantage. No developing country, Smith asserts, should try to nurture particular "strategic" (as we now say) industries:

> By means of such regulations, indeed, a particular manufacture may sometimes be acquired sooner than it could have been otherwise, and after a certain time may be made at home as cheap or cheaper than in the foreign country. But though the industry of the society may be thus carried with advantage into a particular channel sooner than it could have been otherwise, it will by no means follow that the sum total, either of its industry, or of its revenue, can ever be augmented by any such regulation. . . . Though for want of any such regulations the society should never acquire the proposed manufacture, it would not, upon that account, necessarily be the poorer in any one period of its duration.

This is from perhaps the most influential section of *The Wealth of Nations*, the one containing the reference to the "invisible hand" and the now hoary old chestnut, "What is prudence in the conduct of every private family can scarce be folly in that of a great kingdom."

But Smith was wrong. Every successful economy—without exception—has prospered by subsidizing key industries and protecting them from foreign competition. And nearly without exception, every developed society has then, with consummate hypocrisy, preached free trade to less-developed countries.

Friedrich List first refuted Smith's development theory. For a thorough review of this issue, see the work of the contemporary Oxford economist Ha-Joon Chang, in particular *Kicking Away the Ladder* and *Bad Samaritans*.

The other important matter about which Smith was influentially wrong was his notion of indefinite progress. He recognized that only economic growth could sustain high wages and widely diffused prosperity without society-wide planning and cooperation. But unsurprisingly, he failed to recognize that there are inescapable limits to growth.

Whatever his failures of vision, Smith at least *had* a moral and social imagination, unlike most of those who now claim his legacy. Perhaps the finest tribute to Smith came from his noblest successor, John Stuart Mill:

> For practical purposes, political economy is inseparably intertwined with many other branches of social philosophy . . . Smith never loses sight of this truth . . . [A] work similar in its object and general conception to that of Adam Smith, but adapted to the more extended knowledge and improved ideas of the present age, is the kind of contribution which political economy at present requires.

It still is.

3

Are We All Liberals Now?

Edmund Burke and Thomas Paine

In the mid-seventeenth century, to think for oneself and determine one's fate were the prerogatives of a tiny hereditary elite. The rest of humanity did not even aspire to those things. By the mid-nineteenth century, the aspiration, at least, was near-universal in Europe and North America, and beginning to be felt elsewhere; and reality had begun, gradually, fitfully, and still incompletely, to shift in that direction everywhere. The arc of history had been bent toward democracy.

What accomplished that most momentous of alterations was, of course, the Enlightenment. The Enlightenment was not a doctrine, or a set of doctrines; it was an attitude. The best definition remains Kant's in his essay "An Answer to the Question: What Is Enlightenment?" (1784):

> Enlightenment is humankind's emergence from its self-imposed immaturity. . . . This immaturity is self-imposed when its cause lies not in a lack of understanding but in a lack of resolve and courage to use it without guidance from another. "*Sapere aude!* Have the courage to use your own understanding!"—that is the motto of enlightenment.

Or, as the New Left of the 1960s and '70s put it, "Question authority!"

Why, one may ask, did it take courage in the seventeenth and eighteenth century to use one's own understanding? Because from time immemorial, virtually everywhere, the prevailing structures of power and privilege had been arbitrary and patently unjust. The beneficiaries of this state of affairs discouraged critical reflection on it, by indoctrination and by the threat of temporal and eternal punishment. Where authority has no justification, to ask for one is sedition.

Some, probably most, of those who opposed self-determination cared only about preserving their privileges. But others have always believed, more or less sincerely, that freedom is too great a burden for ordinary people and that governing is beyond their capacity. Even to choose their rulers or their form of government is too much for them. On these subjects they must not, for their own good, "use their understanding without guidance" from wiser others.

The revolutions in America and France were the first large-scale assertions of popular sovereignty, and they gave rise to a great debate on the question of self-determination. It was a somewhat lopsided debate; the opponents of popular sovereignty mainly replied with force rather than with arguments. Only one thinker of stature tried to rebut the advocates of self-determination (though he too called for forcibly suppressing them): Edmund Burke. In *The Great Debate*, Yuval Levin, editor of *National Affairs* and a frequent contributor to the *Weekly Standard* and *National Review*, reconstructs the supreme agon of that controversy, Burke's angry *Reflections on the Revolution in France* and Thomas Paine's incandescent reply, *Rights of Man*.

Burke was Anglo-Irish, the private secretary (we would now say chief of staff) of a leading Whig politician, and eventually a member of Parliament. The Whigs favored limiting the prerogatives of royalty in favor of those of aristocracy. They were (or claimed to be) something of a "good government" party; that is, not so egregiously corrupt, cruel, or tyrannical as the Tories; and Burke made a reputation early on as an opponent of some of the more flagrant abuses of the time, including the criminal justice system, religious discrimination, the administration of Ireland, and the plundering of the colonies, particularly India and America.

But as a dangerous radical observed in our own time, it is one thing to give food to the poor and quite another thing to ask why the poor have no food. Burke was willing to acknowledge abuses and mitigate them, but he rejected all talk of structural injustice, equal rights, or radical reform. Paine (and Burke's other contemporary critics, Joseph Priestley, Mary Wollstonecraft, James Mackintosh, and William Godwin) scoffed that Burke's defense of the status quo (the "British constitution," he called it reverently) was a tissue of fallacies, sophistries, and evasions, camouflaged by gorgeous rhetoric. This might have been posterity's verdict as well if the French Revolution had turned out differently. But the Terror and Napoleon's dictatorship appeared to vindicate Burke. An alliance of counterrevolutionary powers, led (as Burke had urged) by England, defeated France militarily, and the controversy subsided. In the latter half of the twentieth century, the Cold War roused American conservatism from its long intellectual slumber. Interest in Burke revived. The Great Debate is still hardly a burning, or even a smoldering, issue for most twenty-first-century Americans. But Levin's good-tempered, evenhanded book will no doubt persuade many readers of its continuing relevance.

"Burke and Paine," Levin writes, "each offer a coherent and, for the most part, internally consistent case about the character of society and politics." He summarizes their opposing cases very handily:

Burke's objection to total revolution draws on his horror at the prospect of abandoning all that has been arduously gained over centuries of slow, incremental reform and improvement. He sees it as a betrayal of the trust of past generations and of the obligation to future ones. Paine's objection to such plodding reform, meanwhile, is that it gives credence to despotism and is motivated more by the desire to sustain inequity than to address injustice.

Burke believes that human nature and the rest of nature make themselves known in politics through long experience, that human beings are born into a web of obligations, and that the social problems we confront do not lend themselves to detached scientific analysis. For all these reasons, he believes that improvements in politics must be achieved by cumulative reform—by building on success to address failure and by containing the effects of innovation within a broader context of continuity.

Paine, on the other hand, believes that nature reveals itself in the form of abstract principles discovered by rational analysis, that human beings are entitled to choose their government freely, that government in turn exists to protect their other choices, and that reason can help people see beyond the superstitions that have long sustained unjust regimes. For all these reasons, he believes that improvements in politics must be achieved by thoroughgoing revolution—by throwing off the accumulated burdens of the past and starting fresh and properly.

This sounds plausible enough. It is certainly the standard account of the Great Debate. But look at these alternatives a little more closely. On the one hand, Paine champions "rational analysis"; on the other, Burke insists that we learn from "long experience." Paine declares that "human beings are entitled to choose their government freely"; Burke counters that "human beings are born into a web of obligations." Paine advocates "throwing off the accumulated burdens of the past"; Burke emphasizes "building on success to address failure."

In each case, the second half of the antithesis is supposed to be incompatible with the first. But in each case, it is no such thing. Every judgment involves *both* rational analysis and the lessons of experience. Why would those who are born into a web of obligations (i.e., everyone) not be entitled to choose their government freely? Why is it impossible to distinguish between past failures and past successes, rejecting the former and building on the latter? Burke's polemical method consists of attributing extreme and implausible positions to his ideological opponents and then refuting them with many expressions of outraged common sense. Enlightenment "radicalism" simply proposed that no tradition or institution be exempt from criticism and that all men and women should have a fair chance to shape the common life. For Burke, this was sheer horror, the world turned upside down. He could not imagine that most human beings would ever attain maturity.

The profound philosophical differences Levin attributes to Burke and Paine are actually superficial ones. Whether reform should be partial or radical, gradual or rapid; whether our ancestors were wise or foolish and the laws they bequeathed us are just or unjust; whether governing well is easy or difficult and most people are or are not capable of or interested in taking part in it; whether we are influenced chiefly by reasons or passions, abstractions or facts, inherited loyalties or ethical reflection—are all beside the main point at issue between Burke and Paine. The main point is: who decides? Shall ordinary men and women be empowered? Does each of us get an equal vote and a chance to be heard? Paine says yes; Burke tries desperately to confuse matters, setting off huge smoke-bombs of rhetorical obfuscation, proceeding from trivially obvious premises to outlandish conclusions by way of grandiloquent non sequiturs. Because an institution or practice has lasted a long time, Burke argues, it deserves to continue. Because none of us can be perfectly objective or impartial, we cannot reason together about fundamentals. Wanting to discuss everything is the same as wanting to abolish everything. Spreading new ideas by persuasion is no different from imposing them by armed conquest. Because variety is a good thing, vast inequalities of wealth and status are desirable. Because inherited privilege bestows special opportunities to become wise and public-spirited, the rest of us can safely assume that the privileged are wise and public-spirited. Because some aspects of our identity are not chosen but given at birth, it follows that, as Jefferson put it with scathing sarcasm, "the mass of mankind have . . . been born with saddles on their backs, [and] a favored few booted and spurred, ready to ride them legitimately, by the grace of God." Stripped of Burkean rodomontade, all these arguments are preposterous. Dressed in it, they have bedazzled generations of conservatives, including Levin.

In the book's concluding chapter, Levin argues, again plausibly enough, for the enduring relevance of the Great Debate. Nowadays, he observes, we all believe, as the Founding Fathers did, in liberty, equality, and innovation. But we also believe, as

they did, in order, continuity, and compromise. We believe in
strong government but also in limited government, in expertise
but also in tradition. We are all liberals, he maintains, though
some of us are progressive, Paine-ite liberals and others are conservative, Burkean liberals.

It is a neat, ingenious, even magnanimous argument. Though
he himself is a down-the-line Republican, Levin seems genuinely
concerned to avoid the appearance of partisanship—he goes so
far as to refrain from so much as naming the two major present-
day political parties. He sincerely believes that a better appreciation
of intellectual history will introduce more comity into contemporary American politics.

But just as Levin exaggerates the importance of philosophical
differences in the Great Debate, he exaggerates the importance
of the Great Debate to contemporary politics. Today, at any
rate, the differences between left and right are not chiefly philosophical; they are cruder, more elemental than that. America is a
plutocracy. The degree to which popular preferences influence
government policy is minimal. (Recently a Princeton political
scientist estimated that the opinions of the bottom 70 percent of
the income scale exercise no influence whatever on policy,
and the next 29 percent not much. That sounds about right.)
"Progressive" vs. "conservative" is one way of describing the
difference between the two major parties, but moderate plutocrats vs. extreme plutocrats is far more accurate. What divides
the 1 percent from the 99 percent is not a different brand of
liberalism.

In reality, the Great Debate ended not long after it began. Within
forty years, the Reform Act expanded the suffrage in England.

Within a century, adult male suffrage was universal in Europe. Within two centuries, adult suffrage was universal. As a source of political legitimacy, the noble birth that Burke so reverenced now ranks somewhere below astrology. The principle of one person/one vote (in practice, alas, one dollar or one Euro/one vote) is as widely accepted as the right to choose one's profession or religion or mate. As for prescription, prejudice, inherited status, and the rest of Burke's fancied "British constitution"— gone and good riddance.

Before the Enlightenment—before even Burke's Glorious (not all *that* glorious) Revolution—the democratic truths that Paine and others vindicated against Burke were memorably asserted by the humble against the haughty. In the Putney Debates of 1647, some of Cromwell's soldiers perceived that their betrayal by the country's large landowners was imminent and spoke out, no less eloquently than Burke. Edward Sexby: "There are many thousands of us soldiers that have ventured our lives . . . But it seems now that except a man hath a fixed estate in this kingdom, he hath no right in it. I wonder that we were so much deceived." John Wildman: "It is the end of Parliament to legislate according to the just ends of government, not simply to maintain what is already established. Every person in England hath as clear a right to elect his Representative as the greatest person in England . . . [for] all government is in the free choice of the people." Thomas Rainsborough: "The poorest he that is in England hath a life to live as the greatest he; and therefore truly, I think it's clear that every man that is to live under a Government ought first by his own consent to put himself under that Government; and I do think that the poorest man in England is not at all bound in a strict sense to that

Government that he hath not had a voice to put himself under. . . . I should doubt whether he was an Englishman or no who should doubt of these things."

For my part, I should doubt whether he or she was a liberal who doubted these things.

4

Shipwrecked

D. H. Lawrence

When D. H. Lawrence died in 1930, E. M. Forster, protesting
the generally obtuse and malicious obituary notices, wrote that
he was "the greatest imaginative novelist of his generation"—a
generation that included Proust, Joyce, Kafka, and Mann. Not
many critics nowadays would go that far; still, Lawrence's standing as a major novelist seems secure.

The opposite is true of his reputation as a thinker. Lawrence
wrote a great deal about politics, psychology, sexuality, and religion (most of it collected in the two volumes of *Phoenix: The
Posthumous Papers*). Insofar as his ideas on these subjects have
been considered at all, it has usually been as a shadowy backdrop
to the fiction, no more intrinsically significant than, say, T. S.
Eliot's royalism. Lawrence's portraits of birds, beasts, and flow-
ers, of rural life, of the growth of individual consciousness, and
of the relations between modern men and women—these are
widely acclaimed. But his ideas are just an embarrassment. Bertrand Russell wrote that Lawrence had "developed the whole
philosophy of fascism before the politicians had thought of it."
Kate Millett in *Sexual Politics* labeled him "the most talented and

fervid" of "counterrevolutionary sexual politicians." According to Philip Rahv, "in the political sphere . . . he was a fantast, pure and simple." Susan Sontag dismissed his notions about sexuality as "reactionary" and "marred by class romanticism." And so it goes: praise for Lawrence the artist, but for Lawrence the prophet, contempt or, at best, tactful neglect.

Every critical consensus contains a measure of truth. Lawrence said a great many foolish things, and there is no point in glossing over them. But there is not much point, either, at this late date, in dwelling on them—as though his ideas have, or ever had, some sort of influence or prestige that urgently needs to be countered. Like Nietzsche, whom he resembles in astonishingly many ways, Lawrence tried to diagnose and oppose an entire civilization, his and ours. He was defeated, even routed. But the attempt deserves more sympathetic attention than it has received. Karl Jaspers lauded Kierkegaard and Nietzsche for having "dared to be ship-wrecked": "They are so to speak, representative destinies, sacrifices whose way out of the world leads to experiences for others. . . . Through them we have intimations of something we could never have perceived without such sacrifices, of something that seems essential, which even today we cannot adequately grasp." To many who are ambivalent about modernity, Lawrence also revealed something "we cannot adequately grasp" that none-theless "seems essential"; and if he often made a fool of himself in the process, it was an indispensable, even a heroic, folly.

Lawrence's starting point was the same problem that had con-fronted Kierkegaard and Nietzsche: nihilism, or the "death of God." The modern age, beginning with the Enlightenment, had seemed to promise a complete liberation from traditional dogmas. Previously unquestioned loyalties—religious, political, racial, familial—were eroded by the spread of philosophical materialism and ethical individualism. But since then (to put the intellectual history of the last 200 years into a single sentence) a question has gradually dawned in those countries where modernity has taken root: If the beliefs that formerly made life seems worth living—beliefs about God, political authority, racial uniqueness, and sexual destiny—if these are seen to be illusions, then what *does* make life worth living?

The question is dramatized memorably in John Stuart Mill's *Autobiography*. The young Mill fell into an intense depression because he had no sustaining illusions—or, as he put it, because "the habit of analysis tends to wear away the feelings." It is hard to think of two thinkers more different than Mill and Lawrence, yet this pithy and poignant phrase of Mill's exactly expresses Lawrence's sense of the modern predicament. Like so many nineteenth-century thinkers, Mill had discovered that criticism could liberate but not motivate. There were plenty of traditional dogmas left to criticize in his time, so he kept at criticism and made an honorable career of it. But things were different for Lawrence.

It may be difficult nowadays to appreciate just how enlightened early twentieth-century England was, at least compared with late twentieth-century America. "Bloomsbury" is now a byword for ultra-sophistication; but it's also true that intellectual and moral emancipation were far more widely diffused—the prosperity and stability of the Victorian era had produced an extraordinary cultural flowering. As regards anything that deserves to be called liberation, Ursula Brangwen, Lawrence's most notable heroine, was miles ahead of most contemporary feminists; and the same relation holds between her counterpart, Rupert Birkin, and male feminists today. Both are, like most of Lawrence's protagonists, like Lawrence himself, aiming neither to defy traditional values nor to resurrect them, but rather to imagine a way of life that takes their disappearance for granted.

So much has been written about Lawrence's "neo-primitivism" and "nostalgia" that it seems worth stressing how far in advance he was of most present-day progressives, at least in one respect. He saw all the way to the end of modern emancipation; and though he sometimes cursed it, he never expected, or even hoped, that we could avoid it. All he wanted was that we survive it. One of his most striking statements about the modern dilemma occurs in the unpublished prologue to *Women in Love*:

> But if there be *no* great philosophic idea, if, for the time being, man-kind, instead of going through a period of growth, is going through a corresponding process of decay and decomposition from some old, fulfilled, obsolete idea, then what is the good of educating? Decay and decomposition will take their own way. It is impossible to edu-cate for this end, impossible to teach the world how to die away from its achieved, nullified form. The autumn must take place in every individual soul, as well as in all the people; all must die, individually and socially. Education is a process of striving to a new, unanimous being, a whole organic form. But when winter has set in, when the frosts are strangling the leaves off the trees and the birds are silent knots of darkness, how can there be a unanimous movement towards a whole summer of fluorescence? There can be none of this, only submission to the death of this nature, in the winter that has come upon mankind, and a cherishing of the unknown that is unknown for many a day yet, buds that may not open till a far off season comes, when the season of death has passed away.
>
> And Birkin was just coming to a knowledge of the essential futil-ity of all attempt at social unanimity in constructiveness. In the winter, there can only be unanimity of disintegration . . .

This is only a vast and vague intuition, not a fully worked-out philosophy of history. Clearly, though, it is not a lament for the old order or a call to reconstruct it. And whatever the coming "unknown" may turn out to be, the "old, fulfilled, obsolete idea" that we must, according to Lawrence, "die away" from certainly includes political and sexual subjection.

It also, however, includes—and here is the source of Lawrence's doubtful contemporary reputation—their negation: political and sexual equality, mechanically defined. Lawrence criticized equality as an ideal. But not because he wanted property and power to be distributed unequally. He wanted them abolished or, better, outgrown. For capitalist and patriarchal ideology he had only contempt. For socialist and feminist ideology he had instead fraternal impatience, precisely because they seemed to have no higher end in view than more property and power for their constituencies. The undeniable justice of this demand did not, he believed, make it any less a dead end.

Lawrence's poems and essays are full of furious invective against the dominion of money. "The whole great form of our era will have to go," he declared; and he left no doubt that this meant, among other things, private ownership of the means of production. Yet he could also write: "I know that we had all better hang ourselves at once, than enter on a struggle which shall be a fight for the ownership or non-ownership of property, pure and simple, and nothing more." He meant that a new form of ownership is not necessarily a new form of life, and that to live and work in a mass is the death of individuality, even if the mass is well fed. Although Lawrence has been condemned as an authoritarian for saying such things, I think they are just about what William Blake or William Morris would have said (perhaps a touch less stridently) if confronted with twentieth-century liberal democracy.

The case of feminism is more complicated. Lawrence wrote some staggeringly wrongheaded things on this subject, and some wise things. I suspect that when he contemplated the sexual future, he saw Bloomsbury writ large—which meant, to him, the triumph of androgyny as an ideal. That was deepest anathema, for though Lawrence's lifework is a landmark in the demystification of sex, it is also a monument to the mystery of sex, which must disappear, he thought, from an androgynous, hyper-rationalized world. Rilke—whom no one has ever been foolish enough to label a counterrevolutionary sexual politician—included in his *Letters to a Young Poet* several stirring passages on sexual equality but also this cautionary comment: "The girl and the woman, in their new, their own unfolding, will but in passing be imitators of masculine ways, good and bad, and repeaters of masculine professions. After the uncertainty of such transitions it will become apparent that women were only going through the profusion and the vicissitude of those (often ridiculous) disguises in order to cleanse their own most characteristic nature of the distorting influences of the other sex." Lawrence devoted much passionate writing to elaborating kindred insights. They are complex insights, and cost him a great many trials and some appalling errors. But it was a post-revolutionary, not a pre-revolutionary, world that Lawrence, like Rilke, was trying to envisage.

Just what sort of world Lawrence had in mind is difficult to know. He was a prophet without a program, not only because he died too soon but also because it's hard to be explicit about primal realities. He believed that the universe and the individual soul were pulsing with mysteries, from which men and women were perennially distracted by want or greed or dogma. Income redistribution and affirmative action were necessary preliminaries, to clear away the distractions; but if they became ends in themselves, then the last state of humankind would be worse than the first. He thought that beauty, graceful physical movement, unselfconscious emotional directness, and a sense, even an inarticulate sense, of connection to the cosmos, however defined—to the sun, to the wilderness, to the rhythms of a craft or the rites of a tribe—were organic necessities of a sane human life. He thought that reason was not something fundamental to human identity but rather a phenomenon of the surface: "I conceive a man's body as a kind of flame . . . and the intellect is just the light that is shed on the things around." He thought that every free spirit revered someone or something braver or finer than itself, and that this spontaneous reverence was the basis of any viable social order. "Man has little needs and deeper needs," he wrote; and he complained that the workers' and women's movements of his time spoke chiefly to our little needs and could therefore lead only to universal mediocrity and frustration.

Lawrence did not despise socialism or feminism, but he despaired of them. It is this despair that accounts for his frequent, complementary excesses of bitterness and sentimentality. He had so few comrades, and such urgent intimations of catastrophe. "We have fallen into the mistake of living from our little needs till we have almost lost our deeper needs in a sort of madness." Whether or not you accept Lawrence's conception of our deeper needs, it is hard to deny the madness. "A wave of generosity or a wave of death," he prophesied, shortly before his own death. We know which came to pass.

Like all the other great diagnosticians of nihilism, Lawrence recognized that though the irrational cannot survive, the rational does not suffice. We live, he taught, by mysterious influxes of spirit, of what Blake called "Energy." Irrationalists make superstitions out of these mysteries, rationalists make systems, each in a futile, anxious attempt at mastery. Lawrence wanted us to submit: to give up the characteristic modern forms—possessive individualism, technological messianism, political and sexual *ressentiment*—of humankind's chronic pretense at mastery. But since that sort of submission is more delicate and difficult than self-assertion, he mainly succeeded in provoking misunderstanding or abuse.

Perhaps only other inspired fools can take his measure. In *The Prisoner of Sex*, Norman Mailer paid Lawrence this exquisite and definitive tribute: "What he was asking for had been too hard for him, it is more than hard for us; his life was, yes, a torture, and we draw back in fear, for we would not know how to try to burn by such a light."

5

The Radicalism of Tradition

T. S. Eliot

Simone de Beauvoir wrote of the twentieth-century conservative thinker: "Gloomy or arrogant, he is the man who says no; his real certainties are all negative. He says no to modernity, no to the future, no to the living action of the world; but he knows that the world will prevail over him." That T. S. Eliot at least partly resembled this imaginary portrait he himself acknowledged; as he wrote to a friend in 1921: "Having only contempt for every existing political party, and profound hatred for democracy, I feel the blackest gloom." In daily life, it is true, Eliot was neither gloomy nor arrogant but serene and gracious, generous and humble. At the height of his fame, his courtesy even to the callow and importunate was legendary. Yet however Eliot achieved this extraordinary equableness (if in fact he did—Randall Jarrell speculated that he was, on the contrary, "one of the most subjective and demonic poets who ever lived, the victim and helpless beneficiary of his own inexorable compulsions and obsessions"), he doubtless saw himself as a man whose vocation was to say no, to stand athwart history strenuously wielding negative certainties.

No to what? Why exactly did Eliot loathe modernity and what exactly did he hope to conserve against its advance? In *After Strange Gods* (which remains, notwithstanding the infamous remark about "freethinking Jews," an important statement of Eliot's beliefs), he refers to "the living death of modern material civilization" and declares "Liberalism, Progress, and Modern Civilization" self-evidently contemptible. (The latter, perhaps, was an echo of the mighty conclusion of Pius IX's *Syllabus of Errors*, which condemned the proposition that "the Roman Pontiff can, and ought to, reconcile himself to, and come to terms with, progress, liberalism and modern civilization.") Elsewhere in the same vein Eliot deplores "the immense panorama of futility and anarchy which is contemporary history" and lays it down that "one can assert with some confidence that our period is one of decline." He praised Baudelaire, who, in an age of "programmes, platforms, scientific progress, humanitarianism, and revolutions," of "cheerfulness, optimism, and hopefulness," understood that "what really matters is Sin and Redemption" and perceived that "the possibility of damnation is so immense a relief in a world of electoral reform, plebiscites, sex reform, and dress reform . . . that damnation itself is an immediate form of salvation—of salvation from the ennui of modern life, because it gives some significance to living."

At the root of this harsh condemnation of modernity lay the conviction of sin—Original Sin. Eliot believed that most people have very little intelligence or character. Without firm guidance from those who have more of both, the majority are bound to reason and behave badly. Eliot made this point frequently: sometimes gently, as in the well-known line from "Burnt Norton": "Humankind cannot bear very much reality"; sometimes harshly, as in "The Function of Criticism," where he derided those in whom democratic reformers place their hopes as a rabble who "ride ten in a compartment to a football match at Swansea, listening to the inner voice, which breathes the eternal message of vanity, fear, and lust."

The obtuseness and unruliness of humankind in the mass meant that order, the prime requisite of social health, could only be secured by subordination to authority, both religious and political. "For the great mass of humanity . . . their capacity for *thinking* about the objects of their faith is small"—hence the need for orthodoxy and an authoritative church rather than an illusory Inner Voice. Likewise, "in a healthily stratified society, public affairs would be a responsibility not equally borne"—hence the need for a hereditary governing class. Underlying these social hierarchies is a hierarchy of values. "Liberty is good, but more important is order, and the maintenance of order justifies any means."

Order, long preserved, produces tradition: "all the actions, habits, and customs," from the most significant to the most conventional, that "represent the blood kinship of 'the same people living in the same place.'" Eliot's best-known discussions of tradition are found in his literary essays: "Tradition and the Individual Talent," "The Metaphysical Poets," and others. His poetry was, of course, revolutionary as well as conservative, and his criticism explains this apparent paradox. Artistic originality emerges only after a lengthy assimilation of many traditions. The artist surrenders his individuality, and it is returned to him enriched. The tradition, too, is enriched. "The whole existing order" is "if ever so slightly, altered; and so the relations, proportions, values of each work of art toward the whole are readjusted; and this is conformity between the old and the new. . . . The past [is] altered by the present as much as the present is directed by the past."

A continually altering tradition is not an unchanging magisterium. In politics and religion as well as in poetry, Eliot's conception of tradition is surprisingly dynamic. Our "danger," he wrote, is "to associate tradition with the immovable; to think of it as something hostile to all change; to aim to return to some previous condition which we imagine as having been capable of preservation in perpetuity." On the contrary, "tradition without intelligence is not worth having." We must "use our minds" to discover "what is the best life for us . . . as a particular people in a particular place; what in the past is worth preserving and what should be rejected; and what conditions, within our power to bring about, would foster the society that we desire." This does not sound like Condorcet or Godwin; but neither does it sound much like Burke or de Maistre.

Eliot was too subtle not to recognize (and too honest not to acknowledge) that his more general pronouncements about political philosophy were unsatisfactory. Like all general pronouncements (in my William James-ian view, at least), they reduce to truisms. Continuity is best, except where change is necessary. Much tradition, some innovation. Firm principles, flexibly adapted. His often-cited remark (in praise of Aristotle) that "the only method is to be very intelligent" helps in estimating his own political criticism.

Concerning two matters of large contemporary relevance, Eliot was profoundly, though unsystematically, intelligent. Eliot's political utterances were, for the most part, fragmentary and occasional: occurring in essays, lectures, and the regular "Commentaries" in his great quarterly the *Criterion*. His compliment to Henry James—"he had a mind so fine no idea could violate it"—applied to Eliot as well, for better and worse. He was never doctrinaire; but on the other hand, he was rarely definite. As one commentator observes: "To gesture toward, but not to reveal; to pursue, but not to unravel, this is Eliot's procedure." But although he eschewed programs, there is much matter in his asides.

About economics, he repeatedly professed theoretical incomprehension. But just as often, he professed skepticism that any immutable laws of political economy proved that extremes of wealth and poverty were inevitable or that state action to counter disadvantage must be futile. Disarmingly, he acknowledged:

> I am confirmed in my suspicion that conventional economic practice is all wrong, but I can never understand enough to form any opinion as to whether the particular prescription or nostrum proffered is right. I cannot but believe that there are a few simple ideas at bottom, upon which I and the rest of the unlearned are competent to decide according to our several complexions; but I cannot for the life of me ever get to the bottom.

Nevertheless, "about certain very serious facts no one can dissent." For "the present system does not work properly, and more and more are inclined to believe both that it never did and that it never will."

What were some of these "very serious facts"?

> ... the hypertrophy of Profit into a social ideal, the distinction between the *use* of natural resources and their exploitation, the advantages unfairly accruing to the trader in contrast to the primary producer, the misdirection of the financial machine, the iniquity of usury, and other features of a commercialized society.

Sometimes he wondered whether Western society was "assembled round anything more permanent than a congeries of banks, insurance companies and industries, and had any beliefs more essential than a belief in compound interest and the maintenance of dividends." On one occasion he sounded almost like a communist:

> Certainly there is a sense in which Britain and America are more democratic than [Nazi] Germany; but on the other hand, defenders of the totalitarian system can make out a plausible case for maintaining that what we have is not democracy but financial oligarchy.

Indeed, Eliot was full of surprises on the subject of communism. Try to imagine his drearily predictable acolytes at the present-day *New Criterion* saying something like this:

> I have . . . much sympathy with communists of the type with which I am here concerned [i.e. "those young people who would like to grow up and believe in something"]. I would even say that . . . there are only a small number of people living who have achieved the right *not* to be communists.

Eliot did not think much of most anticommunists, who "abhor extreme socialism for motives in which a very little Christianity is blended with a great deal of self-interest and prejudice." For "no one is any more justified in a general condemnation of the principles of the extreme Left than he is in a general condemnation of those of the extreme Right. The principle of Justice affirmed by the intellectuals of the Left is at least analogous to Christian justice."

In fact, Eliot feared and despised unrestrained capitalism (something you would not gather from Russell Kirk's relentlessly one-dimensional *Eliot and His Age*). He associated himself with those who "object to the dictatorship of finance and the dictatorship of bureaucracy under whatever political name it is assembled." Try to imagine the words "dictatorship of finance" appearing in the *New Criterion* or *Commentary* or even *First Things*. Ditto for Eliot's tart verdict on the Masters of the Universe:

> Unrestrained industrialism, then (with its attendant evils of over-production, excessive "wealth," an irrelevance and lack of relation of production to consumption which it attempts vainly to overcome by the nightmare expedient of "advertisement"), destroys the upper classes first. You cannot make an aristocrat out of a company chairman, though you can make him a peer.

The indictment continues. Capitalism "is imperfectly adapted to every purpose except that of making money; and even for money-making it does not work very well, for its rewards are neither conducive to social justice nor even proportioned to intellectual ability." It "tends to divide the community into classes based upon differences of wealth and to occasion a sense of injustice among the poorer members of society." During World War II he wrote a friend that he was willing to join a "revolution" whose "enemies" would include "popular demagogues and *philosophes*" on the one hand, and on the other "those who want after this war to revert to money hegemony, commercial rivalry between nations, etc."

Even when deploring the consequences of Original Sin, Eliot could not help acknowledging the social scaffolding of moral and cultural questions. He supported censorship of pornography, though not of "books possessing, or even laying claim to, literary merit." But, he went on, "what is more insidious than any censorship is the steady influence which operates silently in any mass society organized for profit, for the depression of standards of art and culture." He was no feminist and posed these scandalously sexist rhetorical questions: "Might one suggest that the kitchen, the children, and the church could be considered to have a claim upon the attention of married women? Or that no normal married woman would prefer to be a wage-earner if she could help it?" But at least he remembered to add: "What is miserable is a system that makes the dual wage necessary."

The incompatibility between untrammeled capitalism and Eliot's conception of the good society went deep. "Stability is obviously necessary," he insisted—indeed it would seem to be the alpha, if not the omega, of any intelligible conservatism. "You are hardly likely to develop tradition, except where the bulk of the population is so well off where it is that it has no incentive or pressure to move about." But without precisely that incentive, the labor market of neoclassical economic theory cannot function. Stable communities or "efficient" labor markets— one must choose.

Eliot was ready to choose. An Anglican committee report he co-authored in the late 1930s called for the "thorough reconstruction of the present economic and political system." Eliot was careful with words, so he probably meant this, bromidic as it sounds. A few years earlier he co-signed a letter to *The Times* arguing that there was enough wealth in the world "to give every individual a certainty of adequate provision," but that "there appears to be lacking some machinery of distribution" to accomplish this. Eliot was a redistributionist.

What kind of "system" did Eliot want? A Christian society, of course—his critique of capitalism strikingly parallels that of *Rerum Novarum*, *Centesimus Annus*, and other papal encyclicals. But like those venerable documents, Eliot's writings, though they could be pointedly negative, were not vividly affirmative. He thought there should be a lot more people living on the land. He thought people should have to spend fewer hours working for a living. He enthusiastically endorsed this description of the goal: a "new type of society, which would give fullest scope both to the individual—thus securing the utmost variety in human affairs— and to the social whole—thus stimulating the rich, collective activities which would surely come to life in a society free to express its invention, its mechanical skill, its sense of the earth in agriculture and crafts, its sense of play." This sounds much more like William Morris than like Margaret Thatcher. But beyond these, he offered virtually no details. He was neither a visionary nor an activist but a critic.

I said above that Eliot had much to teach us about two matters of contemporary relevance. About the first, distributive justice, he wrote much, directly if not programmatically. About the other, he wrote scarcely a word; not surprisingly, since it was hardly visible on the horizon before his death. I'm referring to the steady erosion of inwardness (Eliot would have said "spiritual depth") resulting from the omnipresence of commercial messages (the "nightmare" of "advertisement") and electronic media.

I have no doubt that Eliot would have reacted strongly and negatively to this development, so discordant with his sensibility and practice. As described in his critical essays, the gradual sur- render of the artist's personality to tradition, which is at the same time the mastery and (however modest) transformation of the tradition, resembles the attitude of the narrator of the *Four Quartets* toward Being and history. In both cases, the prescribed motions of the spirit are inward and downward, the virtues prescribed are humility, gravity, receptiveness. The refrain of "Burnt Norton" has become a meme: "the still point of the turning world."

This capacity—as a valiant minority of contemporary critics keep insisting—is what advertising and the cyberworld are, with fearful rapidity, extinguishing. It simply cannot withstand the immediacy, volume, and near-instantaneous succession of stimuli to which all of us outside a monastery are incessantly subjected. The spirit has its rhythm and metabolism; it cannot survive in just any environment. Or, if you prefer: the brain is plastic and may be drastically reshaped. Our world is flat, as we have been (loudly) told. Will the same processes that flattened it also flatten our souls?

The most moving passage I have encountered in all of Eliot's writings occurs in a letter to his dear friend Paul Elmer More:

> To me, religion has brought at least the perception of something above morals, and therefore extremely terrifying; it has brought me not happiness, but the sense of something above happiness and therefore more terrifying than ordinary pain and misery; the very dark night and the desert. To me, the phrase "to be damned for the glory of God" is sense and not paradox; I had far rather walk, as I do, in daily terror of eternity, than feel that this was only a children's game in which all the contestants would get equally worthless prizes in the end. . . . And I don't know whether this is to be labeled "Classicism" or "Romanticism"; I only think that I have hold of the tip of the tail of something quite real, more real than morals, or than sweetness and light and culture.

This revelation has not been vouchsafed to me, but I can recognize here a description of something supremely valuable. I would fight, as I believe Eliot would, to preserve the conditions of its possibility against the encroachment of the electronic hive.

6

Agonizing

Isaiah Berlin

Securus judicat orbis terrarum, says a maxim of Roman law; which means, loosely translated: the *New York Times*, the *New York Review of Books*, and the *Times Literary Supplement* can't all be wrong. Isaiah Berlin is a certified sage, an object of near-universal veneration. "Few writers and intellectuals command the awe and admiration accorded to Sir Isaiah Berlin, and with good reason," declared the *Economist* recently. "There is, arguably, no more admired thinker in the English-speaking world," began the *Boston Globe*'s review of his latest book, *The Crooked Timber of Humanity*. Berlin's career has been a rapid-fire sequence of academic honors: fellow of two Oxford colleges; Chichele professor of social and political theory at Oxford; president of Wolfson College, Oxford; president of the British Academy; the Erasmus, Lippincott, Agnelli, and Jerusalem prizes; and a knighthood for academic distinction.

The Crooked Timber of Humanity is a twilight volume: it revisits longstanding preoccupations and restates long-held positions, not in order to revise or synthesize but to clarify or embellish. As usual, Berlin's essays blend the history of ideas, the philosophy of history, political theory, and moral philosophy. His approach is relaxed and untheoretical; his prose style is weighty and graceful.

The unity of Berlin's thought is not far to seek: he has devoted his career to telling a single story. If the master narrative of modernity recounts the gradual progress of emancipation, the alternate or antinarrative describes the costs of that progress: the blindness of enlightenment and the cruelties of emancipation. No sooner was the autonomy of reason secured than the adequacy of reason began to be questioned. Kant's and Hegel's challenges to Enlightenment rationalism are well known; but Berlin has brought into view, more than any other historian, the full vigor and variety of the anti-Enlightenment tradition. In previous books he showed deep similarities among such marginal and apparently disparate figures as Vico, Herder, Sorel, the nineteenth-century Russian Slavophiles, and Tolstoy as a moral and political thinker. The longest and most substantial essay in *The Crooked Timber of Humanity* adds Joseph de Maistre to this number, though with due allowance for de Maistre's distorting extremisms.

What these thinkers have in common is epistemological and moral pluralism: a conviction that the aims of scientific method— predictiveness, universal applicability, logical simplicity, ontological parsimony—cannot be imported into the study of psychology, history, or politics. Individuals and cultures are radically diverse, ineffably deep, infinitely complex. Only imaginative identification, a renunciation of the urge to theoretical mastery, and a yielding to the sheer particularity of things can produce genuine understanding.

Even more important than this interpretive pluralism is ethical pluralism. Moral no less than aesthetic values are radically diverse. Both within and among human beings, conflict, or at any rate tension, is inevitable. Compromise is possible, but not perfect harmony. This "banality" (his own characterization) is Berlin's constant, almost obsessive, theme. An astonishingly high proportion of his essays, whatever their subject, employ something like the following formula. Enlightenment political thought is said to rest on three premises: first, that every meaningful, properly formulated question has a single correct answer; second, there exists a reliable method for discovering this answer; third, all these answers must be compatible, since truths cannot contradict one another. It follows from these premises that one (and only one) perfectly rational and harmonious way of life is discoverable. This conclusion is deemed to justify unlimited coercion by those who have attained to this discovery against those who have not. And so the tendency of every utopian movement is totalitarian: when perfectibility is the assumption, coercion must be the result.

Of course Berlin's pluralism has more flesh on its bones than this. In his finest essays—on Vico, Hamann, and Herder in *Against the Current*, on Herzen, Belinsky, Turgenev, and Tolstoy in *Russian Thinkers*, and on de Maistre in *The Crooked Timber of Humanity*—he depicts the rebellion against Enlightenment rationalism through marvelously vivid and dramatic intellectual portraits. But the actual arguments, even in his celebrated "Two Concepts of Liberty" and "Historical Inevitability," are thin.

By his own astute and engaging admission, Berlin is not an original thinker. He is, rather, a supremely effective exponent of the conventional moral and political wisdom. This is not entirely, or even in the main, a disparaging judgment. The conventional wisdom is genuine wisdom. Revolutionary, egalitarian, and utopian rhetoric has been put to deplorable uses in the twentieth century; now and for a long time we would do well to be suspicious of it. To have articulated this suspicion comprehensively and, so to speak, genealogically, with large resources of erudition and eloquence, as Berlin has done, is an important service. So is his lifelong admonition that (to quote his approving summary of Montesquieu's position) "durable and beneficial social structures are seldom simple, that large areas of political behavior always remain very complex and obscure, that a radical change of one part of it might easily lead to unpredictable effects in others, and that the end might be worse than the beginning."

This last, however, is a sentence that revolutionary democrats like Michael Harrington or Rosa Luxemburg might have written—it is, at least, a sentiment they would have endorsed. The conventional wisdom had nothing to teach either of them about respect for individual liberty, while they had a great deal of unconventional wisdom to teach Berlin and the civilization that has lionized him. In every society, some truths are convenient and some are not. To those who expound convenient truths (especially with Berlin's incomparable verve) much is given and much forgiven.

Berlin's frequent animadversions on Marx and Marxism are, unfortunately, a contribution to conventional unwisdom. The notion that Marx is responsible for the Gulag is, of course, a terrible simplification. Berlin himself has warned more than once against it. Nonetheless, it's hard to see what other sense to give comments like this:

> [For Hegel and Marx,] a large number of human beings must be sacrificed and annihilated if the ideal is to triumph. . . . The path may lead to a terrestrial paradise, but it is strewn with the corpses of the enemy, for whom no tear must be shed, since right and wrong, good

and bad, success and failure, wisdom and folly, are all in the end determined by the objective ends of history, which has condemned half mankind—unhistorical nations, members of obsolete classes, inferior races—to what Proudhon called "liquidation" and Trotsky . . . described as the rubbish heap of history.

(*The Crooked Timber of Humanity*, p. 198)

Or this:

Marx—and it is part of his attraction to those of a similar emotional cast—identifies himself exultantly . . . with the great force which in its very destructiveness is creative, and is greeted with bewilderment and horror only by those whose values are hopelessly subjective, who listen to their consciences, their feelings, or to what their nurses and teachers tell them. . . . When history takes her revenge . . . the mean, pathetic, ludicrous, stifling human anthills will be justly pulverized. . . . Whatever is on the side of victorious reason is just and wise; whatever is on the other side . . . is doomed to destruction.

(*Four Essays on Liberty*, p. 62)

At one remove from Marx himself, "Marxist sociology" supposedly teaches:

It is idle for the progressives to try to save their reactionary brothers from defeat: the doomed men cannot hear them, and their destruction is certain. All men will not be saved: the proletariat, justly intent upon its own salvation, had best ignore the fate of their oppressors; even if they wish to return good for evil, they cannot save their enemies from "liquidation." They are "expendable"— their destruction can be neither averted nor regretted by a rational being, for it is the price that mankind must pay for the progress of reason itself: the road to the gates of Paradise is necessarily strewn with corpses.

(*The Crooked Timber of Humanity*, pp. 178–9)

All this is fine prose, but as an account of Marx's historical materialism, it is tosh. Marx doubted—correctly, as the bloody history of the European and American labor movements demonstrates—that capitalists would give up without a fight or that they would (even by their own standards) fight fair. That's about all his infamous revolutionary amorality amounted to. To talk darkly of liquidating half mankind or pulverizing human anthills—that is, to assimilate Marxism to Stalinism—is mere mischief.

I do not mean that Berlin tailored his rhetoric to flatter the prejudices of his Establishment audience, or anything of that sort. On the contrary, he seems to me all unselfconscious integrity, incapable of altering an adjective, much less an opinion, for the sake of the Erasmus, Lippincott, Agnelli, and Jerusalem prizes altogether. He obviously believes every word he has written about Marx, some of which are just and penetrating. But if Berlin didn't believe and hadn't frequently and eloquently expounded these damaging half-truths about Marx during the central decades of the Cold War, I doubt he would have been the object of so much institutional affection and gratitude.

The fervent gratitude he inspires is, in a way, the most remarkable thing about Berlin's career. "People are pleased," observes Russell Jacoby (in "Isaiah Berlin: With the Current," *Salmagundi*, Winter 1982), "to find a man of learning who does not accuse them or their society of unspeakable crimes. . . . Berlin reassures his readers in a prose studded with the great names of

Western culture that complexity is inevitable and solutions impossible; the threat is from the utopians and artists who imagine a better world."

The critique of utopia is certainly the nerve of Berlin's writings. Like his critique of Marx, it is surprisingly simplistic for so renowned an evangelist of complexity. Sometimes it is not even minimally informative. Berlin frequently tries to make mere repetition or enumeration do the work of detailed analysis. By and large, his strictures are pronounced rather than proved.

Take this passage from "The Decline of Utopian Ideas in the West":

> Broadly speaking, western Utopias tend to contain the same elements: a society lives in a state of pure harmony, in which all its members live in peace, love one another, are free from physical danger, from want of any kind, from insecurity, from degrading work, from envy, from frustration, experience no injustice or violence, live in perpetual, even light, in a temperate climate, in the midst of infinitely fruitful, generous nature. The main characteristic of most, perhaps all, Utopias is the fact that they are static. Nothing in them alters, for they have reached perfection: there is no need for novelty or change; no one can wish to alter a condition in which all natural human wishes are fulfilled.
>
> (*The Crooked Timber of Humanity*, p. 20)

In short, the Garden of Eden minus original sin. But consider what are perhaps the five most influential utopian fictions in English: More's *Utopia*, Bellamy's *Looking Backward*, Morris's *News from Nowhere*, Wells's *A Modern Utopia*, and Ernest Callenbach's *Ecotopia*. No characteristic from Berlin's list applies categorically to all five; or indeed, arguably, to any of them. All members of all these utopian societies are liable to some danger, want, frustration, envy, violence, insecurity, and tedious work, however insignificant compared with present-day levels. They are cooperative, egalitarian, technically advanced commonwealths, not idylls of static perfection. *Pace* Berlin, no "metaphysical" theories of human nature are required to accept them (with whatever reservations) as inspiring models or programs, only a lively and discriminating moral imagination.

Similarly, in "The Apotheosis of the Romantic Will" Berlin declares that

> thinkers from Bacon to the present have been inspired by the certainty that there must exist a total solution: that in the fullness of time . . . the reign of irrationality, injustice and misery will end; man will be liberated, and will no longer be the plaything of forces beyond his control—savage nature, or the consequences of his own ignorance or folly or vice; that this springtime in human affairs will come once the obstacles, natural and human, are overcome, and then at last men will cease to fight each other, unite their powers, and cooperate to adapt nature to their needs . . .
>
> (*The Crooked Timber of Humanity*, p. 212)

This Berlin regards as an absurdity, a Sorelian "great myth" of perfect harmony through a scientifically-arrived-at "total solution"—the sinister implications of that last phrase are almost certainly intended. To me, on the contrary, it seems an entirely reasonable and humane goal (though patronizingly and tendentiously formulated by Berlin, to be sure)—a goal that implies neither psychological nor intellectual nor moral uniformity, nor any perfect harmony, fortuitous or coerced.

A final example, from the same essay. According to Berlin, the Romantics have done well for humanity by dealing a "fatal blow" to the notion that

> rational organization can bring about the perfect union of such values and counter-values as individual liberty and social equality, spontaneous self-expression and organized, socially directed efficiency, perfect knowledge and perfect happiness, the claims of personal life and the claims of parties, classes, nations, the public interest. If some ends recognized as fully human are at the same time ultimate and mutually incompatible, then the idea of a golden age, a perfect society compounded of a synthesis of all the correct solutions to all the central problems, is shown to be incoherent in principle.
>
> (*The Crooked Timber of Humanity*, p. 237)

If this passage is purged of exaggeration and caricature—or even if one merely removes the words "perfect" and "golden age"— then the incoherence vanishes, or at least requires a good deal more demonstration than Berlin provides, either in this essay or (despite his reputation as *the* theorist of political pluralism) anywhere else.

Would any of those to whom the above beliefs are ascribed—that is, the "many who put their trust in rational and scientific methods designed to effect a fundamental social transformation"—acknowledge them in the form here proffered by Berlin? I doubt it. Again and again—almost without exception, in fact—Berlin trivializes and dismisses utopianism by means of such phrases as "earthly paradise," "the perfect life," "a perfect and harmonious society, wholly free from conflict or injustice or oppression," "a static perfection in which human nature is finally and fully realized, and all is still and immutable and eternal." But has any utopian writer, no matter how deluded, ever really promised perfection? Any influential utopian writer? Most influential utopian writers? Even if the answer to that last question were "Yes" (and if it is not, then Berlin's central claim about utopianism is untrue), the important issue raised by the utopian tradition would not be "Is humankind perfectible?" but "How perfectible is it?" How far can we go? And why can't we even make a start?

Notwithstanding his famously varied interests and extraordinary range, Berlin has never found the occasion to raise, much less come to terms with, these urgent and obvious questions. He has instead devoted himself to addressing continual reminders about the unattainability of perfect harmony to a civilization that cannot rouse itself to legislate a decently progressive income tax or do more than gesture fitfully at homelessness, global hunger, and a score of other evils for which a doubtless imperfect posterity will doubtless curse and despise us. Berlin will not, I'm afraid, win the Scialabba Prize.

He will survive that disappointment; for all his frequent and graceful self-deprecation, he evidently enjoys his own good opinion, along with everyone else's. Near the end of his splendid essay on Turgenev is a passage of what is unmistakably self-description:

> the small, hesitant, not always very brave band of men who occupy a position somewhere to the left of center, and are morally repelled both by the hard faces to their right and the hysteria and mindless violence and demagoguery on their left. Like the men of the [18]40s, for whom Turgenev spoke, they are at once horrified and fascinated. They are shocked by the violent irrationalism of the dervishes on the

left, yet they are not prepared to reject wholesale the position of those who claim to represent the young and the disinherited, the indignant champions of the poor and the socially deprived or repressed. This is the notoriously unsatisfactory, at times agonizing, position of the modern heirs of the liberal tradition.

(*Russian Thinkers*, p. 301)

This is a perfectly honorable position, but it is not, as far as I can see, an agonizing one. It seems, in fact, quite a comfortable one. Turgenev, it is true, was not comfortable. But then, he tried long and hard to find common ground with the "indignant champions of the poor," rather than merely informing them that not much, alas, could be done. Berlin is naturally in favor of whatever *can* be done; but what in particular that might be, and why not more, never seems to be his immediate concern. "The concrete situation is almost everything," he advises, concluding an essay titled "The Pursuit of the Ideal." The concrete situation is just what Berlin has rarely had a word to say about.

Forty years ago Irving Howe wrote: "But if the ideal of socialism is now to be seen as problematic, the problem of socialism remains an abiding ideal. I would say that it is the best problem to which a political intellectual can attach himself." So it was, and still is. And Berlin still hasn't.

7

Still Enlightening after All These Years

Leo Strauss and Eric Voegelin

Most Americans dislike neoliberalism: the technocratic, managerial ethos of the Democratic Party since the early 1990s. They believe, rightly, that it exists to administer the decline of the post–World War II, New Deal–mediated industrial order and to ratify the extinction of an older, producerist way of life. Neoliberal economics plus consumerism, the culture of celebrity, and rights-based identity politics is what secular modernity has come to mean to most Americans, and most of them reject it, or at any rate are deeply uneasy about it, whether articulately or not. Those on the left who wish to redeem and vindicate modernity have a great deal of distinguishing and discriminating to do in the years ahead; and they will face competition from conservatives, who have their own reckonings with modernity to proffer.

Of course no one wants—or at any rate will admit wanting—to roll back modernity altogether. Reactionaries get toothaches and are as grateful for modern dentistry as the rest of us. They also have daughters, to whose professional ambitions and achievements they are by no means indifferent. And whether they are of the 1 percent or the 99 percent, most of them understand that capital has no homeland, that nation-states are no match for financial markets, and that those markets do not take the slightest notice of an investor's race, color, or creed, the kink of his hair, or the slant of her eyes. All that is solid has long since melted into air. Nationalism and religion remain excellent ways of motivating us to kill, but they are no longer of much use in showing us how to live.

The libertarian right wastes no tears on religion or nationalism. They are entirely—in fact, exclusively—modern; they have jettisoned all such premodern baggage as charity, loyalty, humility, and self-sacrifice. By and large, they think that pushpin is as good as poetry and Facebook is as good as Tolstoy. Whatever satisfies your utility function.

Still, however perversely, libertarians at least think. The commissars of the Republican Party since 1980 have not allowed an idea into their heads, individually or collectively. Their sole principle is service to the rich; their sole function to be, in Thomas Frank's apt phrase, a "wrecking crew," or as wrecker-in-chief Grover Norquist sniggered, to drown the government in a bathtub. They can scarcely appreciate George Will, much less Charles Krauthammer, who, though reduced by long immersion in the sound-bite culture of television and the opinion pages to a sequence of irritable mental gestures, is nonetheless an intellectual. Even Bill O'Reilly is probably too highbrow for Republican politicians—he writes books, after all, or at any rate puts his name to them. The Democrats, as Frank shows in his latest book, *Listen, Liberal*, are the party of the 2 through 10 percent—the professional class, to whom ideas do matter, though far less than income and status.

It is no use, then, expecting philosophy to shed much light on contemporary American politics. But perhaps, conversely, political history can help adjudicate some philosophical disputes. One such venerable yet evergreen debate centers on the Enlightenment. Has the Enlightenment been a success or a failure—or better, how much of each and in what respects? How much moral progress has humankind made, and how much more can we hope for? How far can we rely on reason, and how much room must we make for tradition, authority, and faith? Two new books by conservatives—Columbia intellectual historian Mark Lilla and Yale political philosopher Steven Smith—examine some well-known (in Smith's case) and little-known (in Lilla's) answers.

The Shipwrecked Mind: On Political Reaction (New York Review Books), like Lilla's 2001 book *The Reckless Mind: Intellectuals in Politics*, is a collection of occasional essays on related themes. The earlier book pondered "tyrannophilia," the regrettable tendency of both left-wing and right-wing intellectuals to lose their bearings and end up defending political violence and oppression. This is a subject of inexhaustible interest to centrist liberals from Isaiah Berlin and Raymond Aron to Michael Ignatieff and Leon Wieseltier, who do not always convey the impression that they fully understand why anyone would become a left-winger or a right-winger or anything but a sensible centrist liberal.

Lilla was far from smug or heavy-handed in *The Reckless Mind*, but he did occasionally overstress the present danger of tyrannophilia and the urgency of responsible moderation. He justifies these emphases in the book's preface, where he laments that "so many admirers of these thinkers [i.e., Heidegger, Schmitt, Benjamin, Foucault, and Derrida] continue to ignore or justify their political recklessness." But do they? The admirers of Heidegger and Schmitt have generally been forthcoming about those authors' obvious and undeniable political recklessness. Some of Foucault's European admirers may have taken seriously his brief infatuations with Maoism and the Iranian Revolution, but not many, and even fewer Americans. And there has not been a Marxist-Leninist above thirty years old in the United States for at least half a century—or if there has, she hasn't published anything. Meanwhile, predatory global capitalism has rolled on, grinding the faces of the poor and destroying the planet, unhampered, indeed virtually unnoticed, by centrist liberals. Lilla at least has the grace to acknowledge, in a footnote to the Afterword in this year's reissue of *The Reckless Mind*, "the countless cases of intellectuals whose political commitments did not pervert their thinking." Perhaps he will join these committed intellectuals before earth's Gini coefficient reaches 1 and Morningside Heights is underwater.

The fauna of *The Shipwrecked Mind* are more exotic than those of *The Restless Mind* and harder to interest us in, though Lilla is a skillful expositor and a graceful writer. Who is "the reactionary," he asks, "this last remaining 'other' consigned to the margins of respectable inquiry"? Intriguingly, he replies: "Reactionaries are not conservatives. That is the first thing to be understood about them." Conservatives like Burke and Tocqueville are satisfied with the status quo, not merely because they are well off in it but because they see the virtue in it and prize stability over an unattainable ideal. Reactionaries are anything but satisfied:

> They are, in their way, just as radical as revolutionaries and just as firmly in the grip of historical imaginings. Millennial expectations of a redemptive new social order and rejuvenated human beings inspire the revolutionary; apocalyptic fears of entering a new dark age haunt

the reactionary. . . . Where others see the river of time flowing as it always has, the reactionary sees the debris of paradise drifting past his eyes. He is time's exile. The revolutionary sees the radiant future invisible to others, and it electrifies him. The reactionary, immune to modern lies, sees the past in all its splendor, and he too is electrified. . . . The militancy of his nostalgia is what makes the reactionary a distinctly modern figure, not a traditional one.

Lilla's portrait of the reactionary as a revolutionary with the polarities reversed is persuasive and illuminating, though it is marred by a spasm of reflexive centrism. He notes the descent from Oswald Spengler of a declinist literature on the American and European right, then adds that nowadays declinism "can also be found on the fringe left, where apocalyptic deep ecologists, antiglobalists, and antigrowth activists have joined the ranks of twenty-first-century reactionaries." This is a false equivalence, or at least two-thirds false. Antiglobalization and antigrowth activists yearn for progress as fervently as Thomas Friedman or Lilla himself but have the wit to recognize that whatever may be the ultimate result of unrestricted capital mobility and unlimited fossil fuel exploitation, it will most certainly not be progress, and may indeed be "apocalyptic." Nostalgia has nothing to do with it.

The first of Lilla's subjects is Franz Rosenzweig, born in 1886 and dead of ALS only forty-three years later. Rosenzweig shared the reaction among early twentieth-century German-speaking philosophers against their Hegelian legacy. Most of them gravitated toward neo-Kantian rationalism or the anti-rationalism of Kierkegaard and Nietzsche. Rosenzweig, spurred by a mystical experience during a Yom Kippur service, turned toward the burgeoning Jewish studies movement. Though never theologically orthodox, he saw in sacred history, both Jewish and Christian, a refuge from and remedy for the spiritual homelessness that afflicted so many cultivated Europeans and Americans in those years. Had he lived, he might have become one of the century's great religious existentialists. But his involved style and his resolute unworldliness limited his influence. Lilla certainly makes him sound interesting but cannot make him sound relevant.

Lilla's next two subjects, Eric Voegelin and Leo Strauss, were far more influential. Both were German refugees, their attention riveted by the extremism and violence that convulsed Central Europe and Russia between the world wars. Both devised esoteric antimodern philosophical systems that found much favor in Cold War America, though in both cases their intellectual seriousness eventually undermined their popularity.

Voegelin naturally blamed the Enlightenment for subverting Western civilization, but he traced the origins of Western decline much further back. The first, fateful step toward the collapse of order was Christianity's distinction between divine and secular authority, the City of God and the City of Man. Until then, humankind had been ruled by god-kings; as a result, everyday life was permeated by, and structurally dependent on, the transcendent, which anchored the individual and society.

Voegelin was best known for his claim that the key to understanding Western history is Gnosticism. An ancient half-Christian, half-pagan heresy, Gnosticism held that the visible world is corrupt, the work of an evil spirit, but might be redeemed by those endowed by a higher, hidden divinity with secret knowledge (gnosis). In Voegelin's view, this was the archetype of millenarian ideologies, in which an elite claiming special inspiration promises to lead the masses to a new and better world.

Strauss too believed that political order required divine sanction, though unlike Voegelin, he had no vestige of belief in the divine. Strauss was a political and religious skeptic but he was convinced that skepticism was bad for non-philosophers—that is, virtually everyone. T. S. Eliot wrote that "human kind/ Cannot bear very much reality"; Nietzsche thought that only supermen could live without "metaphysical comfort." Strauss agreed with them and drew a radical political conclusion: philosophers (actually, since few people pay attention to philosophers nowadays, one should probably say "intellectuals") ought to protect ordinary people from unbearable truths by shoring up whatever myths their society lives by. Of course, different societies may have irreconcilable myths, in which case war is unavoidable. But better war than chaos or anomie.

Better for whom? Not necessarily for ordinary people— Strauss seems to have cared very little about ordinary people. But definitely better for intellectuals, who require to be subsidized (for their useful myth-making) and then left alone to "converse." Lilla describes all this rather more benignly:

> Strauss held [that] all societies require an authoritative account of
> ultimate matters—morality and mortality, essentially—if they are to
> legitimate their political institutions and educate citizens. Theology
> has traditionally done that by convincing people to obey the laws
> because they are sacred. The philosophical alternative to this obedi-
> ence was Socrates's life of perpetual questioning beholden to no
> theological or political authority. For Strauss this tension between
> [philosophy and religion] was necessary and in any case inevitable
> in human society. Without authoritative assumptions regarding

morality, which religion can provide, no society can hold itself together. Yet without freedom from authority, philosophers cannot pursue truth wherever it might lead them.

. . . The philosopher and the city each have something to teach the other. Philosophers can serve as gadflies to the city, calling it to account in the name of truth and justice; and the city reminds philosophers that they live in a world that can never be fully rationalized, with ordinary people who cling to their beliefs and need assurance. The wisest philosophers, in Strauss's estimation, were those who understood that they must be political philosophers, thinking about the common good. But they must also be politic philosophers, aware of the risks they take in challenging false certainties.

This is a good deal too charitable. False certainties, Strauss thought, were indispensable: ordinary people must accept them, since they must have some comforting beliefs to insulate them from the harsh truths that would drive them to despair and disorder; and philosophers must propagate them, since they must rely on benighted ordinary people to support a stable and orderly world, safe for philosophizing. A properly functioning false certainty is the last thing a Straussian political philosopher would want to challenge.

The remainder of *The Shipwrecked Mind* touches briefly on a few widely assorted and (apparently) justly obscure thinkers. First is the mid-twentieth-century theologian Jacob Taubes, an admirer of Carl Schmitt and Walter Benjamin, who declared Saint Paul an apostle from the Jews to the rest of humanity and the first and perhaps greatest revolutionary. Another admirer of Saint Paul is the contemporary philosopher of "the event," Alain Badiou, who considers Mao the greatest of all revolutionaries— readers can profitably skip this chapter. Also included are two essays Lilla wrote while living in Paris during and after the *Charlie Hebdo* murders. The essays take two books by "new reactionaries," Eric Zemmour's right-wing jeremiad *Le Suicide français* and Michel Houellebecq's novel *Soumission,* as starting points for reflections on the appearance of a troubling strain of cultural despair.

Introducing readers to obscure and difficult authors is hard and valuable work. Here and in *The Reckless Mind,* Lilla has done it well and deserves our thanks. Still, although he is not strictly obliged to indicate the degree of his agreement or disagreement with his subjects' opinions, I think he might have seen fit to take exception to some of their more outlandish ones. *The Political Religions* contains, he tells us, "the germ of all Voegelin's major works"; the book's "basic theme" is that "the fantasy of creating a world without religion, a political order from which the divine was banned, led necessarily to the creation of grotesque secular deities like Hitler, Stalin, and Mussolini. . . . When you abandon the Lord, it is only a matter of time before you start worshiping a Fuhrer." It is Voegelin's assertion that seems grotesque to me, a crass libel on the Enlightenment. Historically, the correlation between religious skepticism and democracy is strong, as is the correlation between dogmatic religion and authoritarianism. The nearest contemporary approximation to "a world without religion" is, after all, Scandinavia, where the divine is not exactly banned.

Likewise, historians may be allowed to exaggerate their subjects' continuing relevance—but only up to a point. As evidence that "we have much to learn from Voegelin's grand narratives," Lilla urges that "those concerned with the revival of political messianism in our time would do well to consider his searching reflections on gnosticism." What revival of political messianism?

If messianism is a vision of radical social transformation, it is notable by its absence from today's world. The Chinese are busy getting and spending under the benevolent supervision of the Communist Party. The Indian masses yearn for air conditioners and washing machines. In Russia, Putin is liquidating his barons and enlisting Orthodoxy in a revival of Tsarism. Europe is under the thumb of central bankers and their civil servants. Africa is torn by ethnic and religious violence. Latin America is tending its wounds after decades of American-backed dictatorships. And US politics, pre- and post-Trump, is completely dominated by two parties distinguished only by the degree of their fealty to the plutocracy. Right-wing populism dreams of returning to the day before yesterday, not of transforming anything. But embattled centrism must have something to be embattled about; there must always be dangerous radicals inciting restive masses to imminent apocalypse.

Again, Lilla seems to agree (it's hard to tell) that "the assumption behind [the Enlightenment] was that the world could be reformed on the basis of reason and empirical inquiry. And that assumption, on Strauss's reading of modern history, was wrong. All the [Enlightenment] managed to do was distort philosophy's mission, leaving it and the world worse off." It is a peculiar reading of modern history according to which either the world has not been reformed (notwithstanding the abolition of slavery, religious toleration, universal suffrage, child labor laws, the emancipation of women) or reason and empirical inquiry do not deserve most of the credit. That the Enlightenment "left the world worse off" is either a deep truth or shallow nonsense, but in any case requires a great deal more in the way of argument than Lilla (or Strauss, for that matter) provides.

Steven Smith, a Straussian, undertakes to provide it, or some of it. *Modernity and Its Discontents: Making and Unmaking the Bourgeois from Machiavelli to Bellow* (Yale University Press) is an ambitious survey of the Enlightenment's precursors (Machiavelli, Descartes, Hobbes, Spinoza), interpreters (Kant, Hegel), and critics (Rousseau, Tocqueville, Nietzsche, Schmitt, Berlin, Strauss), with side trips into Franklin's *Autobiography*, Flaubert's *Madame Bovary*, Lampedusa's *The Leopard*, and Bellow's *Mr. Sammler's Planet*. Smith is not as cogent an analyst or as fine a stylist as Lilla, but he is an engaging and good-natured, if occasionally prolix, guide to this vast intellectual territory.

Gallantly, Smith begins by putting the Enlightenment in the best possible light, defining it as "the desire for autonomy and self-direction, the aspiration to live independently of the dictates of habit, custom, and tradition, to accept moral institutions and practices only if they pass the bar of one's critical intellect, and to accept ultimate responsibility for one's life and actions." Politically, it entails "individual rights, government by consent, and the sovereignty of the people." What's not to like about any of that?

Some of the Enlightenment's critics object that human nature is simply not up to it: we are too belligerent or too greedy or too superstitious ever to put war, poverty, and intolerance behind us. Dostoevsky's Grand Inquisitor makes this case memorably. Burke's horror at the thought of any individual's "private stock of reason" challenging the verdict of tradition and Carl Schmitt's insistence that our political loyalties have nothing to do with reason but instead seize us unaccountably and irresistibly are other influential examples of this argument, which we get in vulgar form every day from politicians who remind us that "there is no such thing as society," and certainly no such thing as a free lunch. Other critics think that the universal reign of reason, peace, and justice is, alas, all too probable and will cause any person of spirit to die of boredom (Nietzsche) or at least not find sufficient scope for heroism and grand ambitions (Tocqueville). Smith sums up the "Counter-Enlightenment" very handily:

> For each movement of modernity, there has developed a comprehensive counternarrative. The idea that modernity is associated with the secularization of our institutions has given rise to fears about the rationalization and "disenchantment" of the world; the rise of a market economy and the commercial republic gave way in turn to an antibourgeois mentality that would find expression in politics, literature, art, and philosophy; the idea of modernity as the locus of individuality and free subjectivity gave rise to concerns about homelessness, anomie, and alienation; the achievements of democracy went together with fears about conformism, the loss of independence, and the rise of the "lonely crowd"; even the idea of progress itself gave rise to a counterthesis about the role of decadence, degeneration, and decline.

Smith's own views are—as is often the case with Straussians—hard to pin down. He would not dream of doubting the "immense benefits" brought about by the Enlightenment's "humanitarian project," its belief that "science and the application of scientific method could provide answers to the most pressing problems—war, poverty, ignorance, and disease—facing humankind." Regrettably, however, progress has given birth to "progressivism," an "almost eschatological faith" in humankind's irresistible advance toward a glorious future. Certain that "all the important problems facing civilization are technical in nature," progressives place entire confidence in experts and see no need for "prudence and practical judgment." The social sciences have furnished the tools with which a "new elite" has created an "administrative state," threatening "an end to politics." Perhaps we must entertain the possibility—familiar to the ancients but supposedly anathema to the Enlightenment—that "our seemingly most intractable problems lie beyond our rational capabilities."

This is a fine muddle. To begin with, reason was only half the Enlightenment's program. The other, equally important half was freedom. The intimate, unbreakable connection between the two halves was this principle: every form of authority must be justified to those over whom it is exercised. The motto of the Enlightenment was: "Question authority." That was also the motto of the New Left, which Straussians rate a little below bubonic plague among history's great misfortunes. Allan Bloom was the most hysterical of them in this respect, but all good Straussians loathe the sixties. Questioning authority is something ordinary people— the poor shlubs—should be strongly discouraged from doing.

Of course radical democrats are no friends of the "administrative state." But here is how Smith frames his objection: "the classical idea of the statesman (or what remains of it) gave [way] to the new idea of the expert or policy specialist as the hero of the new age." The Straussians' idea of a heroic statesman is Henry Kissinger, quite possibly the most callous, dishonest, self-serving public figure in American history. To be sure, the administrative state must be made democratically accountable. (At present it is wholly accountable, but only to people with significant power over investment and employment, which are a capitalist society's oxygen supply.) But in that arduous and long-term effort, Straussians will be no help.

There have always been free spirits and critical thinkers, but a critical mass was achieved in the seventeenth and eighteenth centuries, when humankind finally "emerged from its self-imposed dependence" (Kant). That beautiful and decisive episode (chronicled for all the ages in Peter Gay's and Jonathan Israel's masterly, epic histories) is vulnerable, like all other human achievements, to erosion and reversal. The Enlightenment's protagonists had no illusions about the inevitability of progress or the attainability of ultimate perfection. They simply recognized that we would do better to trust to open debate and democratic decision-making than to the prudence of statesmen or the wisdom of philosophers. We owe it to them, of course, to listen patiently to their critics, both friendly (like Berlin) and unfriendly (like Strauss). But we owe it to ourselves and one another to keep clear forever of that "self-imposed dependence."

8

A Whole World of Heroes

Christopher Lasch

"The history of modern society, from one point of view," Christopher Lasch observed in *Haven in a Heartless World* (1977), "is the assertion of social control over activities once left to individuals and their families." This, at any rate, is the point of view from which Lasch constructed his ambitious and provocative critique of American society. From another point of view, of course, modernity is identified with, even defined by, the rise of individualism: economic, political, and ethical. The latter perspective is the once and probably still dominant ideology of progress: of history as the story of freedom, a narrative of individual emancipation from the trammels of communal prescription and superstition.

Whether these two points of view are antagonistic or complementary is not clear, to me at least. It may be that individual freedom and social control have, in different areas or aspects of experience, simply grown up side by side; or that they are intimately and paradoxically (that is to say, dialectically) related. Typically the left has endorsed and the right opposed individualism in the progressive or Enlightenment sense, which denotes the lessened authority of traditional beliefs and practices. But what are the political implications of non-traditionalist anti-modernism—Lasch's brand?

Lasch himself offered little help in answering that question; he was notoriously, exasperatingly wary of programmatic statement and ideological self-definition. He did, for what it's worth, affirm in response to critics (albeit fifteen years before his death):

> Once and for all: I have no wish to return to the past, even if I thought a return to the past was possible. The solution to our social problems lies in a completion of the democratic movement inaugurated in the eighteenth century, not in a retreat to a pre-democratic way of life. Socialism, notwithstanding the horrors committed in its name, still represents the legitimate heir of liberal democracy. Marxism and psychoanalysis still offer the best guides to an understanding of modern society and to political action designed to make it more democratic.

In his last decade, Lasch's alarm and disgust deepened, his tone soured, and his allegiance to socialism faltered. But although his complaints about contemporary society sometimes sounded like the neoconservatives', their origin and import were radically different. To see why—to reconstruct Lasch's intricate and wide-ranging cultural critique and connect it with the neo-populism of *The Revolt of the Elites and the Betrayal of Democracy*—will require a lengthy detour through the labyrinth of psychoanalytic theory.

According to Freud, a newborn infant cannot distinguish between itself and the rest of the world, and therefore between the source of its needs (its own body) and the source of its gratifications (other people, especially its mother). Hence its first mental experience is a sense of omnipotence. Inevitably, some of its needs go unmet, at which time it becomes aware, more or less traumatically, of its separation from the rest of the world. It reacts with rage against the source of its frustration (its parents); but since the source of its frustration is also the source of its gratification and the sole guarantee of its continued existence, the infant cannot tolerate its own impulses of rage and aggression, which would, if realized, annihilate it along with its parents.

This dilemma is unique in the animal world, since only humans are so helpless for so long after birth. The infant's response is fateful—indeed, virtually defines the human condition. The infant represses its rage. But repressed emotions always return. The infant's rage is converted into a variety of fantasies: the fantasy of primal union, in which the irreversibility of separation and dependence is denied; the idealization of the parents, which denies that the parents sometimes frustrate the child and also that it wishes to punish them in return; and the splitting of parental images into all-good and all-bad, which denies the incomprehensible discovery that gratification and frustration come from the same source.

These fantasies have one crucial thing in common: they are all outsized, out of scale. The infant is pictured as either omnipotent or helpless, the parents as either perfectly benevolent or implacably threatening. And the fundamental truth of the infant's situation—its separation from and dependence on the rest of the world—arouses alternating panic and denial.

According to psychoanalytic theory, the repression of infantile rage and the fantasies that result are universal and unavoidable. It is what happens thereafter that determines the degree of the child's—and adult's—maturity or pathology. What must occur, if emotional health is to be achieved, is a gradual scaling down of the superhuman size that the parents have assumed in the infant's fantasies, as well as a gradual softening and displacement ("sublimation") of the intense, overwhelming feelings they have called forth. How?

In Lasch's account, there are several ways. First, through the child's continual experience of love and discipline from the same source, i.e., its parents. The actual experience of discipline—of limited but not token punishment—slowly breaks down the archaic fantasy that the parents' displeasure means the infant's annihilation. Next, through what Lasch called "optimal frustrations." In sharp contrast to the awkward and excessive solicitude of the contemporary over-anxious mother, the instinctive confidence of a woman immersed in a kin community or "biological stream" allows the child to experience simultaneously the lessening of its mother's attentions and its own modest, growing mastery of its immediate environment. Then there is the child's encounter with what Lasch (following the British psychoanalyst D. W. Winnicott) called "transitional objects": playthings, games, and other objects and activities that symbolically express unconscious attachments but at the same time provide the child with reliable links to a stable, comprehensible external world. And finally, there is everyday contact with the father, whom infants of both sexes formerly envied, hated, and feared because of his superior access to the nurturing mother. When the child is part of the father's work environment, it observes two things: first, that he is fallible; and second, that he possesses important and satisfying skills, which he is able and willing to pass on to the child, thus earning its gratitude. Both insights help reduce him to human size in the child's psyche.

To the extent that these several experiences occur, the child can overcome its archaic terror at the discovery of its separateness from the world as well as its unconscious fear and hatred of those who forced this discovery upon it. It can also abandon its chief defense against those feelings: the fantasy of overcoming separateness and regaining primal, undifferentiated union with the world. In other words, it can become a self, distinct from others and comfortable with the distinction. It can grow up.

But if these maturational experiences do not occur, no secure self emerges. The growing child's unconscious mental life is still haunted by boundless rage over infantile helplessness, by the fear of parental retaliation that this rage induces, by the simultaneous idealization and demonization of the parents, and by the infant's only available defense against these impulses and fears: the fantasy of a return to oneness and omnipotence.

The result is a neurotic adult. Neurotic, Lasch asserted, in specific and predictable ways: wary of intimate, permanent relationships, which entail dependence and thus may trigger infantile rage; beset by feelings of inner emptiness and unease, and therefore ravenous for admiration and emotional or sexual conquest; preoccupied with personal "growth" and the consumption of novel sensations; prone to alternating self-images of grandiosity and abjection; liable to feel toward everyone in authority the same combination of rage and terror that the infant felt for whoever it depended on; unable to identify emotionally with past and future generations and therefore unable to accept the prospect of aging, decay, and death. This constellation of symptoms is known within psychoanalytic theory as narcissism: the lack of an autonomous, well-defined self. It is currently, as Lasch claimed and the clinical literature attests, the most common form of emotional pathology—the neurotic personality of our time.

It was not always so. The neurotic personality of Freud's time was quite different—acquisitive, fanatically industrious, self-righteous, sexually repressed. Then the typical symptom was obsessional (an inexplicable compulsion, e.g., incessant handwashing) or hysterical (chronic excitability or, conversely, non-somatic paralysis of a limb or faculty, e.g., frigidity). These symptoms stood out in sharp relief against the background of a stable personality, something like a "bug" in an otherwise well-functioning computer program. To simplify for the sake of contrast: the Victorian/Viennese neurosis was localized and discrete; contemporary narcissism is systemic and diffuse. To simplify even more dramatically: the character of selfhood has changed, from a strong (often rigid) self, in secure possession of fundamental values but riddled (often crippled) with specific anxieties, to a weak, beleaguered self, often full of charms and wiles, and capable, but only fitfully, of flights of idealism and imagination.

Why? What can account for this subtle but immensely significant shift? In three strikingly original books, *Haven in a Heartless World* (1977), *The Culture of Narcissism* (1979), and *The Minimal Self* (1984), Lasch formulated an answer. He posited a connection between two of the deepest, broadest phenomena of modern history: the change in personality described above, and the change from early, developing capitalism (relatively small-scale, still permeated with pre-industrial values and work practices, and largely concerned with expanding production to satisfy basic needs) to mature capitalism (dominated by huge, bureaucratic organizations, "rationalized" by the reduction of workers' initiative, autonomy, and skills, and concerned with expanding consumption through the creation of new needs). Modernization, according to Lasch, is the introduction of new, parallel forms of domination into work life and family life. In a sweeping but closely argued passage in

The Minimal Self he makes the central link in his complex argument:

> The socialization of reproduction completed the process begun by the socialization of production itself—that is, by industrialization. Having expropriated the worker's tools and concentrated production in the factory, industrialists in the opening decades of the twentieth century proceeded to expropriate the worker's technical knowledge. By means of "scientific management," they broke down production into its component parts, assigned a specific function on the assembly line to each worker, and kept to themselves the knowledge of the productive process as a whole. In order to administer this knowledge, they created a vastly enlarged managerial apparatus, an army of engineers, technicians, personnel managers, and industrial psychologists drawn from the same pool of technical experts that simultaneously staffed the "helping professions." Knowledge became an industry in its own right, while the worker, deprived of the craft knowledge by which he had retained practical control of production even after the introduction of the factory system, sank into passive dependence. Eventually, industry organized management itself along industrial lines, splitting up the production of knowledge into routinized operations carried on by semiskilled clerical labor: secretaries, typists, computer card punchers, and other lackeys. The socialization of production—under the control of private industry—proletarianized the labor force in the same way that the socialization of reproduction proletarianized parenthood, by making parents unable to provide for their own needs without the supervision of trained experts.

How does industrialization produce a culture of narcissism? Lasch argued that the evolution of capitalism has affected family structure and the socialization of children in a number of ways.

In reorganizing the production process, it has removed the father from the child's everyday experience and deprived him of the skills that formerly evoked the child's emulation and gratitude. This means that the child's archaic, punitive fantasies about the father persist unchecked. In encouraging geographic mobility, it has uprooted families from kin communities and replaced inter-generationally transmitted folk wisdom about child rearing with social-scientific expertise dispensed by professionals. This undermines parental confidence and replaces face-to-face authority over the child with the impersonal, bureaucratic authority of schools, courts, social-welfare agencies, and psychiatrists. In promoting mass consumption, advertisers (like social-science professionals) have convinced parents that their children are entitled to the best of everything but that, without expert assistance, parents are helpless to determine what that might be. In generating a mass culture glutted with rapidly obsolescing commodities and transient images, it blurs the distinction between reality and illusion and renders the world of objects unstable and bewildering. This makes it difficult for the child to locate "transitional objects" that would help it find its way from infantile attachments into the external world of culture and work. And in promising an endless supply of technological marvels, it evokes grandiose fantasies of absolute self-sufficiency and unlimited mastery of the environment, even while the quasi-magical force that conjures up those marvels—i.e., science—becomes ever more remote from the comprehension or control of ordinary citizens. This is a recipe for regression to psychic infancy: fantasies of omnipotence alternating with terrified helplessness.

One of the prime tenets of psychoanalysis is that pathology and normality are not sharply demarcated but continuous. So these secular developments—the sundering of love and discipline in the child's experience, the invasion of family life and work life by professional and corporate elites, the blurring of distinctions by mass culture—not only produce more narcissistic individuals than formerly but also create a new psychic environment. A world populated by rigid selves is a world of sublimation and its derivatives: aggression, greed, cruelty, hypocrisy, unquestioning adherence to inherited values and restraints. A world of weak selves is more fluid, corruptible, blandly manipulative, sexually easygoing, uncomfortable with anger and rivalry, and leery of defining constraints, whether in the form of traditional values or future commitments. The distinction between the early capitalist self and the late capitalist self is, roughly, the distinction between Prometheus and Narcissus, the Puritan and the swinger, the entrepreneur and the corporate gamesman, the imperial self and the minimal self. That these distinctions bespeak profound change is obvious; that they represent progress is less so.

For Lasch, then, modernization was not the solution but a new form of the problem—the problem, that is, of domination. This belief was the source of his longstanding quarrel with his fellow socialists and feminists. Much, perhaps most, of the left has always been convinced that industrialization, technological development, and the erosion of traditional forms of authority are intrinsically progressive. Modernization has had its costs, admittedly, but the answer to the problems of modernity was usually held to be more of the same, preferably under democratic auspices. In socialism's glorious youth, Marx called for "a ruthless criticism of everything existing"; few of his successors doubted that the decline of Christianity, patriarchy, possessive individualism, and everything else existing would be followed directly by something better. But, Lasch argued, these things have by and large declined; the result is not a radical extension of political and sexual autonomy but rather a bureaucratically mediated war of all against all.

Lasch's most intimate and intense disagreements were with cultural radicals: critics of education, sports, religion, sexuality, the family, and the work ethic, and proponents of a new, "liberated" ideal of expressiveness and self-realization. What these radicals ignore, Lasch charged, is that Christianity, competitive individualism, and the patriarchal family are already obsolescent, at least in those social strata where modernization is most advanced. These values and institutions have been undermined not by leftist opposition but by capitalists themselves, for their own purposes: to promote mass consumption and to regiment the work process. By espousing an ideal of personal liberation largely confined to leisure time and heavily dependent on the consumption of goods and services, cultural radicals have conceded defeat. Instead of adapting to industrialization and mass culture, Lasch contended, the left should oppose them. Only a change to human scale—to local, decentralized control in workplaces, communities, and families—can halt the spread of commodity relations and the bureaucratization of the self.

But what, if anything, can motivate so drastic a reversal of the direction of modern history? *The True and Only Heaven* (1991), Lasch's *chef d'oeuvre*, addressed this question. In that book Lasch opposed the philosophy of "progress" to the tradition of "virtue," a universalistic moral psychology to a particularist one, the "ethos of abundance" to the "ethos of the producer." It was the latter, he argued—the ethos of the artisan, the small proprietor, the yeoman farmer; of civic virtue, civic equality, and a broad diffusion of wealth, culture, and competence—that sustained the "moral economy"—the character, worldview, and social relations—that mass production and political centralization have decisively undermined. "The history of popular movements," he concluded, "shows that only an arduous, even a tragic understanding of life can justify the sacrifice imposed on those who seek to challenge the status quo."

To the majestic edifice of argument in his previous books, *The Revolt of the Elites* adds numerous elegant flourishes, though no new structural features. Lasch's death last year at sixty-one was, in the obvious sense, sadly premature; in another sense, this posthumous collection nicely rounds off his oeuvre. Forcefully written, erudite, and topical, it achieves a public voice; while those who have followed Lasch's long and complex intellectual development will be glad of a few more clues to what, in the end, his thought comes to politically.

The title essay and its companion, "Opportunity in the Promised Land," are a critique of two pillars of progressive ideology: meritocracy and social mobility. Though frequently considered essential features of a democratic society, they are best understood, Lasch argues, as an efficient method of elite recruitment and legitimation. Meritocratic elites, he points out, are in some ways even less publicly accountable than hereditary ones. The latter usually had local roots and loyalties, and their caste ideology emphasized civic responsibility and *noblesse oblige*. Even more important, their superiority was obviously arbitrary. They were therefore far less prone to the pernicious delusion—which Lasch, drawing on the work of Robert Reich and Mickey Kaus, shows is alarmingly prevalent among the newer managerial/cognitive elites—that they deserved their relative immunity from social ills.

A high degree of upward mobility is in fact quite compatible with sharp social stratification. Nor does it have much historical connection with democracy in the United States. That anyone with enough energy, talent, cunning, and ambition could become president, or become rich, or otherwise escape the common lot is not at all what most eighteenth- and nineteenth-century Americans meant by democracy. What "defined a democratic society, as Americans saw it, [was] not the chance to rise in the social scale so much as the complete absence of a scale that clearly distinguished commoners from gentlemen." The egalitarianism that so profoundly impressed generations of European visitors derived "not merely from the distribution of wealth or economic opportunity but, above all, from the distribution of intelligence and competence."

> Citizenship appeared to have given even the humbler members of society access to the knowledge and cultivation elsewhere reserved for the privileged classes. Opportunity, as many Americans understood it, was a matter more of intellectual than of material enrichment. It was their restless curiosity, their skeptical and iconoclastic turn of mind, their resourcefulness and self-reliance, their capacity for invention and improvisation that most dramatically seemed to differentiate the laboring classes in America from their European counterparts.

Readers who are not professional historians may wonder whether this is an idealized portrait, though enough evidence is included in *The True and Only Heaven* and *The Revolt of the Elites* to place the burden of proof on those who would reject it. If it is even approximately accurate, it argues powerfully for Lasch's contention that we can aim either at maximum economic efficiency (conventionally defined) or robust democracy, but not at both.

Lasch's dissatisfaction with present-day political culture was intense and comprehensive. It extended to the supplanting of neighborhoods by networks and "lifestyle enclaves"; of public parks, cafes, taverns, general stores, community centers, and other informal gathering places that "promote general conversation across class lines" by shopping malls, health clubs, and fast-food chains; of schooling based on patriotic myths and stories of heroic virtue by a sanitized, ideologically innocuous curriculum "so bland that it puts children to sleep instead of awakening feelings of awe and wonder"; of the torchlight parades and oratorical eloquence, the impassioned debates before vast audiences, the scrappy, partisan newspapers and high voter turn-out associated with nineteenth-century politics by the apathy and gullibility of the contemporary electorate and the intellectual and moral poverty of contemporary political speech. Of course, lots of people complain about such things. But without a plausible account of their origins, that sort of complaint merely exasperates and demoralizes. It is just because Lasch convincingly connects these phenomena with the rationalizing imperatives of the market and the state that, even though the latter seem all but irresistible, his criticism energizes.

Lots of people talk about "virtue" these days. The preaching of virtue to the poor and beleaguered by such court philosophers as William Bennett, Gertrude Himmelfarb, and George Will has unfortunately done much to discredit the word among the friends of equality. Lasch's conception strikes a better balance than theirs between self-denial and self-assertion. It includes an emphatic lack of deference toward wealth, office, and professional credentials; contempt for luxury and greed; a strong preference for economic independence and for face-to-face relations in business and government; a sense of place; a lively curiosity about science, art, and philosophy; and perhaps most of all, a passion for vigorous debate and splendid rhetoric. A lot more, in short, than diligence and chastity, which seem to be mainly what the neoconservatives have in mind. Lasch's notion of virtue is strenuous and classical; his ideal of a democratic society is, in a magnificent phrase of Carlyle's that he quoted often, "a whole world of heroes."

A whole world of heroes—this ideal has at least two radical implications. The first is that democracy requires a rough equality of condition. Dignity and virtue cannot survive indefinitely amid extremes of wealth and poverty; only someone with a paltry conception of virtue could believe otherwise. The second is that the democratic character can only flourish in a society constructed to human scale. Just as modern war has made military valor more or less superfluous, a world dominated by large corporations and bureaucracies offers little scope for the exercise of civic virtue; nor even, in the long run, for psychic autonomy and integrity—i.e., for selfhood, as we currently understand it.

It may very well be, as Lasch recognized, that these and other prerequisites of full, rather than merely formal, democracy cannot be reestablished. The "assertion of social control" by capital and the state, which Lasch identified as the thrust of modern history, may not be reversible. It certainly will not be reversed unless more people begin to think as passionately, rigorously, and imaginatively about democracy as Christopher Lasch, like very few others in our time, has done.

9

The Wages of Original Sin

Philip Rieff

"Isn't it curious," my theology teacher used to say with a sly smile, "that beyond good and evil is always . . . evil?" This is traditionally the last resort, the trump card, of the orthodox: that there is no virtue among unbelievers, or at least no security for their virtue. Why should someone who doesn't love God, or at least fear His judgment, be moral? In *God Is Not Great*, Christopher Hitchens recalls a debate between the philosopher A. J. Ayer and an Anglican bishop about the existence of God. Apparently out of arguments, the bishop exclaimed: "But if you really believe all that, why don't you immediately go out and commit every sort of depraved act?" It hadn't occurred to His Grace that a skeptic, even a skeptical Oxford philosopher, could be anything but wicked.

Contemporary social science has pretty well established that believers and unbelievers commit every sort of depraved act in roughly equal proportions. Nevertheless, the assumption that one cannot be reliably good without God persists in the United States, explicitly or implicitly, to the extent that a declared unbeliever almost certainly cannot be elected to national office.

Around half the population identify themselves as born-again Christians and believe in angels, miracles, the inerrancy of the Bible, and the special creation of the earth within the last 10,000 years. So if (as everyone seems to agree) America is in decline morally, an excess of skeptical rationalism is probably not to blame. Still, the modern world is undeniably more secular than the premodern one, especially among the educated, and that fact must surely have large psychological, if not behavioral, consequences. What have been, and will be, the effects of the Enlightenment on the individual and collective moral psychology of the West?

For five decades, until his death in July 2006, Philip Rieff pondered that question intently, learnedly, and eccentrically. Though Rieff was a sociology professor, he was not a social scientist; he was a social theorist in the line of Durkheim and Weber, an erudite synthesist. All three were social psychologists of religion, but Rieff was a social psychologist of irreligion as well. Equally important, he had an analytical resource they did not: Freudian psychoanalysis.

Rieff's first book (by far his best, perhaps because it's said to have been written in collaboration with his then wife, Susan Sontag) was a penetrating and imaginative study, *Freud: The Mind of the Moralist* (1959). At the time, most people considered Freud an immoralist—a proponent of liberation. Morality was supposedly what made us ill, posing unreasonable demands on behalf of "civilization" and forcing our healthy instinctual passions underground, into the unconscious, from which they tried to escape by way of "symptoms." These symptoms were strangled protests against the tyranny of culture over nature. The psychoanalytic cure was a protracted guerrilla campaign, aiming to take over one inner stronghold after another without provoking an all-out counterattack in the form of a nervous breakdown.

Freudian therapy was an indifferent success, but Freudian theory was enormously influential. The lesson most people took from it was a strong suspicion of moral authority and a reluctance to exercise it over young children. Inhibition, repression, and conformity were assumed to be unhealthy; spontaneity, individualism, and self-expression to be healthy. The prestige of "order" plummeted; that of "freedom" soared.

The Mind of the Moralist was a vigorous dissent from this standard interpretation. Rieff's point was not just that, unlike his noisier disciples, Freud was temperamentally conservative, rating order as highly as freedom and restraint as highly as expression. This stance could be (and regularly was) dismissed as reflexive Victorian/Viennese caution. On the contrary, Rieff argued, Freud's caution was well founded. He understood that he had not really explained away our primal, nameless sense of guilt, which lay beneath the more superficial and intelligible constraints imposed by culture, with the implausible hypothesis of a primal crime. And yet, for this resolute unbeliever, such guilt could have no rational basis—who, after all, was humankind accountable to?

Rieff's explanation of what there is to be guilty about was repeated in many books over many years, with increasing urgency (and, it must be said, portentousness). Human possibilities are limitless; about this he seemed to agree with Freud's liberationist successors. But what excited them terrified him— and, he claimed, everyone else, at least before the triumph of the therapeutic ethos. Our primal endowment—formless, destructive, uncontrollable instinct—paralyzes and isolates us. We cannot trust ourselves or one another until a firm structure of interdictions has been installed in everyone's psyche. These must be expounded by an interpretive elite, ratified through a calendar of rituals, and enforced by stern authority. Every culture is a dialectic of prohibition and permission, renunciation and release. Freud would have agreed; but whereas his followers concluded that the original "yes" of instinct was silenced, or at least muted, by the "no" of repressive authority, Rieff countered that instinct was cacophonous and only the original, creative "no" gave it a distinct voice. As he put it in *The Mind of the Moralist*—his style, already a little melodramatic, foreshadowing his later, full-blown apocalyptic abstractions—the primal self is "in a panic to express the fecundity of its own emptiness" and must be mastered by "unalterable authority." For if "everything could be expressed by everyone identically," then "nothing would remain to be expressed individually." Hence the "irreducible and supreme activity of culture" is to "prevent the expression of everything," thereby precluding "the one truly egalitarian dominion: nothingness."

For most educated (even many uneducated) Westerners, however, all formerly unalterable authorities now lie in the dust, like Ozymandias. Science has banished the supernatural, technology has vanquished scarcity, and so, having lost its parents, ignorance and misery, morality is now an orphan. This is the triumphalist view of modernity, and Rieff shared it; only instead of a triumph, he thought it a catastrophe. The dimensions of this catastrophe dawned on him gradually. The last chapter of *Freud* is "The Emergence of Psychological Man," a tentative sketch of what modernity had wrought. Until the twentieth century, in Rieff's account, three character types had successively prevailed in Western culture: political man, the ideal of classical times, dedicated to the glory of his city; religious man, the ideal of the

Christian era, dedicated to the glory of God; and a transitional figure, economic man, a creature of Enlightenment liberalism. Economic man believed in doing good unto others by doing well for himself. This convenient compromise did not last long, and what survived of it was not the altruism but the egoism. Psychological man was frankly and shrewdly selfish, beyond ideals and illusions, a charming narcissist at best, at worst boorish or hypochondriacal, according to his temperament.

But the worst thing about psychological man was his children. Raised without repressions, they were incapable of renunciation and regarded all authority as illegitimate. Rieff's second book, *The Triumph of the Therapeutic* (1966), raised the alarm about their "devastating illusions of individuality and freedom." A society without hierarchy, whose members "cannot conceive any salvation other than amplitude in living itself," must end in moral squalor, chaos, anomie, and universal boredom. Nor will it help to "disguise their rancorous worship of self in the religion of art," for art too depends on renunciation. Here Rieff quotes Nietzsche at length (in what is for me the most illuminating passage in Rieff's entire corpus):

> Every system of morals is a sort of tyranny against "nature" and also against "reason"; that is, however, no objection, unless one should decree, by some other system of morals, that all kinds of tyranny and unreasonableness are unlawful. What is essential and invaluable in every system of morals is that it is a long constraint. . . . The singular fact remains that everything of the nature of freedom, elegance, boldness, dance, and masterly certainty, which exists or has ever existed, whether in thought or administration, in art or in conduct, has only developed by means of the tyranny of such arbitrary law; and in all seriousness, it is not at all improbable that precisely this

is "nature" and "natural" and not *laisser-aller*! . . . The essential thing is apparently (to repeat it once more) that there should be long obedience in the same direction; there results thereby, and has always resulted in the long run, something which has made life worth living.

(Beyond Good and Evil, #188)

Muscular strength is built gradually, for example by overcoming the resistance of progressively heavier weights. Moral and psychological strength also require resistance—the pressure of cultural interdicts, dictating what is not to be done or even thought of. Such discipline simplifies our lives and economizes our energies. Without an unquestioned moral demand system, based on guilt, fear, and faith and generating obedience, trust, and dependence, there can be no spiritual hygiene, no communal purpose. And that is what the triumph of the therapeutic ethos makes impossible. Nowadays "the religious psychologies of release and the social technologies of affluence do not go beyond release and affluence to a fresh imposition of restrictive demands. This describes, in a sentence, the cultural revolution of our time. The old culture of denial has become irrelevant to a world of infinite abundance and reality." In the absence of strict, even harsh, limits (to use a plain word Rieff himself, puzzlingly, so seldom used that one is led to wonder whether his elaborately artificial prose style was itself meant as a discipline), we cannot thrive.

While Rieff was writing *The Triumph of the Therapeutic* in the early 1960s, the New Left and the counterculture were still gathering force. When the storm broke in the mid- and late sixties, he was aghast. In 1971 he gave an interview to the editors of *Salmagundi*. When they asked him to edit the transcript for publication, he responded with a book-length open letter, *Fellow Teachers* (1973), denouncing students and teachers alike, the former for their ignorant impatience of all discipline and sacred authority, the latter for their irresponsible acquiescence.

> Students can bring us no hope at all until the protest style, as Love of Humanity and Power to the People, is seen through. With the vision of this horror, we will see in true light the craven aping and inter-minable apologies for the transgressive types at the bottom: the perverts, the underclass, all those who can do no wrong because they have been wronged. . . . I repeat what I have said often: immediately behind the hippies are the thugs. They occupy the remissive space opened up by the hippies, deepening it from an aesthetic into a poli-tics. The self-absorbed therapy of the hippies clears the way for the mass-murder therapy of the thugs.

He could not refrain from the ultimate epithet: "Released from sacred fear by our remissive teaching elites, transgressives carry their peculiar authority with more right and less shame than ever before in the history of our misery. Hence Hitler and Holocaust. . . . Gulag and Dachau, torture and terror, are the dry-eyed children of our enlightenments."

Despairing, Rieff fell silent until his death thirty-three years later. (One of his students, Jonathan Imber, published *The Feeling Intellect*, a valuable collection of Rieff's occasional writings, in 1990.) He did not, however, cease working. He left behind a mass of manuscripts, which several former students were helping him ready for publication. One of them, *My Life among the Death-works*, appeared in 2006. The remaining manuscripts make up a trilogy, *Sacred Order/Social Order*, of which *My Life among the Deathworks* is the first volume.

Charisma is not Rieff at his best. The book is repetitive, dense with jargon, impatient of exposition, and more than occasionally intemperate. In form, it is an extended quarrel with Max Weber's sociology of religion, which relies on the concept of charisma but, according to Rieff, radically misunderstands it. Weber conceived charisma as one of three kinds of authority—traditional, charismatic, and bureaucratic—that characterize all organizations, including religious ones. Traditional authority, typical of primitive societies, derives from inertia and aims at continuity. Bureaucratic authority, typical of modern societies, derives from methodical reasoning and aims at efficiency. Charismatic authority is untypical and unpredictable; it derives from a singularly compelling, dynamic figure, seemingly gifted by God, and aims at radical reform or innovation. The charismatic figure arises when a tradition or bureaucracy stagnates, and his legacy is inevitably regularized by his uncharismatic successors. Since Weber, the term has been drastically vulgarized and is now mostly employed by journalists or publicists to puff politicians and pop-culture personalities.

Rieff deplores this progressive secularization of charisma and insists on its fundamentally religious significance. "My position is . . . no charisma without creed." For Rieff, a creed is not primarily theological but moral: a "particular order of interdicts and remissions." Genuine charisma is not transgressive; it does not abolish limits or license lawlessness. Rather, it imposes new interdicts, a "new organization of avoidances and of salvations through avoidances." Charismatics satisfy "the need for love in its prototypical form, as a craving for authority, reorganizing its expression within a fresh content of ambivalences." As he writes, in one of all too many suggestive but obscure passages:

The suffering that is the predicate for a charismatic situation is therefore not material suffering as such, but the deprivation of that authority that is inseparable from the love relation. The revolutionary authority of the charismatic is not a cure when viewed from the perspective of a therapeutically sophisticated culture, but rather, another symptom of the prototypal series with the resistances reorganized to express yet different repressions.

Besides Weber, Rieff engages with the Old Testament prophets, Saint Paul, and Kierkegaard. His exegeses are ingenious and original, and they all yield the same conclusion: religion is prohibition, culture is inhibition, authority is salvation, submission is wisdom, liberation is folly, and criticism of anything but the pretensions of critical reason is impiety. Modern American society has so completely forgotten these lessons that one is constantly expecting to hear Rieff exclaim, like Heidegger: "Only a God can save us."

In all his books—indeed, on virtually every page—Rieff propounded a single thesis: the urgent necessity of a "sacred order," promulgated by a "creedal organization," consisting of "interdicts and remissions," admitting of no appeal and no criticism—except, if it should decay, from prophets who either purify and reaffirm the old interdictory order or establish a new one. Without this, he warned continually, no greatness of soul, no lasting happiness, no common life is possible.

And yet Rieff never—not once—suggested what the basis of a plausible sacred order might be. The old faiths, he acknowledged, have lost their hold on Western elites; but he offered no hint, scarcely even any hope, of a new one. It is as though a prophet came among the people, foretold a terrible future, and admonished: "You must believe and obey, or you are lost." And when the people cried out in earnest: "We cannot abide that future; tell us what to believe and whom to obey," he replied: "It matters not what or whom; only believe and obey."

Prescribing religion without specifying any particular theology has become commonplace among social critics, particularly communitarians. They have a point. No society—for that matter, no individual—can flourish without a great deal of trust, devotion, solidarity, and self-discipline. Religion often fosters these things, and not only among co-religionists. But although untrammeled sexual freedom is not a requirement of human flourishing, any more than the untrammeled freedom to accumulate money, untrammeled intellectual freedom most certainly is. Unquestioned authority is not merely undesirable, it is impossible, a contradiction in terms. Authority is what remains after all questions have been asked, all objections posed, all doubts explored. Until then, there is only superstition or cowed silence. Religious orthodoxy, and in particular the theistic hypothesis, has had many centuries to establish its intellectual authority. Its prospects are dwindling. If trust, devotion, and the other requisites of community depend on a general belief in supernatural agencies, then the triumph of the therapeutic is probably permanent.

Well, then, can we be good without God? Certainly some people can. Marcus Aurelius, David Hume, George Eliot, John Stuart Mill, and William James—my candidates for the most perfect of human beings—were not theists. But of course, the existence of exceptions has never been at issue. The question is about the rest of us, run-of-the-mill humanity. What can motivate ordinary men and women to behave decently most of the time and heroically in emergencies?

Perhaps it might help to reduce the many temptations to behave otherwise. Chief among these in twenty-first-century America are the relentless sexualization of advertising and entertainment, the pervasive economic insecurity engineered by business and governmental (especially Republican) policies, and the enfeeblement of civic life entailed by extreme laissez-faire ideology. These things make it harder to maintain dignity or restraint and to trust or care about other people. None of them are necessary consequences of skepticism or intellectual freedom, and some of them are promoted most vigorously by people who loudly proclaim themselves religious. Only the first has provoked any organized religious opposition, however, and even then has generated only a fraction of the energy and resources wasted on opposing sex education and the teaching of evolution—not to mention the antiabortion movement, which would surely prevent more abortions by helping to lower the sexual temperature of consumer marketing than by proselytizing unwed mothers and harassing their physicians.

Just as important as avoiding temptation is acquiring the strength to subdue it. Ordinary people must become heroes, and we can. The deepest determinant of contemporary social psychology is not mass unbelief but mass production. Industrialism has decisively undermined the republican ideals of independence, self-sufficiency, and proprietorship—the "modest competence" postulated by early democratic theorists as the basis of civic virtue and civil equality. It is the practice of demanding skills, rather than fragmented and routinized drudgery, that disciplines us and makes mutual respect and sympathy possible. Work that provides scope for the exercise of virtues and talents; a physical, social, and political environment commensurate in scale with our authentic, non-manufactured needs and appetites; and a much greater degree of equality, with fewer status distinctions, and those resting on inner qualities rather than money—these are the requirements of psychic health at present. The alternative is infantilism and authoritarianism, compensated—at least until the earth's ecology breaks down—by frantic consumption.

Tracing a society's predicament to its historical and political roots is more difficult than endlessly excoriating or mocking its most outlandish manifestations. It is also more rewarding. That is why, after reading *Freud: The Mind of the Moralist* and perhaps also *The Triumph of the Therapeutic*, those in sympathy with Rieff's complaint should turn to the writings of Christopher Lasch. In a series of invaluable books, notably *The Minimal Self* (1984), *The True and Only Heaven* (1991), and *The Revolt of the Elites* (1994), Lasch diagnosed contemporary narcissism far more rigorously and persuasively than Rieff. It is the worker's loss of autonomy, Lasch showed, his dependence on a remote, centralized economic authority, that has produced a culture of unlimited consumption and ersatz self-expression; and it is the disappearance of the household economy, which removed the father's work life from the child's experience, that has produced the characteristic modern ambivalence about authority, which Rieff can only blame on rationalist hubris and original sin. This exceptional historical insight, along with his robust, unflagging concern with democracy and equality, set Lasch, morally as well as intellectually, above all other recent critics of modernity.

Lasch has also, it happens, written the best essay I have encountered about Rieff, a chapter in *The Revolt of the Elites*. After much agreement and praise, he gently rebuked Rieff for falling into a practice the older man had himself rightly criticized: i.e., recommending religion for purely instrumental reasons. "The issue," Lasch reminded Rieff, "is not whether religion is necessary but whether it is true." For that reason, "an honest atheist is always to be preferred to a culture Christian." Notwithstanding Rieff's uncompromising anathemas, honest believers and honest unbelievers will need one another if contemporary American society is to be redeemed.

10

Against Everything

Ivan Illich

The 1950s, '60s, and '70s—*les trentes glorieuses*, the French call them—were indeed fat years in Western Europe and the United States. Unions were strong, unemployment was low, and a lot of jobs still came with health insurance, pensions, and a fair chance of not either migrating at any moment to lower-wage countries or suddenly being replaced by software/hardware. Notwithstanding an ugly racist backlash to the Civil Rights Movement and an unjust, hideously destructive war in Indochina, it was possible, for a few brief years, to believe that the American economy and polity were sound in their fundamentals, however much in need of reform.

And yet, radical social criticism flourished in those decades as never before in America, not even in the Great Depression: Mills, Marcuse, Goodman, Baldwin, Harrington, Lasch, Kozol, Norman O. Brown, Wendell Berry, Shulamith Firestone, the Port Huron Statement, among others. Perhaps there's something to the idea that revolutions are a response to rising expectations: that economic success and apparent security liberate the radical imagination, while widespread insecurity cramps it, inducing a defensive crouch. At any rate, an awful lot of people back then professed themselves—ourselves, I must acknowledge sheepishly—revolutionaries.

Ivan Illich was an idiosyncratic revolutionary. Fundamentally, most radical critics object that our institutions unfairly allocate good and services—education, health care, housing, transportation, consumer goods—or jobs, or respect, or, simply, money. Illich nicely summarized the left's perennial program as "more jobs, equal pay for equal jobs, and more pay for every job." For Illich, these demands were beside the point. He thought that, by and large, the goods, services, jobs, and rights on offer in every modern society were not worth a damn to begin with. In fact, he thought they, and the way of life they constituted, were toxic. He was not a reactionary in any useful sense of that term, but he was a fervent antiprogressive.

Illich was born in Vienna in 1926 of Jewish and Catholic parents. The family fled the Nazis in 1941, and after the war, Illich studied cell biology and crystallography in Florence, theology and philosophy in Rome, and medieval history in Germany. He was ordained a Roman Catholic priest and in 1951 was sent to a poor Puerto Rican parish in New York City. He was very successful, both as a parish priest and also, somewhat more surprisingly, in charming the ultra-conservative Cardinal Spellman. In 1956 he became vice-rector of the Catholic University of Puerto Rico. By then he was a fairly outspoken critic of pre–Vatican II Catholic orthodoxy, and his new superiors were not charmed. He spent 1959 wandering around Latin America, then settled in Cuernavaca, Mexico, where he founded a freewheeling language school and research center, the Center for Intercultural Documentation (CIDOC), which became, like Berkeley and Greenwich Village, a seedbed of sixties radicalism.

At some point the Vatican became alarmed—it's rumored that the CIA had complained about him—and Illich was summoned to Rome to explain himself. Apparently the Church authorities satisfied themselves that this retiring polyglot cleric was not actively subversive. But CIDOC had become a distraction, as had his own growing celebrity. Illich had no taste for empire-building, so he phased out the center in 1976 and became an itinerant scholar, living from course to lecture series to research grant, with occasional royalties as well. He wrote a dozen books (or fifteen, depending on how strict your definition is) and died in 2002.

The first of Illich's books, *Deschooling Society* (1971), made him very famous. It caught the crest of a wave of critique and experiment in American education: Paul Goodman, John Holt, Paulo Freire, free schools, community control. Illich shared his contemporaries' antiauthoritarianism but not their reasons. For most educational radicals, the enemies were tradition—the age-old authority of church and state, bosses and parents—and inequality—the gap between resources devoted to rich and poor children. From this point of view, the remedies were plain: practice emancipatory social relations in all schools and lavish more resources on those serving poorer children.

To Illich's mind, those remedies missed the point. He thought the educational system had no good reason to exist. It was, like every modern service industry, in the business of creating and defining the needs it purported to satisfy—in this case, certification as an expert—while discrediting alternative, usually traditional, methods of self-cultivation and self-care. The schools' primary mission was to produce people able and willing to inhabit a historically new way of life, as clients or administrators of systems whose self-perpetuation was their overriding goal. Thus schools produce childhood, a phenomenon that is, Illich claimed, no more than a few centuries old but is now the universal rationale for imposing an array of requirements, educational and medical, on parents and for training people as lifelong candidates for credentials and consumers of expertise.

It is not *what* schools taught that Illich objected to; it is *that* they taught:

> To understand what it means to deschool society, and not just to reform the educational establishment, we must focus on the hidden curriculum of schooling. . . . [It is] the ceremonial or ritual of schooling itself [that] constitutes such a hidden curriculum. Even the best of teachers cannot entirely protect his pupils from it. Inevitably, this hidden curriculum of schooling adds prejudice and guilt to the discrimination which a society practices against some of its members and compounds the privilege of others with a new title to condescend to the majority. Just as inevitably, this hidden curriculum serves as a ritual of initiation into a growth-oriented consumer society for rich and poor alike.

> Once young people have allowed their imaginations to be formed by curricular instruction, they are conditioned to institutional planning of every sort. . . . Neither ideological criticism nor social action can bring about a new society. Only disenchantment with and detachment from the central social ritual and reform of that ritual can bring about radical change.

What school teaches, first and last, is "the need to be taught."

In a series of subsequent books—*Tools for Conviviality* (1973), *Energy and Equity* (1974), *Medical Nemesis* (1974), *Toward a History of Needs* (1978), *The Right to Useful Unemployment* (1978), and *Shadow Work* (1981)—Illich formulated parallel critiques of medicine, transportation, law, psychotherapy, the media, and other social spheres. The medical system produces patients; the legal system produces clients; the entertainment system produces audiences; and the transportation system produces commuters (whose average speed across a city, he liked to point out, is less than the average speed of pedestrians or bicyclists—or would be, if walking or bicycling those routes hadn't been made impossible by the construction of highways). In this process, far more important than merely teaching us behavior is the way these systems teach us how to define our needs. "As production costs decrease in rich nations, there is an increasing concentration of both capital and labor in the vast enterprise of equipping man for disciplined consumption."

Why do we have to be taught to need or disciplined to consume? Because being schooled, transported, entertained, etc.—consuming a service dispensed by someone licensed to provide it—is a radical novelty in the life of humankind. Until the advent of modernity only a century or two ago (in most of the world, that is; longer in "advanced" regions), the default settings of human nature included autonomy, mutuality, locality, immediacy, and satiety. Rather than being compulsorily enrolled in age-specific and otherwise highly differentiated institutions, one discovered interests, pursued them, and found others (or not) to learn with and from. Sick care was home- and family-based, far less rigorous and intrusive, and suffering and death were regarded as contingencies to be endured rather than pathologies to be stamped out. Culture and entertainment were less abundant and variegated but more participatory. The (commercially convenient) idea that human needs and wants could expand without limit, that self-creation was an endless project, had not yet been discovered.

This is perhaps obvious; but can Illich seriously doubt that the great changes since then constitute progress? It's a question to which he cannily declined to give a direct answer, even while he assailed the self-satisfaction of the age. He insisted that he was a historian and diagnostician, not an advocate or a prophet. He at any rate fleshed out the diagnosis amply and eloquently, especially in *Medical Nemesis*, his longest book. "The pain, dysfunction, disability, and anguish resulting from technical medical intervention rival the morbidity due to traffic and industrial accidents and even war-related activities, and make the impact of medicine one of the most rapidly spreading epidemics of our time." Partly this was malpractice, or what he called "clinical iatrogenesis": "The Department of Health, Education, and Welfare calculates that 7 percent of all patients suffer compensable injuries when hospitalized. . . . One out of every five patients admitted to a typical research hospital acquires a iatrogenic disease. . . . The frequency of reported accidents in hospitals is higher than in all industries except mines and high-rise construction." But these defects were reformable; more intractable was "cultural iatrogenesis": the destruction of "the potential of people to deal with their human weakness, vulnerability, and uniqueness in a personal and autonomous way." The difficulty of giving birth or dying at home is an obvious example.

Even more fundamental was "social iatrogenesis," the damage that results from the institutional shape medicine takes in modern society. "When the intensity of biomedical intervention crosses a critical threshold, clinical iatrogenesis turns from error, accident, or fault into an incurable perversion of medical practice. In the same way, when professional autonomy degenerates into a radical monopoly and people are rendered impotent to cope with their milieu, social iatrogenesis becomes the main product of the medical organization."

The notion of "radical monopoly" plays an important role in Illich's critique of professionalism:

> A radical monopoly goes deeper than that of any one corporation or any one government. It can take many forms. When cities are built around vehicles, they devalue human feet; when schools preempt learning, they devalue the autodidact; when hospitals draft all those who are in critical condition, they impose on society a new form of dying. Ordinary monopolies corner the market; radical monopolies disable people from doing or making things on their own. The commercial monopoly restricts the flow of commodities; the more insidious social monopoly paralyzes the output of nonmarketable use-values. Radical monopolies . . . impose a society-wide substitution of commodities for use-values by reshaping the milieu and by "appropriating" those of its general characteristics which enabled people so far to cope on their own.

Professions colonize our imaginations; or as Foucault (whom Illich's language sometimes recalls—or anticipates) might have said, they reduce us to terms in a discourse whose sovereignty we have no idea how to contest or criticize.

Unlike Foucault, who sometimes seemed to take a grim satisfaction in demonstrating how cunningly we were imprisoned in our language and institutions, Illich was an unashamed humanist. His ties to the *barrios* and *campesinos* of North and South America were deep and abiding. His "preferential option for the poor" (the slogan of Catholic liberation theology) was a peculiar one: he hoped to save them from economic development at the hands of Western-trained technocrats. Illich had hard words for even the best Western intentions toward the Third World. (It is possible that what annoyed the CIA was Illich's advice to the Peace Corps volunteers who came to Cuernavaca for Spanish-language instruction that they should leave Latin American peasants alone, or perhaps even try to learn from them how to de-develop their own societies.) Religious and ecological radicals, however generous and respectful, still wanted to bring the poor a poisoned gift.

> Development has had the same effect in all societies: everyone has been enmeshed in a new web of dependence on commodities that flow out of the same kind of machines, factories, clinics, television studios, think tanks. . . . Even those who worry about the loss of cultural and genetic variety, or about the multiplication of long-impact isotopes, do not advert to the irreversible depletion of skills, stories, and senses of form. And this progressive substitution of industrial goods and services for useful but nonmarketable values has been the shared goal of political factions and regimes otherwise violently opposed to one another.

Illich might have said more about those fugitive "stories, skills, and senses of form"; he might have tried harder to sketch in the details of a society based on "nonmarketable values." But in *Tools for Conviviality* and elsewhere, he at least dropped hints. He certainly did not idealize the primitive—he might have welcomed the term "appropriate technology" if he had encountered it. He enthused over bicycles and the slow trucks and vans that moved people and livestock over the back roads of Latin America before the latter were "improved" into useless and dangerous highways. He was a connoisseur of the hand-built structures cobbled together from cast-off materials in the *favelas* and slums of the global South. He thought phone trees and computer databases that would match learners and teachers were a very plausible substitute for the present educational system. He thought the Chinese "barefoot doctors" were a promising, though fragile, experiment. He was friendly to any gadget or technique or practice—he called them "convivial" tools—that encouraged initiative and self-reliance rather than smothering those qualities by requiring mass production, certified expertise, or professional supervision.

Illich proposed "a new kind of modern tool kit"—not devised by planners but worked out through a kind of society-wide consultation that he called "politics," undoubtedly recognizing that it bore no relation to what currently goes by that name. The purpose of this process was to frame a conception of the good life that would "serve as a framework for evaluating man's relation to his tools." Essential to any feasible conception, Illich assumed, was identifying a "natural scale" for life's main dimensions. "When an enterprise [or an institution] grows beyond a certain point on this scale, it first frustrates the end for which it was originally designed, and then rapidly becomes a threat to society itself."

A livable society, Illich argued, must rest on an "ethic of austerity." Of course he didn't mean by "austerity" the deprivation imposed by central bankers for the sake of "financial stability" and rentier profits. Nor, though he rejected affluence as an ideal, did he mean asceticism. He meant "limits on the amount of instrumented [i.e., technical or institutional] power that anyone may claim, both for his own satisfaction and in the service of others." Instead of global mass society, he envisioned "many distinct cultures . . . each modern and each emphasizing the dispersed use of modern tools."

Under such protection against disabling affluence . . . tool ownership
would lose much of its present power. If bicycles are owned here by
the commune, there by the rider, nothing is changed about the essentially convivial nature of the bicycle as a tool. Such commodities
would still be produced in large measure by industrial methods,
but they would be seen and evaluated . . . as tools that permitted
people to generate use-values in maintaining the subsistence of their
respective communities.

Whether one calls this revolution or devolution, it clearly requires,
he acknowledged, "a Copernican revolution in our perception of
values." But there was nothing quixotic or eccentric about it. On
the contrary, this affirmation of limits aligns Illich with what is
perhaps the most significant strain of social criticism in our time:
the antimodernist radicalism of Lewis Mumford, Christopher
Lasch, and Wendell Berry, among others.

Any assessment of Illich's thought requires at least a footnote
about his curious, controversial late work, *Gender* (1983). Like
many antimodernists, Illich had an uneasy relationship with
feminism. He thought about sexual inequality much as he did
about economic inequality: its injustice was too obvious to need
much arguing, but more money and power for women and the
poor amounted to, in effect, better seats at the banquet table when
all the food was unhealthy and unpalatable. He was, unlike most
political and sexual radicals, disenchanted with money and power
altogether.

Illich claimed that sex, like childhood, was a modern invention. When production moved out of the household, life was
sundered into two spheres: one where the means of life were
gained, and another which supported those efforts. Marxists
called these two realms the sphere of production and the sphere

of social reproduction. Illich called them wage labor and "shadow work." The latter included all unpaid efforts that made the former possible: not only housework, shopping, and child care but also what has come to be called "emotional labor," and even the family's liaison with external caregivers. The great majority of this shadow work is done by women, increasingly alongside their own wage labor. Sex as a role, an attribute of a being abstractly conceived as a laboring subject, evolved as a rationale for this division into *homo economicus* and *femina domestica*, which Illich condemned as heartily as any feminist could wish.

Before sex, there had been only gender. Every premodern society, according to Illich, assigned every object and every task—and sometimes each stage of each task—either exclusively to men or exclusively to women. "From afar, the native can tell whether women or men are at work, even if he cannot distinguish their figures. The time of year and day, the crop, and the tools reveal to him who they are. Whether they carry a load on their head or shoulder will tell him their gender." The specific assignments varied from one society to another; what never varied was that some activities and objects were only for women or only for men.

What to do with this historical and anthropological fact—if it is a fact—was not clear, even to Illich. But he was sure it mattered deeply, and he tried to say why in a remarkable passage that can serve as well as any to summarize his view of modern life. (It will help the reader to know that "vernacular" was a term of art for Illich: it meant "untaught," with overtones of "colloquial," "customary," "instinctual," and perhaps most usefully, "amateur.")

The distinction between vernacular gender and sex role is comparable to that between vernacular speech and taught mother tongue, between subsistence and economic existence. Therefore, the fundamental assumptions about the one and the other are distinct. Vernacular speech, gender, and subsistence are characteristics of a morphological closure of community life on the assumption, implicit and often ritually expressed and mythologically represented, that a community, like a body, cannot outgrow its size. Taught mother tongue, sex, and a life-style based on the consumption of commodities all rest on the assumption of an open universe in which scarcity underlies all correlations between needs and means. Gender implies a complementarity within the world that is fundamental and closes the world in on "us," however ambiguous and fragile this closure might be. Sex, on the contrary, implies unlimited openness, a universe in which there is always more.

Criticism of this breadth and depth illuminates everything. Exactly how to turn it against everything is usually, as in this case, more than even the critic can say.

11

Back to the Land?

Wendell Berry

An antimodernist is someone who stands in the path of progress and yells "Stop!" Of course, different antimodernists want
to stop different things. The first antimodernists, the Luddites
of early nineteenth-century England, wanted to stop power
looms from replacing (and thereby starving) weavers, to the
considerable profit of textile industrialists. John Ruskin and
William Morris in late nineteenth-century England wanted to
stop the comely landscapes and buildings of the English countryside from being razed to make way for cheap and ugly but
profitable new construction, both commercial and residential.
William F. Buckley Jr., who coined the above phrase about
standing in the path of progress, wanted to stop democracy,
racial and sexual equality, and pretty much everything else
humane and good, but above all, progressive taxation. (He was
rich.) Ivan Illich wanted to stop expertise, which he thought
had trapped modern men and women in universal dependence.
Christopher Lasch wanted to stop mass society, which he
showed, with a wide-ranging critique spanning history, sociology, and psychoanalysis, produces people who are less able

to resist authority than those who grow up in a human-scale, largely face-to-face society.

Wendell Berry is probably the best-known and most influential antimodernist alive today, at least in the English-speaking world. Besides being a prolific essayist, novelist, story writer, and poet, Berry is a farmer in the Kentucky River Valley, an experience that has provided him with his material, his message, and his pulpit. He did not come to farming in midlife, as a novelty or a pastoral retreat. He grew up where he now farms, and his family has been farming in the area for many generations. Farming is the deepest layer of his mind; writing—learned at state colleges and then at Stanford in a famous seminar with Wallace Stegner—is the upper layer. That upper layer itself is divided: the fiction and poetry (a selection was issued last year by the Library of America) are slow-moving and deep-gauged, beautifully observed and full of interior incident, never loud or didactic. The essays, by contrast, though full of elegantly phrased and powerfully rhythmic sentences, are intensely earnest, aiming not to entertain or even to instruct but to convince and move.* It's been a feat, writing a dozen or so novels, several books of stories, several more of poems, and hundreds of lengthy essays and occasional pieces, all while managing a 200-acre farm, with only his wife and (occasionally) his children to help him. It's an equal feat traversing registers: the droll, meditative equanimity of his fiction, and the ardor, sometimes anger, of his nonfiction.

What is Berry angry about? In 1950 there were 20 million farms in the United States. Today there are 1 million. What forced those millions of farmers and their families off their land

---

* Wendell Berry, *Essays 1969–1990*, ed. Jack Shoemaker, Library of America. Wendell Berry, *Essays 1993–2017*, ed. Jack Shoemaker, Library of America.

was a "free market" pincer movement. Many farm communities had lost young men to World War II. They could not immediately go back to traditional, labor-intensive, self-sufficient farming. The federal government stepped in, aggressively promoting radical consolidation, mechanization, and specialization in one or two crops. Giant trading companies bought the farmers' crops cheap and sold them dear. Giant chemical companies, with the help of university schools of agriculture, sold them fertilizers, herbicides, and pesticides, which the new monocultures required, unlike the traditional diversified and rotated crops. The banks did their part: they were uninterested in extending credit to small traditional farms, preferring to finance purchases of distressed farms and of shiny new tractors, pickers, and combines. By the 1970s, the US Department of Agriculture declared victory, boasting that only 4 percent of America's labor force fed the other 96 percent, with a surplus left over for export and humanitarian food aid. Berry sees it differently: "What we have called agricultural progress has, in fact, involved the forcible displacement of millions of people."

The industrialization of agriculture did not merely uproot lives, bad as that was. It went far toward destroying the land itself. Topsoil is a complex substance, home to thousands of microscopic organisms. It is a fragile balance of elements and requires steady attention from an experienced eye. When it is doused with heavy chemicals and repeatedly plowed, it dries up and blows away. Millions of tons of topsoil have washed or blown away under the regime of industrial agriculture.

Along with the soil, a culture has been washed away: the culture of agrarianism. A society whose main products are a few crops grown in enormous quantities on huge farms and estates and then exported: this may be an agricultural society, but it is not an agrarian one. In an agrarian society, farming is an art and a discipline. The soil, the watercourses, the animals are treated with care—what Berry calls "kindly use"—and preserved from one generation to another, rather than as "inputs" to be depreciated according to a commercial schedule. A farm is full of idiosyncrasies, over which an industrial farmer will ride roughshod but which a genuine farmer will take the time to learn. For this reason, farms in agrarian societies tend to be of middling size—giantism is alien. In an agrarian society, farming is a kind of self-expression, with more of the craft spirit than the business spirit. Though independent, conscientious farmers are becoming rarer, Berry finds enough of them to compose a kind of master class illustrating the good farming practices he's constantly preaching.

Every culture shapes a corresponding character. The industrial farmer tends to be calculating, single-minded, forward-looking (anxiously as much as providently), unsentimental, given to uniformity and routine. He accepts that he's a cog in a machine, dependent on impersonal market forces. He assumes that bigger is better and that all problems have technical solutions. He's a manager: his skills and attitudes are as relevant to making widgets as to growing crops.

In an agrarian culture, by contrast:

A competent farmer is his own boss. He has learned the disciplines necessary to go ahead on his own, as required by economic obligation, loyalty to his place, pride in his work. His workdays require the use of long experience and practiced judgment, for the failures of which he knows he will suffer. His days do not begin and end by rule, but in response to necessity, interest, and obligation. They are not measured by the clock, but by the task and his endurance; they last

as long as necessary or as long as he can work. He has mastered
intricate formal patterns in ordering his work within the overlapping
cycles—human and natural, controllable and uncontrollable—of the
life of a farm.

Importantly, their socialization is also different. The commercial
farmer usually takes an Agricultural Extension course or two,
emerging with a couple of loose-leaf binders and a few phone
numbers at the Ag faculty and the Farm Bureau. The agrarian
farmer does not scorn academic instruction, but his deepest
orientation toward farming "does not come from technique or
technology. . . . It does not come even from principle." Instead it
comes, mysteriously, "from a passion that is culturally prepared—
a passion for excellence and order that is handed down to young
people by older people whom they respect and love." This sort
of face-to-face induction into a complex tradition is an example
of the wisdom of human scale—one of Berry's obsessions.

The Unsettling of America (1977), from which I've been quot-
ing and which is included whole in these Library of America
volumes, is Berry's most ambitious and influential book, tracing
the dire society-wide consequences of the decline of agriculture.
It's been a long decline. In 1785 Thomas Jefferson, the tutelary
genius of *Unsettling*, wrote to another Founding Father, the New
York banker John Jay: "Cultivators of the earth are the most
valuable citizens. They are the most vigorous, the most independent, the most virtuous, and they are tied to their country,
and wedded to its liberty and interests, by the most lasting bonds."
Ten years later he advocated education for farmers, "so much as
may enable them to read and understand what is going on in the
world, and to keep their part of it going on right, for nothing
can keep it right but their own vigilant and distrustful

superintendence." That last, embattled phrase presages the long history of agriculture's undermining by commerce and finance. Perhaps Jefferson already had an inkling of Alexander Hamilton's schemes to introduce capitalism into the fledgling United States. He had probably also drawn the right conclusions from the crushing by the propertied faction (with the hearty approval of Washington, Adams, Hamilton, and other grandees) of protests by indebted small farmers, such as Shays' Rebellion.

The link between smallholding and American democracy lasted for a century or so. In 1820 around 80 percent of Americans were self-employed as farmers, craftsmen, or shopkeepers. Lincoln gave that ethos moving expression in a well-known passage: "The prudent, penniless beginner in the world labors for wages awhile, saves a surplus with which to buy tools or land for himself, then labors on his own account another while, and at length hires another new beginner to help him." But after the Civil War, just as they had after the Revolutionary War, financial and mercantile vultures preyed on distressed farmers, driving them into debt and into highly disadvantageous marketing arrangements.

The result was the late nineteenth-century Populist movement, the high point of radical democratic politics in American history. A mass movement of farmers, the Populists won many state offices in the South and Midwest, but they allowed themselves to be absorbed into the Democratic Party. They were decisively defeated by the Republicans, already the party of big business (and of industrial-scale graft), in the election of 1896 and subsequently faded away. Curiously, Berry has nothing to say about the Populist movement, even though it was the first and only organized entrance by farmers onto the national political stage.

Perhaps it's not so curious. Berry's is a politics of individual virtue. Personal responsibility is his watchword, rather than solidarity. Here are his thoughts on political strategy:

> For most of the history of this country our motto, implied or spoken, has been Think Big. A better motto, and an essential one now, is Think Little. That implies the necessary change of thinking and feeling, and suggests the necessary work. Thinking Big has led us to the two biggest and cheapest political dodges of our time: plan-making and law-making. The lotus-eaters of this era are in Washington, D.C., Thinking Big. Somebody perceives a problem, and somebody in the government comes up with a plan or a law. The result, mostly, has been the persistence of the problem, and the enlargement and enrichment of the government.
>
> But the discipline of thought is not generalization; it is detail, and it is personal behavior. While the government is "studying" and funding and organizing its Big Thoughts, nothing is being done. But the citizen who is willing to Think Little, and accepting the discipline of that, to go ahead on his own, is already solving the problem.

This is splendid prose. It is disastrous advice. Leave aside the implicit belittling of Social Security, Medicare, Medicaid, unemployment insurance, and other examples of "plan-making" and "law-making" that tens of millions of Americans have felt very grateful for. Look at the present balance of forces: the structures of legislative, electoral, ideological, and financial control in the United States are deeply entrenched, highly resistant to citizen initiative, and virtually without exception geared to the needs of the country's largest industries and banks. Nothing those plutocrats do not wish to be done will be done in America, even if a hundred million Little Thinkers "go ahead on their own."

Only if that hundred million organize themselves and coordinate their efforts—in other words, become Big Thinkers—is there the slightest hope for wresting control of our country from this corporate/financial oligarchy. Berry himself has been an exemplary activist in his day, especially in opposing the strip mining that has disfigured much of his lovely region. Unfortunately, the coal industry out-strategized the activists—not to mention deploying vastly greater financial resources. But would any degree of uncoordinated private individual virtue have had better luck stopping them?

No amount of recycling, farming right, eating right, being neighborly, or being personally responsible in other ways will matter much if we don't subsidize solar and wind power, raise mileage requirements, steeply tax carbon, drastically reduce plastic production, kill coal, and provide jobs for all those whom these measures would disemploy. (We could put them to work on infrastructure and renewables, which we would invest in with the proceeds of steep wealth and corporate—especially energy— taxes.) In a face-to-face society, virtue is the right lever. Unfortunately, we live in a mass society, thoroughly bureaucratized and institutionalized, dense with complex systems, which only large aggregations of people (or money) can move. We need more, not fewer, plans, laws, and policies, but democratically formulated ones.

Berry has almost (not quite; he hedges) given up on the possibility of democracy in mass society. It is an entirely understandable reflex: virtually every governmental institution in our society is corrupt or ineffectual, and even many well-meaning people have been infected by consumerism, overreliance on experts, and other character defects of a massified, technologized population. But cultivating our own gardens and learning the virtues we have forgotten will not suffice to save the world and is probably not even feasible. Surveying the erosion in some nearby farms, Berry laments that it takes 50,000 years to build five feet of topsoil. While building character by cultivating our gardens, as Berry recommends, is probably not quite so slow a process, it will surely take a few generations at least. But within a few generations, our gardens will be inundated, some literally and others by the tens of millions of climate refugees tramping across the earth. The World Bank has estimated that up to 216 million people may be forced to migrate by 2050 due to drought, declining crop productivity, sea level rise, and other climate-related causes. No amount of uncoordinated individual action can succor hundreds of millions of refugees.

"If we are to hope to correct our abuses of each other and of other races and of our land, and if our effort to correct these abuses is to be more than a political fad that will in the long run be only another form of abuse, then we are going to have to go far beyond public protest and political action. We are going to have to rebuild the substance and the integrity of private life in this country." This may sound obviously right, but in fact it's wrong, at least in implication. We only have so much time and energy, after all, and if we go "far beyond" political action, we will almost certainly shortchange it. Berry's prescription underestimates the opposition—the plutocrats really have closed off every path to change except the most difficult one: sustained, society-wide, decentralized popular mobilization. For all Berry's humane rootedness, and however attractive the way of life he expounds, Ralph Nader, the indefatigable organizer, networker, and advocate—the wholly public man—is a better model right now for those who want to spare the earth and its inhabitants.

~

Like most antimodernists, Berry is very good at reminding us what we have sacrificed by embracing modernity. One such sacrifice is a sense of place. Only a few generations ago, a sizeable fraction of humankind lived where their ancestors had lived for hundreds or thousands of years. Now almost no one does. To the extent we take any notice of this change, we probably think it is all to the good. Mobility is highly valued in contemporary culture. The idea of an organic and permanent connection to a single place strikes most people as archaic, even oppressive.

But our current, historically new life pattern, in which most children leave home in late adolescence and never return to that place to live, has its costs. For the rest of that young person's life, her internalized focus of authority will be institutional and abstract: university, corporation, profession, government. Abstractions are hard to have human-scale emotions about. The place one grew up in, if one returns there with a degree of mastery (or achieves it in place), makes it easier to grasp that one has changed—there's a detailed, familiar background to see oneself against, rather than the nebulous grid of a shadowy bureaucracy. Belonging to a place, as Berry repeatedly emphasizes, can be anchoring and liberating at the same time. "It is only in the place one belongs to, intimate and familiar, long watched over, that the details rise up out of the whole and become visible: the hawk swoops into the clearing before one's eyes; the wood drake, aloof and serene in his glorious plumage, swims out of his hiding place."

Berry is a serious Christian, and also a serious reader of poetry. His prose is studded with quotations from the Bible and the poetic canon. It may be surprising (though it shouldn't be, really) how easy it is to find a text in Homer, Virgil, Dante, Shakespeare, Blake, or Wordsworth celebrating humility, fortitude, magnanimity, chastity, marital fidelity, or some other Christian (though not exclusively Christian) virtue. Character and virtue are indeed fragile, and it's reasonable to exploit all the resources of human culture to shore them up. But although it lends his writing gravity and grace, I'm sorry that Berry insists on giving the agrarian ethos a religious framework and on situating human flourishing within a "Great Economy," by which he means not Gaia but the "Kingdom of God." As a result, he speaks less persuasively than he might to those of us who feel that our civilization has somehow gone wrong and that at least some part of traditional wisdom is indeed wisdom, but who cannot believe that this universe is the work of the Christian God, or of any God. And yet we need Berry's preaching as much as anyone. Jesus came, after all, to call sinners, not the just, to good farming practices.

Our culture's great need today is for a pious paganism, a virtuous rationalism, skeptical and science-loving but skeptical even of science when necessary, aware that barbarism is as likely as progress and may even arrive advertised as progress, steadily angry at the money-changers and mindful of the least of our brethren. I don't see how anyone who shares Berry's Christian beliefs could fail to adopt his ideal of stewardship. But if those religious beliefs are necessary as well as sufficient—if there is no other path to that ideal, as he sometimes seems to imply—then we may be lost. One cannot believe at will.

Berry is often compared with Thoreau, and one can see why: both of them ardent and amazingly prolific, both outdoor thinkers, both wary of technological progress. But unlike Berry, Thoreau sometimes played with ideas; he also did not believe the world was going altogether badly. I think Paul Goodman might be a better comparison. Goodman was thoroughly urban, but he was hands-on, keenly interested in designing and building, insatiably curious about the details of whatever subject he was theorizing about. He was also very eloquent about virtue and character, though wholly secular. It would have been tremendously interesting—perhaps even culture-changing—to hear them trying to reach common ground. Their lives didn't overlap, unfortunately; but we can try the thought experiment.

12

Preserving the Self

Matthew Crawford

Aristotle and Marx may not have agreed on much else, but they agreed on the purpose of life. Aristotle defined the highest happiness as "the pursuit of excellence to the height of one's capacities, in a life affording them full scope." For Marx, the mark of a rational, humane society is that free, creative labor has become "not only a means to life, but life's prime want." Not leisure, not entertainment, not consumption, but creative activity is what gives human beings their greatest satisfaction: so say both the sage of antiquity and the prophet of modernity.

How much creative activity does work life in the contemporary United States encourage or allow? "Creative" is not a well-defined word, so no precise answer is possible. But it's hardly controversial that the "de-skilling" of the workforce has been the goal of scientific management since the beginning of the industrial age and is accelerating. In *Mindless: Why Smarter Machines Are Making Dumber Humans* (2014), journalist Simon Head tracks the rapid spread of computerized business systems (CBS): job-flow, business-process software designed to eliminate every vestige of initiative, judgment, and skill from the lives of workers and even middle managers. CBS, he writes, "are being used to marginalize employee knowledge and experience," so that "employee autonomy is under siege from ever more intrusive forms of monitoring and control." Head cites a 1995 report that "75–80 percent of America's largest companies were engaged in Business Process Reengineering and would be increasing their commitment to it over the next few years," as well as a 2001 estimate that 75 percent of all corporate investment in information technology that year went into CBS. They're expensive, but they're worth it: insecure, interchangeable workers mean lower labor costs.

The end result of de-skilling was foreseen nearly 250 years ago by one of capitalism's earliest and most penetrating critics:

> The man whose whole life is spent in performing a few simple operations, of which the effects are perhaps always the same, or very nearly the same, has no occasion to exert his understanding or to exercise his invention in finding out expedients for removing difficulties which never occur. He naturally loses, therefore, the habit of such exertion, and generally becomes as stupid and ignorant as it is possible for a human creature to become. The torpor of his mind renders him not only incapable of relishing or bearing a part in any rational conversation, but of conceiving any generous, noble, or tender sentiment, and consequently of forming any just judgement concerning many even of the ordinary duties of private life. . . . But in every improved and civilized society this is the state into which the labouring poor, that is, the great body of the people, must necessarily fall, unless government takes some pains to prevent it.
>
> (Adam Smith, *The Wealth of Nations*)

Prescient though he was, Smith did not foresee the degree to which the state would become a largely owned subsidiary of business, with no interest in preventing the stultification of "the great body of the people."

In recent years de-skilling has been joined by omni-directional saturation advertising in a pincer movement aimed at turning our non-work as well as our work lives into profit centers. Matthew Crawford's brilliant and searching new work of social criticism begins with a familiar modern ordeal: boarding an airplane. Those plastic bins you put your shoes, wallet, and keys into? It dawned on some marketing genius that the insides of them could be plastered with ads. The tubes of lipstick advertised on the bottom of Crawford's bin resembled flash drives, so he almost failed to retrieve the flash drive containing the lecture he was flying somewhere to give. Once past security, he looked for a quiet place to sit and think. Forget it—shops, huge ad posters, TVs, "the usual airport cacophony." Virtually every inch of this public space made a claim on his attention for private commercial purposes. Except one: the business class lounge, the only place in the airport quiet enough to work, where the samurai of commerce sit devising the innovative marketing and business-process strategies that appropriate and direct the attention of the poor shlubs in the rest of the terminal.

These banal frustrations give rise to some original reflections on the political economy of attention in *The World beyond Your Head*. Though we rarely think of it this way, control of our attention is both a public good—a commons—and an individual right. In public places like airports, subways, buses, stadiums, streets, and schools, and even more in quasi-public spaces like television, newspapers, and social media, our attention is sold to advertisers in ever finer increments. This is, Crawford suggests, strictly analogous to environmental pollution and the plundering of public resources.

There are some resources that we hold in common, such as the air we breathe and the water we drink. We take them for granted, but their widespread availability makes everything else we do possible. I think the absence of noise is a resource of just this sort. More precisely, the valuable thing that we take for granted is the condition of not being addressed. Just as clean air makes respiration possible, silence, in this broader sense, is what makes it possible to think. We give it up willingly when we are in the company of other people with whom we have some relationship, and when we open ourselves to serendipitous encounters with strangers. To be addressed by mechanized means is an entirely different matter.

But for those who hold to the psychological model of rational choice that underlies neoclassical economics, it is not a different matter. On that view, decisions are made by ranking all available options on a single, unidimensional scale of utility or desirability. Ads, however seductive, are simply information, and the more information we have, the better—the freer—our choices. Consumers have a right to be bombarded with solicitations, however distracting, just as workers have a right to accept any conditions of employment, however degrading or unhealthful. Any government interference between seller and buyer or employer and employee is paternalism, the bane of American liberty.

Although even economists are beginning to abandon these simplistic notions of individuality and freedom, they continue to inform the official ideology of our governing parties and are entrenched in law and policy (to the advantage, not coincidentally, of sellers and employers). Crawford proposes a different model of individuality and choice, at once traditional and radically new. Expounding it, with richly informative excursions into neuroscience, experimental psychology, intellectual history, mass culture, skilled crafts, and sports, is the main business of *The World beyond Your Head*.

The detached, autonomous self of rational choice theory assumes the possibility of what philosophers call "the view from nowhere." In quest of epistemological certainty, we "take a detached stance toward our own experience, and subject it to a critical analysis from a perspective that isn't infected with our own subjectivity." Analogously, moral autonomy requires (paraphrasing Kant) that we "abstract from all objects . . . they should be without any influence at all on the will, which should not bend to outside forces or attractions but rather manifest its own sovereign authority."

These formulations did much useful work historically, asserting and defining human freedom against oppressive traditional authority. But they don't, when pushed to the limit, hold up. There are always initial conditions, presuppositions, things our previous experience has primed us to notice or overlook; there are always pre-existing appetites, values, commitments. We can't abstract from all these things when making judgments or choices, because they are, taken together, us. Our selves do not exist apart from circumstances, accidents, constraints. We are situated beings. "How we act is not determined in an isolated moment of choice; it is powerfully ordered by how we perceive the situation, how we are attuned to it, and this is very much a function of our previous history of shaping ourselves to the world in a particular way."

What this means in practice is illustrated by Crawford's superbly detailed, psychologically astute descriptions of motorcycle riding and repair (the subject of his previous, best-selling *Shop Class as Soulcraft*), glass blowing, short-order cooking, organ-making, and other demanding skills. In each case, a beginner submits to the rules and traditions of some practice. A sustained narrowing of focus and intensification of discipline gradually yield a wider vision of possibilities and an increase in freedom of action. Internalizing the past of the activity and identifying with the community of its practitioners make one capable and desirous of carrying it forward—of creating something new. The joint attention required by any shared effort creates a new viewpoint, in which our genuine individuality is more accurately perceived and more reliably confirmed. Rootedness, obedience, and self-limitation are thus the conditions of autonomy and mastery. Crawford summarizes:

> Genuine agency arises not in the context of mere choices freely made (as in shopping) but rather, somewhat paradoxically, in the context of submission to things that have their own intractable ways, whether the thing be a musical instrument, a garden, or the building of a bridge. . . . When we become competent in some particular field of practice, our perception is disciplined by that practice; we become attuned to pertinent features of a situation that would be invisible to a bystander. Through the exercise of a skill, the self that acts in the world takes on a definite shape. It comes to be in a relation of *fit* to a world it has grasped.

But does individual character matter in a liberal democracy? On the neoclassical model, work, culture, and politics are mutually independent. In the political marketplace as in every other, we are presented with an array of options, inform ourselves about them, compute our preferences, and select one. We decide in much the same way as IBM's Deep Blue decides on chess moves: we start from scratch every time and calculate. Of course the analogy is imperfect: computers don't have habits, prejudices, impulses, or

memory lapses; and their capacity for attention is virtually unlimited. The neoclassical model needs quite a number of simplifying
assumptions, like pre-Copernican epicycles. But the alternative—
to acknowledge that humans are not simple utility maximizers
with arbitrary preferences and unbounded desires, but rather that
there is a hierarchy of human goods, with limits on the scale and
rhythms within which we can flourish—would upend our current political economy.

It would mean, among other things, revulsion against what
work has become, or is becoming, for all too many of those
Americans lucky enough to have jobs: not merely ill paid and
insecure but also repetitive, stressful, and wholly scripted. The
only way workers can resist this degradation is (as Adam Smith
pointed out) collectively. But neoclassical economics frowns on
unions, committed instead to the fiction that fully autonomous
individuals can negotiate freely and on equal terms with large
corporate employers; and likewise to the dogma that the only
proper subject of this negotiation is the price of the employee's
labor, not its meaning.

Seeing past the liberal model of individual autonomy might
also mean recognizing that consumerism can have civic consequences. Just as atmospheric fine particles can clog our lungs
and impair our society's physical health, an unending stream of
commercial messages, some overwhelming and some barely per-
ceptible, can clog our minds, fragment our attention, and in the
long run, impair our society's mental and civic health. Even intelligent and straightforward ads, in sufficient quantities, might do
this to us; the dumb and manipulative ones we are daily subjected
to are surely accelerating our moronification. "Please," Crawford
pleads, at once jokingly and in earnest, "don't install speakers in
every single corner of a shopping mall, even its outdoor spaces.

Please don't fill up every moment between innings in a lazy college baseball game with thundering excitement. Please give me a way to turn off the monitor in the backseat of a taxi. Please let there be one corner of the bar where the flickering delivery system for Bud Lite commercials is deemed unnecessary, because I am already at the bar."

This—and no doubt a great deal more of *The World beyond Your Head*—is just what John Ruskin, William Morris, Ivan Illich, Christopher Lasch, Wendell Berry, and other great conservative radicals, or radical conservatives, would say to our over-managed, ad-choked, out-of-scale society. They were all skeptical of inevitable progress, alert to the costs as well as the benefits of new technology, able to distinguish the blessings from the cruelties of tradition, and as anxious to preserve the former as to abolish the latter. We're lucky that Matthew Crawford has updated this invaluable dissenting thread of cultural commentary. But our ecologies—of attention, of imagination, of civic virtue—are eroding ever faster. All too soon, it may no longer matter what anyone says.

13

Last Men and Women

We all know Nietzsche's parable of the last man. Certain that democracy, science, and secular humanism would definitively reshape civilization, Nietzsche—or more precisely, Zarathustra—asked what kind of human being would result. His answer, dripping with sarcasm and contempt, was that ordinary humans would become a kind of insect, "a race as ineradicable as the flea-beetle," a creature that would "make the earth itself small." Here is Zarathustra's lament:

"Alas, the time of the most despicable man is coming, he that is no longer able to despise himself. Behold, I show you the *last man*.

"'What is love? What is creation? What is longing? What is a star?' the last man asks, and he blinks.

"'We have invented happiness,' say the last men, and they blink. They have left the regions where it was hard to live, for one needs warmth. One loves one's neighbor and rubs against him, for one needs warmth.

"No shepherd and one herd! Everyone wants the same, everyone is the same; whoever feels different goes voluntarily into a madhouse.

"One has one's little pleasures for the day and one's little pleasures for the night, but one has a regard for health.

"'We have invented happiness,' say the last men, and they blink."

(*Thus Spoke Zarathustra*, I, 5)

Plenty of others besides Nietzsche have expressed misgivings about the likely character structure of democratic citizens, and these critics have not all been opponents of democracy. (I'm using "democracy" here to mean the whole Enlightenment program: not just political equality but also feminism, pacifism, human rights, and the welfare state, along with a chastened belief in, and modest hopes for, moral and material progress.) Tocqueville's reservations are well known: "The general character of past society was diversity," he wrote; "unity and uniformity were nowhere to be met with. In modern society, however, all things threaten to become so much alike that the peculiar characteristics of each individual will be entirely lost in the uniformity of the general aspect." Even John Stuart Mill fretted that "the general tendency of things throughout the world is to render mediocrity the ascendant power among mankind. . . . At present individuals are lost in the crowd." Criticisms of mass society and mass man swelled to a roar in the twentieth century: Durkheim, Spengler, Schmitt, Ortega, Walter Lippmann, Heidegger, the Frankfurt School, Foucault, Alasdair MacIntyre, Allan Bloom, and many, many others.

Most of these criticisms I reject, not for their often powerful diagnoses but for the illiberal prescriptions that usually accompany them. I agree with Richard Rorty's admirably forthright solution to the supposed dilemma of democratic mediocrity: to wit, "even if the typical character types of liberal democracies *are* bland, calculating, petty, and unheroic, the prevalence of such people may be a reasonable price to pay for political freedom." We can and should separate the private from the public, self-creation from tolerance, the pursuit of perfection from democratic politics. As Rorty famously elaborated:

> From Plato through Kant down to [Habermas and Derrida], most philosophers have tried to fuse sublimity and decency, to fuse social hope with knowledge of something big . . . My own hunch is that we have to separate individual and social reassurance, to make sublimity [unlike tolerance] a private, optional matter. That means conceding to Nietzsche that democratic societies have no higher aim than what he called "the last men"—the people who have "their little pleasures for the day and their little pleasures for the night." Maybe we should just make that concession, and also concede that democratic societies do not embody anything, and cannot be reassured by anything, larger than themselves (e.g., by "rationality"). Such societies should not aim at the creation of a new breed of human being, or at anything less banal than evening out people's chances of getting a little pleasure out of their lives. This means that citizens of those societies who have a taste for sublimity will have to pursue it on their own time, and within the limits set by *On Liberty*. But such opportunities might be quite enough.

That, broadly, is where I also stand—with the Enlightenment and its contemporary heirs, and against Straussians, religious conservatives, national greatness neoconservatives, Ayn Randian libertarians, and anyone else for whom tolerance, civic equality, international law, and a universal minimum standard of material welfare are less than fundamental commitments. But without, I hope, contradicting myself, I'd like to work the other side of the street for a while: to acknowledge the force of at least some criticisms of modernity and progress.

Perhaps the most important, though also the most fragile, success Enlightenment liberalism has had is the delegitimation, however partial, of war. The perception that the arbitrary power of absolute rulers facilitated needless and vastly destructive wars was a powerful impetus to popular sovereignty in the nineteenth and twentieth centuries, culminating in the United Nations Charter. Though the Charter has been repeatedly violated by the great powers—and not only by them—it is not quite a dead letter, and a global culture of respect for international law may be the most urgent cause any activist could devote her life to.

Even so, biology has its rights. In 1910, the last year of his life and only a few years before the First World War put an end to the long European peace, William James wrote a pamphlet for the Association for International Conciliation, one of the many pacifist groups whose prominence in that period convinced many people that war between nations, being so obviously irrational, was therefore impossible. James's essay, titled "The Moral Equivalent of War," is a work of supreme pathos and wisdom. James himself was a pacifist, a founding member of the Anti-Imperialist League, a group formed to protest America's military interventions in Cuba, Haiti, and the Philippines, and one of the most humane and generous spirits America—or any other nation—has ever produced.

James understood perfectly the folly—the "monstrosity," as he called it—of war, even in those comparatively innocent, pre-nuclear days. But he also acknowledged the place of the martial virtues in a healthy character. "We inherit the warlike type," he pointed out, "and for most of the capacities of heroism that the human race is full of we have to thank [our bloody] history." "The martial virtues," he continued, "although originally gained by the race through war, are absolute and permanent human goods. . . . Militarism is the supreme theater of strenuousness, the great preserver of our ideals of hardihood; and human life with no use for strenuousness and hardihood would be contemptible." "We pacifists," he wrote with characteristic intellectual generosity, "ought to enter more deeply into the aesthetic and ethical point of view of our opponents." To militarists, a world without war is "a sheep's paradise," flat and insipid. "No scorn, no hardness, no valor any more!" he imagines them saying indignantly. "Fie upon such a cattleyard of a planet!" This, remember, was the era of Teddy Roosevelt, preacher of the strenuous life and instigator of splendid little wars. James's pacifism may be common sense to you and me, but when he wrote, the common sense of Americans was mostly on Roosevelt's side.

How to nourish the martial virtues without war? James resolved this apparent dilemma with a suggestion many decades ahead of its time: universal national service, every youth to be conscripted for several years of hard and socially necessary physical work, with no exceptions and no class or educational discrimination. This army without weapons would be the moral equivalent of war, breeding, James argued, some of the virtues essential to democracy: "intrepidity, contempt of softness, surrender of private interest, obedience to command." I am sure James would have agreed that these are not the only virtues essential to democracy—he himself, with his anti-imperialist activism, exemplified an equally essential skepticism and resistance to authority. But I wonder if twenty-first-century intellectuals, most of whom need no convincing about the necessity of skepticism and resistance to authority, would also agree with James about the importance of valor, strenuousness, and self-sacrifice.

James wrote in America before World War I, a situation of almost idyllic innocence compared with that of the next writer I want to cite, D. H. Lawrence. The Great War, as contemporaries called it, was a soul-shattering experience for English writers. The complacent stupidity with which Europe's governing classes initiated, conducted, and concluded that war, the chauvinism and bloodlust with which ordinary people on all sides welcomed it, and above all, the mindless, mechanical grinding up of millions of lives by a war machine that seemed to go of itself—these things infuriated Lawrence almost to madness. Like many others, Lawrence saw the facelessness, the impersonality, the almost bureaucratic character of this mass violence as something new and horrifying in human history. As a pre-eminent champion of the body and the instincts against the abstract, impersonal forces of modernity, he marshalled torrents of impassioned prose against the apparently inexorable encroachments of progress. Here is a passage from "Education of the People," published posthumously in the two volumes of *Phoenix*.

We are all fighters. Let us fight. Has it come down to chasing a poor fox and kicking a leather ball? Heavens, what a spectacle we should be to the ancient Greek. Rouse the old male spirit again. The male is always a fighter. The human male is a superb and god-like fighter, unless he is contravened in his own nature. In fighting to the death, he has one great crisis of his being.

What is the fight? It is a primary, physical thing. It is not a horrible, obscene, abstract business, like our last war. It is not a ghastly and blasphemous translation of ideas into engines, and men into cannon-fodder. Away with such war. A million times away with such obscenity. Let the desire of it die out of mankind. . . . Let us beat our plowshares into swords, if we will. But let us blow all guns and explosives and poison-gases sky-high. Let us shoot every man who makes one more grain of gunpowder, with his own powder.

And then let us be soldiers, hand-to-hand soldiers. Lord, but it is a bitter thing to be born at the end of a rotten, idea-ridden machine civilization. Think what we've missed: the glorious bright passion of anger and pride, reckless and dauntless.

In other words: fight when you must, when your blood boils over and your anger won't be gainsaid. But fight face to face, hand to hand, in your own quarrels and in your own skin, as a responsible human being and not a machine, or worse, a machine-operator. I think William James would have agreed with that. More: I think Mary Wollstonecraft, Margaret Fuller, Grace Paley, perhaps even Dorothy Day would have agreed. I believe that one can be—*must* be—both a feminist and an upholder of the martial virtues, just as James showed that one must be both a pacifist and an upholder of the martial virtues.

Modernity imperils another set of virtues, which are a little harder to characterize than the martial virtues, but are even more important. I don't mean the bourgeois virtues, though there's some overlap. I suppose I'd call them the yeoman virtues. I have in mind the qualities we associate with life in the early American republic—the positive qualities, of course, not the qualities that enabled slavery and genocide. In 1820, 80 percent of the American population was self-employed. Protestant Christianity, local self-government, and agrarian and artisanal producerism fostered a culture of self-control, self-reliance, integrity, diligence, and neighborliness—the American ethos that Tocqueville praised and that Lincoln argued was incompatible with large-scale slave-owning. Today that ethos survives only in political speeches and Hollywood movies. In a society based on precarious employment and feverish consumption, on debt, financial trickery, endless manipulation, and incessant distraction, such a sensibility seems archaic.

According to the late Christopher Lasch, the advent of mass production and the new relations of authority it introduced in every sphere of social life wrought a fateful change in the prevailing American character structure. Psychological maturation—as Lasch, relying on Freud, explicated it—depended crucially on face-to-face relations, on a rhythm and a scale that industrialism disrupted. The result was a weakened, malleable self, more easily regimented than its preindustrial forebear, less able to withstand conformist pressures and bureaucratic manipulation—the antithesis of the rugged individualism that had undergirded the republican virtues.

In an important recent book, *The Age of Acquiescence*, the historian Steve Fraser deploys a similar argument to explain why, in contrast with the first Gilded Age, when America was wracked by furious anticapitalist resistance, popular response in our time to the depredations of capitalism has been so feeble. Here is Fraser's thesis:

> During the first Gilded Age the work ethic constituted the nuclear core of American cultural belief and practice. That era's emphasis on capital accumulation presumed frugality, saving, and delayed gratification as well as disciplined, methodical labor. That ethos frowned on self-indulgence, was wary of debt, denounced wealth not transparently connected to useful, tangible outputs, and feared libidinal

excess, whether that took the form of gambling, sumptuary displays, leisured indolence, or uninhibited sexuality.

How at odds that all is with the moral and psychic economy of our own second Gilded Age. An economy kept aloft by finance and mass consumption has for a long time rested on an ethos of immediate gratification, enjoyed a love affair with debt, speculation, and risk, erased the distinction between productive labor and pursuits once upon a time judged parasitic, and become endlessly inventive about ways to supercharge with libido even the homeliest of household wares.

Can these two diverging political economies—one resting on industry, the other on finance—and these two polarized sensibilities—one fearing God, the other living in an impromptu moment to moment—explain the Great Noise of the first Gilded Age and the Great Silence of the second? Is it possible that people still attached by custom and belief to ways of subsisting that had originated outside the orbit of capital accumulation were for that very reason both psychologically and politically more existentially desperate, more capable, and more audacious in envisioning a non-capitalist future than those who have come of age knowing nothing else?

If this argument is true—and I find it painfully plausible—where does that leave us? An individual's or a society's character structure cannot be willed into or out of existence. Lost virtues and solidarities cannot be regained overnight, or even, perhaps, in a generation. Even our ideologies of liberation may have to be rethought. A transvaluation of values may be in order: faster, easier, and more may have to give way to slower, harder, and less—not only for ecological reasons but also for reasons of mental and moral hygiene. And even if we bite that bullet and decide, as a society, to spit out the poisoned apple of consumerism and technological addiction, is there a path back? If individual self-sufficiency and local self-government are prerequisites for human flourishing, then maybe it is too late.

I know of only one book that takes the full measure of the dilemmas I've been hinting at and goes on to show one way to a sane and stable future. It's a utopian novel by Ernest Callenbach, called *Ecotopia*. It was published in 1975 and had a brief vogue but seems to have disappeared along with the rest of the counter-culture of that era. It deserves better: it's politically and psychologically astute, and ecologically far ahead of its—or our—time. But the utopian society it depicts, located in the Pacific Northwest, is made possible by the survival in that region of some of the very cultural traits and virtues whose obsolescence in the rest of the country I've been lamenting.

Do my apparently disparate-sounding worries have anything in common? Possibly this: they all result from one or another move on the part of the culture away from the immediate, the instinctual, the face-to-face. We are embodied beings, gradually adapted over millions of years to thrive on a certain scale, our metabolisms a delicate orchestration of innumerable biological and geophysical rhythms. The culture of modernity has thrust upon us, sometimes with traumatic abruptness, experiences, relationships, and powers for which we may not yet be ready—to which we may need more time to adapt.

But time is short. "All that is solid melts into air"—Marx meant the crust of tradition, dissolving in the acid bath of global capitalism. Now, however, the earth itself is melting. Marx's great metaphor has acquired a terrifying second meaning.

And so has Nietzsche's. If we cannot slow down and grow cautiously, evenly, gradually into our new technological and political possibilities and responsibilities—even the potentially liberating ones—the last recognizably individual men and women may give place, before too many more generations, to the simultaneously sub- and super-human civilization of the hive.

PART II

The Left

14

South of Eden

Leonardo Sciascia

In Giuseppe Tomasi di Lampedusa's novel *The Leopard*, the philosophical Prince Fabrizio explains sadly to a visitor, a liberal reformer urging Italian national unity, why nineteenth-century Sicily will not join the modern world: "The Sicilians never want to improve, for the simple reason that they think themselves perfect; their vanity is stronger than their misery." A curious and pathetic illusion, this. Mortification would seem a more appropriate response to Sicilian history and culture than vanity. The guiding principles of Sicilian society, at least as it is portrayed in nineteenth- and early twentieth-century Italian literature, are envy, jealousy, superstition, avarice, low cunning, unremitting suspiciousness, and everlasting vindictiveness. The stubbornly adhered-to—and frequently romanticized—Sicilian ideals of *onore, vendetta,* and *omertà* mean, in practice, that all women are property, that all grievances are mortal, and that all outsiders are untrustworthy. D. H. Lawrence, who knew and loved Sicily as well as any other non-Italian, was aghast at the mores of the Sicilian village: "so squalid, so pottering, so despicable; like a crawling of beetles." At their worst, Sicilians of the traditional

stripe can make the wiliest and most grasping of Balzacian villains seem like the most ethereally pure of Dickensian heroines.
The Mafia and the Inquisition, the two most successful institutions in the island's history, are about what they (being only a
couple of generations removed, perhaps I should say "we")
deserve.

Nevertheless, from this unpromising human material some
enduring literature has been fashioned. Giovanni Verga, one of
the founders of European naturalism, produced several
renowned novels and stories set in Sicily, as did the young Luigi
Pirandello, for all his later cosmopolitanism. Southern Italy,
with its similar social and cultural conditions, was the setting
of Ignazio Silone's widely admired fiction, including his masterpiece, *Bread and Wine*. And one of the most popular Italian
books of this century, Carlo Levi's *Christ Stopped at Eboli*,
chronicles the encounter of an urban intellectual from the
North, exiled by Mussolini to a remote village in the rural
South, with his premodern countrymen.

To this slender but distinguished line one may add the contemporary Sicilian writer Leonardo Sciascia. Born in 1921, he
spent most of his life as a schoolteacher. In the 1950s he began to
write historical/political sketches of his native region, which
were collected in his first book, *Salt in the Wound*. Around the
same time, he began writing fiction; *Sicilian Uncles* is his first
collection. His subsequent fiction became progressively more
playful, allusive, and oblique. *Candido* is an updated version,
with modern Italian characters, of Voltaire's fable. *The Council
of Egypt* is a historical tale about a forged manuscript; though
not quite as baroque as *The Name of the Rose*, it is nearly as erudite and as epistemologically suggestive. *Mafia Vendetta*, *A
Man's Blessing*, *Equal Danger*, and *One Way or Another* are

detective novels, all of them featuring murder, political conspiracy, and an ambiguous outcome in which, true to Sicilian reality, something less than justice is done. *The Wine-Dark Sea* is a collection of short stories, Pirandellian in their combination of whimsy and melancholy. Although Sciascia is one of Europe's most eminent living writers, English translations of all his works have been in and out of print; so every new translation or reissue, like this one from Carcanet, is an event.

Sicilian Uncles is the most political in content and the most conventionally realistic in form of Sciascia's fiction, and it is arguably his best. It consists of four novellas. In "The American Aunt," a boy observes the arrival of the occupying American army and the subsequent metamorphosis of his town—a ritual of Sicilian history—from hostility to hospitality. He cadges cigarettes from the soldiers and sells them to his layabout uncle, who mourns for the "respect" and "glory" that Mussolini's conquests had brought Italy. Along with the soldiers, there begins to arrive a stream of parcels from the townspeople's American relatives. It is like a first installment of the Marshall Plan, and like the later installments, it is accompanied by frequent exhortations to vote against the Communists in the postwar elections.

Eventually the boy's aunt arrives from Brooklyn with her family and a trunkful of gifts, whose distribution is supervised by the Sicilian uncle, formerly pro-Fascist but now staunchly pro-American. The aunt's triumph is a little muted: she finds the island not quite so poor and primitive as in her girlhood memories and her fantasies of benevolence. But she finds something else, too: a husband for her daughter in the canny, courtierlike uncle. This encounter between New World wealth and Old World subtlety is, in its way, reminiscent of Henry

James—though nothing could be less Jamesian than Sciascia's laconic style.

The Italian post–World War II elections, in which the Communists lost to the Christian Democrats (with a little help from the CIA), took place in 1948. Exactly a century earlier, the specter of revolution had likewise haunted Sicily, and was likewise beaten back. The narrator of "Forty-Eight" is also a boy. His father is the gardener of Baron Garziano of Castro, who, along with the Bishop and the Prefect, incarnates the traditional triple nemesis of the Sicilian peasantry: Church, state, and landed aristocracy. When the European revolution of 1848 sets off tremors even in Castro, the terrified Baron and the wily Bishop manage to ride out the storm and return to their customary pursuits: the Baron to adultery and the Bishop to embezzlement. But twelve years later the specter returns in the form of Garibaldi, whose troops (including the narrator, now a young man) are in the process of unifying Italy. Ever a survivor, the Baron welcomes and abjectly flatters Garibaldi—though enough of the Red Shirts see through his cajolery to suggest that the old order in no longer invulnerable.

In both these stories, the ingenuousness of the child-narrator highlights the ubiquitous, ineffable rascality of Sicilian adults. This contrast is the source of much of Sciascia's humor. For example, the pro-Fascist uncle in "The American Aunt," who grumbles that Mussolini is too soft on political opponents, is full of terrors when the tide turns:

> "The Communists!" he said. "Neither you nor your father understand anything of what's going on. They're coming now. You'll see those murderers arrive right here, burning the churches, destroying families, pulling people from their beds and shooting them."

My uncle was thinking of himself. He was in bed at least sixteen hours a day. I pictured him being dragged from his bed by the feet—which pleased me—but I wasn't so pleased at the thought he might be shot.

The note of compassion in that last sentence is characteristic of Sciascia. Notoriously, Sicilian speech is sly and melodramatic by turns; the effect is ridiculous but endearing. Sciascia renders it sardonically, unsentimentally, with affection but without condescension.

"The American Aunt" and "Forty-Eight" are exquisitely wrought stories, in part because their author maintains his aesthetic distance: the comic invention is so exuberant that moral and political meaning remain latent. The other two tales in *Sicilian Uncles*, "Antimony" and "The Death of Stalin," are more directly political; Sciascia's wry humanism is closer to the surface. But if they are not quite so coolly elegant, they are even more affecting.

In "The Death of Stalin," the shoemaker Calogero Schirò is a loyal Communist and a fervent admirer of Stalin, whom he defends against the continual imprecations of the parish priest. The Nazi-Soviet Pact of 1939 tests his faith and gives the priest something to gloat over. But, helped by the appearance of Stalin in a dream, he reasons it out: the Non-Aggression Pact is a trap for Hitler; Stalin is biding his time. The priest is skeptical, but Calogero is gleeful at his discovery: "'Stalin's the greatest man in the world,' he said. 'To think of traps like that you need a brain as big as a fifty-pound sack of flour.'"

There are other troubling developments—the annexation of Poland, the invasion of Finland, the liquidation of Stalin's generals, the loss of the postwar elections—but Calogero keeps the faith. Then the hardest blow falls: Stalin dies and his "mistakes" come to light. Even the party admits them. Calogero is shaken; the priest exults. Again he tries to reason it out: Stalin's "brain was beginning to crumble with always having to think about the benefit of mankind: at a certain point he became eccentric." But he's too honest not to end up dissatisfied and confused.

"The Death of Stalin" is extremely funny. But even more important, Sciascia shows that although Calogero was deceived, he was something more dignified than a dupe. To acknowledge the horrible crimes of Stalinism, and at the same time do justice to the honorable aspirations it exploited, is difficult; it has rarely been done better than here. As the Germans retreat before the victorious Russian armies, Calogero has a reverie:

Stalin was coming down into the very heart of Europe, bringing Communism and Justice. Thieves and usurers were trembling, and all those spiders who wove the world's riches and its injustices. In every city that the Red Army reached, Calogero imagined dark swarms in flight: the men of oppression and injustice convulsed with animal terror; while in the light-filled piazzas the workers mobbed Stalin's troops. Comrade Stalin, Marshal Stalin, Uncle Joe, everybody's uncle, protector of the poor and weak, the man with justice in his heart. Calogero closed out every reasoning about the things wrong with Regalpetra and the world by pointing to the portrait, "Uncle Joe'll take care of it," and he thought it had been he who had invented the familiar nickname, which by that time all the comrades in Regalpetra were using. On the contrary, all the farm laborers and sulfur miners in Sicily, all the poor who believed in hope, used to call him "Uncle Joe," as they once had done to Garibaldi. They used the name "Uncle" for all the men who brought justice or vengeance, the hero or the *capomafia*: the idea of justice always shines when vindictive thoughts are decanted. Calogero had been interned, his comrades there had instructed him in doctrine, but he couldn't think of Stalin as anything other than an "Uncle" who could arm for a vendetta and strike decisively *a baccagliu*, that is, in the slang of all Sicilian "Uncles," against the enemies of Calogero Schirò: Cavaliere Pecorilla, who had sent him into internment; Gangemi, the sulfur miner, who had refused to pay him for resoling a shoe; and Dr. La Ferla, who had distrained him of over two hundredweight of wheat to pay for an operation on his groin, which a butcher could have done better.

There is no need to detail the ironies in this passage, or the fate of Calogero's hopes; I could hardly bear to, in any case. Still, this homely vision—this jumble of ancient grievances, local prejudice, and personal pain—seems to me as worthy of respect as the loftiest flights of Gramsci.

Stalinism and Fascism had another fateful encounter: the Spanish Civil War. George Orwell's *Homage to Catalonia* begins with a now famous anecdote: his brief meeting with an illiterate Italian militiaman, who symbolized for him everything brave and decent about the Republican cause—everything that, like Calogero Schirò's vision, was frustrated and betrayed by Stalinism. The protagonist of "Antimony" is also a young militiaman, this time on the Fascist side, one of the many unemployed Italians shipped to Spain by Mussolini to fight for Franco. But the Fascist firing squads nauseate him, and he comes to realize that the people he is fighting in Spain and the people he lives among in Sicily—the peasants and the sulfur miners—have a common enemy. "I would say that the least peasant in my home district, the most 'benighted,' as we say, that is, the most ignorant, the one most cut off from a knowledge of the world, if he had been brought to the

Aragon front and had been told to find out which side people like himself were on and go to them, he would have made for the Republican trenches without hesitation." It is a memorable political education. Despite its brevity, "Antimony" ranks with *Homage to Catalonia* and André Malraux's *Man's Hope* as one of the finest imaginative products of the Spanish Civil War.

By the end of that war W. H. Auden was to write, in deepest disillusionment, that "intellectual disgrace/Stares from every human face." Very few politically engaged writers have emerged from this century's ideological wars with their intellectual honor intact. Sciascia may be numbered among them. The humanism that shines through the fiction of Silone, the films of de Sica, the essays of Chiaromonte, Camus, Orwell, and Dwight Macdonald—this, leavened with the bittersweet humor of the immemorially defeated Sicilian, is Sciascia's sensibility as well. The miracle, even more in his case than in theirs, is that so much disillusionment and defeat could yield so much generosity and hope.

"All my books taken together form one," Sciascia has written: "a Sicilian book which probes the wounds of past and present and develops as the history of the continuous defeat of reason and of those who have been personally overcome and annihilated in that defeat." Defeat, yes; but there is hope in Sciascia's "Sicilian book" too. In *Politics and the Novel* Irving Howe paid tribute to Silone in terms that will do equally well to sum up Sciascia's achievement: "He remains hopeful, with a hopefulness that has nothing to do with optimism, that from the hidden inarticulate resources of the poor, which consist neither of intelligence nor nobility, but rather of a training in endurance and an education in ruse—that from all this, something worthy of the human may yet emerge."

15

A Critical Life

Irving Howe

To be universally respected at the close of one's career can be a bitter fate. For nearly five decades Irving Howe has scolded and coaxed, reasoned with and preached to, American society—on the whole futilely, as he would be the first to admit. McCarthyism, the Cold War, the Vietnam War, the Reagan regression, the conformism of intellectuals, and the commercialization of culture have rolled along unaffected by the forceful, eloquent, scrupulously nuanced criticism perseveringly produced by Howe and his democratic-socialist comrades in their journal, *Dissent*, and elsewhere. Though radical in substance, that criticism has generally been moderate in tone; so American society, impervious to enlightenment but sensitive to ridicule, has gratefully accorded Howe a measure of moral prestige as an elder statesman of the "responsible" left. Even veteran radicals cherish respectability. But I don't doubt that Howe would gladly trade his for, say, the prospect of a modest national health-insurance program or a slight reduction in arms sales abroad.

Howe is by no means exclusively a political writer. Most of *Selected Writings: 1950–1990* is in fact literary criticism: Howe was a professor of English for thirty years and has published books on Hardy, Faulkner, and Sherwood Anderson, besides several collections of essays and reviews. Nor are his literary interests and approach limited by ideology. Predictably, he has written with sympathy and insight about Zola, Dreiser, and Silone; less predictably but equally well about Wharton and Frost, Leskov and Pirandello, Whitman and Stevens, Edward Arlington Robinson and T. E. Lawrence. And his three major essays on modernism (two of them, "The Idea of the Modern" and "The City in Literature," are included in *Selected Writings*; the other, "Mass Society and Post-Modern Fiction," is not) are definitive.

But Howe's first love, or first vocation, was politics. The East Bronx in the 1920s and '30s, where he grew up, was an ideological hothouse, from which the children of immigrant Jewish unionists generally emerged as one or another variety of socialist. At City College, this cohort of young radicals—Howe, Daniel Bell, Irving Kristol, and a couple of hundred others—sharpened their dialectical skills debating each other about *Capital*, current events, and, above all, Trotskyist schism and Stalinist orthodoxy. (There's a piquant sketch of this milieu in Howe's 1982 memoir, *A Margin of Hope*.)

Howe was an active member of a small Trotskyist group, editing its journal and speaking at its forums, when he was drafted in 1942 and sent to Alaska. There he sat out World War II in an undemanding clerical job and read greedily. This enforced turn inward, and perhaps also the postwar collapse of revolutionary fervor throughout the American left, accelerated Howe's ideological evolution. After a brief spell of renewed party activity, he abandoned Trotskyism for a non-sectarian, unaffiliated radicalism—moved, so to speak, from agitation to dissent. In 1954, with $2,000 and a few like-minded radicals, he started *Dissent*.

Meanwhile, on the strength of his freelance literary criticism in *Partisan Review* and *Commentary*, he was offered a job teaching at newly founded Brandeis University. Eventually he returned to New York, teaching at his alma mater and at Hunter College. Like many other children of immigrants, Howe returned also to his ethnic roots, editing and writing about Yiddish literature even as it became virtually extinct in the 1960s and '70s, and producing *World of Our Fathers*, a panoramic and best-selling portrait of Jewish immigrant life.

The world of the children has, however, attracted even more attention. In the last decade or so, a spate of histories, biographies, and memoirs has traced the career of the New York intellectuals, from their spectacular debut in the 1930s and '40s via *Partisan Review*, through their ascent to cultural prominence, their reconciliation with American society in the 1950s, and (sometimes) their re-radicalization or (more often) conservative turn in the 1960s and '70s. The research has been assiduous, the interpretations ingenious, the polemics fierce. And with reason: they were an unusually coherent and distinguished group, including Lionel Trilling, Dwight Macdonald, Sidney Hook, Meyer Schapiro, Philip Rahv, Hannah Arendt, Mary McCarthy, Harold Rosenberg, Delmore Schwartz, Bell, Kristol, Howe, and quite a few others equally or only slightly less eminent. For a brief Golden Age, they seem to have attained or at least approached an intellectual ideal: a union of independence and community, integrity and commitment, cosmopolitanism and authority. All this, in turn, made their political evolution especially significant, as though it marked the inevitable trajectory of intellectual radicalism in America.

There was not, of course, only one trajectory, or even two. But there was a general movement that had, if not a common destination, at least a common point of departure. The illusions painfully and publicly shed by one after another of the New York intellectuals were, first, that a socialist revolution was possible in the foreseeable future; and second, that a pseudo-socialist or Leninist revolution, which would leave a single party in control of the state and the economy, was desirable, if only as a step toward genuine socialism.

Renouncing these beliefs did the New York intellectuals credit. But where did it leave them politically? It left most of them in an apolitical limbo, from which they sallied forth only for an occasional *Partisan Review* symposium or *cause célèbre*, such as the controversy over Hannah Arendt's 1963 report on the trial of ex-Nazi Adolf Eichmann or the student strike at Columbia in 1968. Some let themselves be carried by the momentum of their rejection all the way into neoconservatism. Howe took the path of most resistance, determined to avoid the simplicities of ortho- doxy and apostasy alike, to keep faith both with socialism's original vision and with the victims of those who have falsely claimed to be realizing that vision in the twentieth century.

It has been a struggle. In a much-quoted anecdote from Howe's autobiography, a friend observes that although Howe's politics are entirely admirable, they are, alas, "boring"; an abashed Howe agrees. I don't, on either count. Howe's politics have at times been less than admirable, but his political development has been a complicated, continuously interesting moral drama.

The essence of drama is conflict. Howe's career has been marked by a symmetrical pair of conflicts: with the older intel- lectuals who, after World War II, made an ignoble peace with American society; and with the young radicals who, in the late 1960s, made incoherent war on it. "This Age of Conformity" (1954) was occasioned by the intellectuals' response, or lack of response, to McCarthyism, and more particularly by the famous *Partisan Review* symposium, "Our Country and Our Culture." The willingness of Sidney Hook, Irving Kristol, and other proto-neoconservatives to minimize McCarthy's threat to civil liberties; the pseudo-religious vagaries of many New Critics; even Lionel Trilling's Olympian nods of approval at mid-century American civilization—for Howe, these were symptoms of a subtle abdication of the critical spirit. "We have all," he wryly lamented, "even the handful who still try to retain a glower of criticism, become responsible and moderate."

"This Age of Conformity" was an effective polemic. Even the middlebrow journals, Howe noted ruefully a few years later, were soon "alive with chatter about conformity." But the essay transcends polemic. Concisely and cogently, Howe identified the historical processes that had produced inescapable pressures toward conformism—above all, the advent of mass society, "a society in which ideology plays an unprecedented part." Intellectuals were recruited en masse into administration, advertising, education, and entertainment. Appearances notwithstanding, the resulting gain in status was not a gain in real social power: it was in fact a loss, not of power (critical intellectuals had none to lose) but of autonomy:

> The institutional world needs intellectuals because they are intellectuals but it does not want them *as* intellectuals. It beckons to them because of what they are but it will not allow them, at least within its sphere of articulation, to either remain or entirely cease being what they are. . . . A simplified but useful equation suggests itself: the relation of the institutional world to the intellectuals is like the relation of middlebrow culture to serious culture. The one battens on the other, absorbs and raids it with increasing frequency and skill,

subsidizes and encourages it enough to make further raids possible—
sometimes the parasite will support its victim.

Resistance to these pressures was undermined by the disappearance of bohemia, a casualty of prosperity and urban renewal.
Three decades before Russell Jacoby's acclaimed *The Last Intellectuals*, Howe's essay described the integration of the literati
into the universities and the transformation of the man of letters
into the academic critic. The result was a "gradual bureaucratization of opinion and taste," the creep of massification into the
realm of the spirit.

"This Age of Conformity" was a masterpiece, one of the pearls
in *Partisan*'s crown. Combining a rhetorical verve equal to anything of Sartre's, a historical penetration akin to Trotsky's (with
a far more restrained and effective deployment of sarcasm), and
an unsentimental humanism reminiscent of Orwell, it was not
just astute but exciting. Not boring at all.

Howe's reputation for tedious correctness is mostly derived,
though, from his other major public controversy, with the New
Left. As readers of Maurice Isserman's *If I Had a Hammer*, Todd
Gitlin's *The Sixties*, or any other serious account of the period
will know, relations were not always hostile. *Dissent* welcomed,
even celebrated, the early New Left. Why things turned sour in
the mid-sixties has lately been the subject of almost as much
research and debate as the political peregrinations of the New
York intellectuals. The protagonists—Howe, Michael Harrington, Tom Hayden—all wrote memoirs during the eighties in
which each one graciously assumed a large share of blame. But
the issues remain.

What the older radicals—Howe, Harrington, and others
from *Dissent* and the League for Industrial Democracy—wanted

from the younger ones was a consistent, explicit, comprehensive anticommunism. The younger ones—Hayden and other leaders of SDS—demurred. Because they had learned anticommunism from J. Edgar Hoover and *Reader's Digest* rather than Rosa Luxemburg and Victor Serge, they mistrusted it. Because Castro and Ho Chi Minh were targets of imperial violence, the younger radicals saw them as victims (which they were) but not as dictators (which they also were). It is notoriously difficult to keep two opposing truths in one's mind at the same time, let alone figure out how to act on them. The young radicals couldn't manage it, and the older ones were no help.

They were even, at times, a hindrance. It's true the young were terribly provoking—the leadership's swaggering arrogance eventually produced an open revolt among New Left women, which was the Lexington and Concord of contemporary American feminism. But although most of Howe's strictures throughout the sixties were justified in tone and content, he finally, fatally, stopped complaining *to* the young radicals and started complaining *about* them. The result, predictably, was a deterioration of relations and escalation of angry rhetoric, and sometimes petty malice, on both sides. The episode was one of Howe's few lapses from political grace.

Another is his apparently invincible antipathy to Noam Chomsky, the leading left-wing critic of American foreign policy, with whom Howe has, as far as I can tell, few or no fundamental political differences. Chomsky's criticisms of some of Howe's more embattled formulations about the New Left and the Middle East, while largely correct in substance, have been excessively harsh in tone. Still, Howe edits a journal and Chomsky does not, a circumstance that imposes unequal obligations. That the best journal of the American left is, in effect, closed to the most important writer on the American left, however personally difficult; that Chomsky's awesome logical powers and appetite for facts and Howe's verbal, psychological, and moral subtlety and tact have, instead of supplementing each other, reacted on each other like gasoline and water—this is a large misfortune. And that the embargo, or at least inhospitality, extends to Gabriel Kolko, Michael Klare, Thomas Ferguson, Joel Rogers, and other talented radicals who might both improve *Dissent*'s foreign policy coverage and themselves benefit from comradely criticism by its editors and other contributors—this is a small tragedy.

Howe's politics have never been more admirable than in his frequent restatements of the socialist ideal. From "Images of Socialism" (1954) to *Socialism and America* (1985), Howe has anxiously but unflinchingly demanded: "Can one still specify what the vision of socialism means or should mean?" After Stalinism and Maoism, it's obvious what socialism doesn't mean. Less obviously, perhaps, but just as surely, it doesn't mean merely the electoral triumph of a socialist party, as Mitterrand's painful experience showed. The only way to answer Howe's question is to gather up fragments from the tradition—cries of protest and invocations of solidarity, heroic lives and utopian fantasies, analytic strands and programmatic patches—and fuse them imaginatively. The resulting unity will be only temporary; the ideal will need to be reimagined in every generation. But this is how traditions live. In our time, Howe's efforts, as much as anyone else's, have kept the socialist tradition alive.

A volume of selected writings, especially one covering four decades, invites a summing up. After all his political positions are noted and literary judgments weighed, what kind of writer/ critic/intellectual has Howe been? Anyone considering Howe's work must first of all be impressed—whether favorably or unfavorably, as superb ambition or absurd presumption—by its extraordinary range. Howe has lived by his own dictum: "By impulse, if not definition, the intellectual is a man who writes about subjects outside his field. He has no field." Howe has in fact characterized his work better than anyone else could, in yet another brilliant, definitive essay, "The New York Intellectuals":

> The kind of essay they wrote was likely to be wide-ranging in reference, melding notions about literature and politics, sometimes announcing itself as a study of a writer or literary group but usually taut with a pressure to "go beyond" it subject, toward some encompassing moral or social observation. It is a kind of writing highly self-conscious in mode, with an unashamed vibration of bravura. Nervous, strewn with knotty or flashy phrases, impatient with transitions and other concessions to dullness, calling attention to itself as a form or at least an outcry, fond of rapid twists, taking pleasure in dispute, dialectic, dazzle . . .
>
> At its best, [this style] reflected a certain view of the intellectual life: free-lance dash, peacock strut, daring hypothesis, knockabout synthesis. For better or worse it was radically different from the accepted modes of scholarly publishing and middlebrow journalism. It celebrated the ideal of the intellectual as anti-specialist, or as a writer whose specialty was the lack of a specialty: the writer as dilettante-connoisseur, *Luftmensch* of the mind, roamer among theories.

The New York style, like every other, had the defects of its virtues. "Impatience with dullness" could decline into smugness and condescension; an exquisite sense of the problematic could turn into a fetish of complexity. "No easy certainties," Howe once wrote about the responsibility of intellectuals, "and no easy acceptance of uncertainty." The later failing is rarer and in a way more honorable. But it is still a failing, one to which Howe himself was prone. His frequent thrusts at the "crude simplicities of left and right" occasionally sounded reflexive—as though it's the energy rather than the crudity of his opponent's formulation that really annoyed him. Howard Zinn, for example, may be incapable of Howe's analytic and strategic virtuosity. But Zinn's comparative simplicity nevertheless produced the magnificent saga of suffering and struggle that is *A People's History*. *Dissent* aims to produce a refined and complicated political awareness among its readers. It's a noble aim. But someone or something else must first have produced an elemental political awareness.

The New York intellectuals have passed from the scene, along with the conditions that produced their distinctive style: the immigrant background, fascism, Stalinism, and global depression; the innovations of the great modernists. So much is inevitable and even desirable. No style can remain fresh and original for long. But as Howe, Jacoby, and many others by now have lamented, the very ideal of cosmopolitanism, of the intellectual as "antispecialist," uniting political and aesthetic interests and able to speak with some authority about both, is obsolescent.

It's a troubling prospect, and an ambiguous one. The cult of professionalism and expertise, the "bureaucratization of opinion and taste," are not merely mechanisms of social control or a cultural failure of nerve. They are also in part a response to genuine intellectual progress. There's much more to know now than in the thirties, and more people have joined the conversation. Perhaps the demise of the "public intellectual," of the "dilettante-connoisseur," is a symptom of crisis: a sign that intellectual wholeness is no longer attainable; that the classical ideals of wisdom as catholicity of understanding, and of citizenship as the capacity to discuss all public affairs, must be abandoned. Perhaps we'll have to learn to live with that.

If so, then those who come after, when reckoning the costs of progress, will want to consider a few exemplary specimens from the world they have lost. Among twentieth-century American intellectuals, they could hardly do better than to choose Irving Howe.

16

The Common Fate

Victor Serge

A stanza from Bertolt Brecht's poem "To Those Born Later" might have served as an epigraph for Victor Serge's memoir:

> I came to the cities in a time of disorder
> When hunger reigned there.
> I came among men in a time of revolt
> And I rebelled with them.
> So passed my time
> Which had been given me on earth.

Victor Kibalchich ("Serge" was a nom de guerre) was born in 1890 to Russian revolutionary exiles—in Brussels because "my parents, in quest of their daily bread and of good libraries, were commuting between London (the British Museum), Paris, Switzerland, and Belgium." His upbringing insured that he would be a rebel and outsider from early youth: "On the walls of our humble and makeshift lodgings there were always the portraits of men who had been hanged. The conversations of grown-ups dealt with trials, executions, escapes, and Siberian highways, with great ideas incessantly argued over, and with the latest books about those ideas." It was a hard life; his eight-year-old brother starved to death.

Like other young rebels (I. F. Stone and Seymour Hersh, for example), Serge left school early and hung about on the fringes of journalism. At twenty he began editing an anarchist newspaper in Paris. When a group of anarchist acquaintances staged a robbery and were caught, Serge was arrested, framed, and sentenced to five years of solitary confinement. On his release he traveled to Barcelona, where an unsuccessful anarchist uprising was in preparation, after which he was again arrested. Serge's early chapters on the pre–World War I European ultra-left milieu and French and Spanish prison camps are, like the rest of the book, wonderfully vivid, but they also have a charm and occasional lightness that the later chapters, more sublime but shadowed by the darkness of the Russian years, lack.

At the end of the war Serge was transferred to France and, along with some other political prisoners, sent to newly revolutionary Russia in exchange for captured French military officers. He arrived in 1919, during the Civil War. With the monarchist and aristocratic officer corps—supplied and reinforced by the British, French, and American governments—attacking on several fronts and the peasantry torn between promises of land and residual loyalties to the old regime and the church, the Bolsheviks' survival was in grave doubt. Serge threw himself into the battle for Petrograd, for several months on the verge of being conquered by White (i.e., counterrevolutionary) forces. Besides helping organize the defense of the city (an experience depicted in one of his several superb novels, *Conquered City*), he acted as a liaison to European parties and publications and also took charge of the archives of the Tsarist secret police, which lent extra authority and keenness of perception to his subsequent analysis of the role of police repression in the decay of Bolshevism.

After the Reds' narrow victory, Serge worked under Zinoviev in the Communist International. The Bolsheviks knew that their hold on power was precarious and believed that the survival of the Revolution depended on successful workers' uprisings in Central and Western Europe. There was plenty of working-class discontent in those countries, and the Russians brought the leadership of foreign revolutionary movements to Moscow for encouragement and advice. Serge was squarely in the middle of this intense activity, both in Moscow and in Berlin, where he worked in the Communist underground. His magnanimous but unsparing portraits of the European revolutionary leadership and intelligentsia, including Gramsci, Lukács, Souvarine, and Andrés Nin, as well as old Bolsheviks such as Trotsky and Radek and Russian writers like Gorky and Yesenin, are a large and unforgettable part of the *Memoirs*.

Revolution failed everywhere, most crucially and disappointingly in Germany. The Soviet Union was isolated—encircled—and the results were catastrophic: a desperate obsession among the leadership with party unity, internal security, and rapid military and economic (in practice, heavy-industrial) development. And by the late 1920s, ten years after the Revolution, the leadership was . . . Stalin.

The descent of the Stalinist darkness on the Soviet Union and the international Communist movement has been described many times, but rarely, perhaps never, with such intimate knowledge and moral discrimination as in Serge's memoirs and novels. Serge the novelist is as lyrical as Pasternak, as shrewd as Koestler, as humane as Silone. *The Case of Comrade Tulayev*—written, like most of Serge's novels, at odd moments, with only remote prospects of publication—is one of the best novels about Stalinism, and indeed one of the best political novels of the twentieth century. The murder of a Communist Party official, in reality a random act of street violence, metastasizes in the imagination of the secret police into an elaborate treasonous conspiracy. Figures of every stature, lofty, middling, and insignificant, all innocent and most of them fervently loyal, are swept into the investigation's maw, while the investigators and their bureaucratic superiors are, without exception, of a chilling mediocrity and cynicism. There is even a scene with Stalin himself, which manages the extraordinary—but for Serge, characteristic—feat of rendering the dictator's ordinary, even impressive, qualities without lessening our horror.

Progressively disillusioned, Serge led for several years the twilight existence of an Oppositionist: still inside the Party, but mistrusted and mistrustful. His wife's family was persecuted, partly on his account; she goes mad, and he is left to care for their young son. He is expelled from the Party. Finally, inevitably, comes his arrest. As usual in such cases, he is presented with fantastic allegations and pressured to confess to at least some of them, for his own good and the good of the Party. Unlike most people in his position, he categorically refuses. He is exiled anyway, to a town in the Urals.

His fellow exiles (portrayed in Serge's novel *Midnight in the Century*, as well as in the *Memoirs*) are a lively bunch, though there are no jobs and hunger is incessant. Here and elsewhere in the book, Serge frequently ends a paragraph with a terse résumé of the subject's eventual fate: "Stetsky disappeared into jail in 1938." "Lominadze will kill himself around 1935; Yan Sten, classed as a 'terrorist,' will be shot around 1937." Very effectively, these individual death knells toll the death of the Revolution as well.

In the mid-1930s, Stalin was courting French intellectuals as part of his Popular Front strategy. Some of Serge's novels and essays had been published in France, so André Gide, Romain Rolland, and others succeeded in winning his release—or rather expulsion. Living first in Belgium, then in France, closely watched by the government, slandered by the Communists, admired by a few free spirits like Orwell and Dwight Macdonald, Serge tried throughout the late thirties simultaneously to defend what the Revolution had started out to be and to criticize what it had become. When France fell to the Nazis, his life was in danger. So dangerous a radical naturally could not be admitted to the United States, so he spent his last years in Mexico, impoverished and isolated, writing his marvelous final novel, *Unforgiving Years*, and this imperishable memoir.

Two passages, one early in the *Memoirs* and one late, give us a sense of the man. In 1917, just released from a French prison, he arrives in Barcelona.

The treadmill that crushed human beings still revolved inside me. I found no happiness in awakening to life, free and privileged alone among my conscript generation, in this contented city. I felt a vague compunction at it all. Why was I there, in these cafés, on these golden sands, while so many others were bleeding in the trenches of a whole continent? Why was I excluded from the common fate? I came across deserters who were happy to be beyond the frontier, safe at last. I admitted their right to safety, but inwardly I was horrified at the idea that people could fight so fiercely for their own lives when what was at stake was the life of everyone: a limitless suffering to be endured commonly, shared and drunk to the last drop. . . . I worked in print shops, went to bullfights, resumed my reading, clambered up mountains, dallied in cafés to watch Castilian, Sevillan, Andalusian, or

Catalan girls at their dancing, and I felt that it would be impossible for me to live like this. All I could think of was the men at war, who kept calling to me.

Twenty-five years later, he looks back over a life of exhilarating struggle and betrayed hopes.

The only meaning of life lies in conscious participation in the making of history. One must range oneself actively against everything that diminishes man and involve oneself in all struggles that tend to liberate and enlarge him. This categorical imperative is in no way lessened by the fact that such an involvement is inevitably soiled by error; it is a worse error merely to live for oneself, caught within traditions which are soiled by inhumanity. This conviction has brought me, as it has brought others, to a somewhat unusual destiny. But we were, and still are, in line with the development of history, and it is now obvious that, during an entire epoch, millions of individual destinies will follow the paths along which we were the first to travel. In Europe, in Asia, in America, whole generations are in upheaval, are . . . [learning] that the egoism of "every man for himself" is finished, that private enrichment is no fit aim for life, that yesterday's conservatisms lead to nothing but catastrophe, and sensing the necessity for a fresh outlook tending towards the reorganization of the world.

It was not "obvious" then; and seventy years later, with plutocracy triumphant nearly everywhere, it is still less obvious. Yet this testimony from someone who, like few others in the twentieth century, never sacrificed either liberty or solidarity deserves profound respect.

Brecht's great poem concludes:

But you, when the time comes at last
And man is a helper to man,
Think of us
With forbearance.

When—if—that time comes at last, few of those born earlier will be remembered with more forbearance, even love, than Victor Serge.

17

A Conservative-Liberal Socialist

Leszek Kołakowski

Ignazio Silone, the novelist and contributor to *The God That Failed* (1949), a hugely influential collection of essays by ex-Communist intellectuals, prophesied that the political future would be fought out between Communists and former Communists, since the latter alone could genuinely understand the Communist threat. Arthur Koestler, another novelist and contributor to *The God That Failed*, said something similar. They and many other ex-Communists—Whittaker Chambers was the most extreme example—took an apocalyptic view: the Cold War was a struggle to the death between two antithetical ideas, two historical and civilizational principles.

In the event, Communism went out not with a bang but a whimper; replacing it, capitalism came in with a bang but has since elicited much whimpering among its unfortunate beneficiaries in Russia, China, and Eastern Europe. It looks, in retrospect, as though Communism was simply forced industrialization by a nationalist bureaucratic elite rather than (as in the Third World) by foreign investors and their local clients, and that the Soviet Empire was largely a way of preventing yet another near-catastrophic invasion of Russia across the flat expanse of Central and Eastern Europe. What did any of that have to do with socialism? In a famous remark, Lenin defined Communism as "soviets plus electricity." That was shortly before he abolished the soviets. It would perhaps be equally accurate to define Stalinism as "Tsarism plus electricity." A drunken Leonid Brezhnev, when asked in 1968 whether the invasion of Czechoslovakia was really compatible with socialist morality, blurted out: "Don't talk to me about socialism. What we have, we keep." *In vino veritas.*

But of course the Communists talked endlessly about socialism to their imprisoned populations. How else could they pretend to justify a harsh one-party dictatorship and an inefficient centrally controlled economy? Most pre–World War I socialists, from Marx and Engels to Mill and Morris to Jaures and Bernstein to Shaw and Wells, said nothing about the revolutionary seizure of power by a self-appointed vanguard. On the contrary, they all preached evolutionary social transformation, mass working-class parties and unions competing for power through elections, strikes, boycotts, and other nonviolent means, and the gradual diffusion of enlightenment and solidarity. If the ruling class used fraud and violence to thwart a democratic transition to socialism—as it undoubtedly will, if that prospect ever threatens—then they might legitimately be resisted and suppressed. (This is the meaning of that perennial bogeyman, the "dictatorship of the proletariat.") But "democratic socialism" would have seemed a tautology to the classical socialists and "authoritarian socialism" a solecism. To them, "socialism" simply meant democratic control of a society's core productive activities.

Still, what a word means in any epoch is an empirical question. If all Communists and the great majority of anti-Communists have agreed for nearly a hundred years to call bureaucratic, one-party dictatorships in underdeveloped countries "socialism," then that is, alas, what the word now means. On the one hand, many Communists were eager to borrow the prestige of a widely cherished ideal; on the other, many anti-Communists were eager to besmirch that ideal by blaming it for the undeniable horrors perpetrated by the Communists. Many others on both sides were no doubt sincerely ignorant of the word's original meaning. I always thought that the scrupulous (and sporting) thing for my fellow anti-Communists to call the sad and malignant entity behind the Iron Curtain would have been "pseudo-socialism." But it never caught on.

Some of Communism's fiercest critics did indeed insist that it was a betrayal of socialism. Orwell emphatically reaffirmed after publishing *1984* that he was a socialist. Silone and Victor Serge were among the better-known ex-Communists who continued to espouse traditional, non-Bolshevik socialism. (Some of the lesser-known ones were Karl Korsch, Paul Mattick, and Anton Pannekoek.) Most ex-Communist intellectuals, however, regarded Communism as a logical development of socialism rather than a hijacking or perversion of it. Whether one agrees with them or thinks they should have known better, it is at any rate easy to understand why they might have preferred to see themselves as victims of a grand tragedy rather than of a wretched travesty.

Among those who have sought to trace twentieth-century totalitarianism back to nineteenth-century socialism and beyond, Leszek Kołakowski is one of the most eminent. He was born in Poland in 1927 and came of age in that epicenter of the mid-twentieth-century European cyclone. After the war he joined the Polish Communist Party and, because of his superior intelligence, was sent to Moscow for ideological grooming. The experience sowed grave doubts in the young Kołakowski's mind. He entered on a career as an academic philosopher but frequently—especially after the Hungarian uprising of 1956, also crushed by the USSR—wrote sharp-edged essays critical of Marxism and pseudo-socialism that attracted the authorities' increasing displeasure, as well as the admiration of many in the West. He was expelled from the Party in 1966 and from Warsaw University in 1968, whereupon he went into exile. He had a distinguished academic career in Berlin, Berkeley, Chicago, and Oxford, received many prizes (including the Erasmus and Jerusalem Prizes and a MacArthur Fellowship), and died in 2009.

The sort of thing that got up the nose of the Polish authorities was "What Is Socialism?" (1956; reprinted in *Is God Happy? Selected Essays* by Leszek Kołakowski, Basic Books, 2013), a satirical broadside that appeared on (and just as quickly disappeared from) bulletin boards around Warsaw University after the student journal that published it was shut down. The essay starts out by asking, innocently, what socialism is not. It never finishes answering. One after another feature of really existing pseudo-socialism is pitilessly catalogued:

- a society in which someone who has committed no crime sits at home waiting for the police;
- a society in which some people are unhappy because they say what they think and others are unhappy because they do not;
- a society in which some people are better off because they do not think at all . . .

and so on and on, with grim humor, through many pages. Finally, socialism is defined: "Socialism is just a really wonderful thing."

It is, in my view, the best thing Kołakowski ever wrote, at any rate about politics.

The rest of Kołakowski's extensive political writings can be summed up in not very many words. Utopias are dangerous folly. Perfect harmony is unattainable. "Socialism" simply means that the state controls the economy—never mind who controls the state—and invariably results in less freedom and efficiency than capitalism. Marx was a clever man, but Marxism is a tissue of sophistries, from surplus-value to historical materialism. Talk of Progress or Necessity is merely a way for ideologues to justify brutality and tyranny. Intellectuals, at least radical ones, should be distrusted. It is a familiar message: Cold War liberalism, ably formulated, with erudition and wit. If the spirit of Marxism-Leninism ever again burns bright, Kołakowski's writings will no doubt serve as a valuable corrective.

Do they, however, have anything to say to twenty-first-century America? Not much, I think. Marxism-Leninism struck no sparks in the United States or Britain, few in Western Europe or South America. For at least thirty years, it has been deader than Arianism or Albigensianism everywhere in the world. Anti-Communism and worship of the "free" market has been America's civic religion for nearly a hundred years. The word "utopia" has scarcely been pronounced (except derisively) in the public square in all that time, and the only fantasies of perfect harmony that have had any effect on public policy are those of neoclassical economists. Since the election of Ronald Reagan in 1980, the United States has seen the rampant financialization of the economy, the pulverizing of organized labor, a drastic increase in economic inequality, the capture by business of the regulatory system, and the growth of the national security state. Internationally, after decades of violent US intervention in Indochina, the Middle East, and Latin America, a corrupt and predatory investor class easily dominates an impoverished, insecure work-force. Global capitalism has, to paraphrase Tacitus, created a wasteland for hundreds of millions of the displaced and exploited—though it has done quite well by a few millions of the enterprising or well-connected—and called it freedom.

No doubt Kołakowski would have more vigorously deplored all this—he did mention it once or twice—if he had not been forced to spend his formative years bravely and eloquently com-bating pseudo-socialist totalitarianism. (And surely it did not help that he spent his first few years of exile in Berlin and Berkeley in the late 1960s and early 1970s, witnessing the worst excesses of the expiring New Left.) It is not easy in mid-life to change gears, alter emphases, play a new tune, especially when one suddenly finds oneself a celebrity. In a famous exchange, the historian E. P. Thompson tried, with enormous tact and discrimination, to suggest to Kołakowski that he might, in his changed circumstances, occasionally turn his attention to a different set of problems, the ones that marginal and beleaguered anticapitalist *and* anti-Stalinist Western leftists like Thompson found most urgent. But Kołakowski simply assumed that his previous arguments had not been absorbed and repeated them. A missed opportunity.

Kołakowski was not, in any case, solely or even primarily a political critic; he was a philosopher and a historian of philosophy. He wrote books on seventeenth-century philosophy, Bergson, Husserl, and positivism, among many others, including several on the philosophy of religion, such as *The Presence of Myth, God Owes Us Nothing, Religion: If There Is No God . . .* , and the middle section of *Is God Happy?*

The Enlightenment plays the same role in Kołakowski's phil-osophical writings as Marxism does in his political writings. It's where modernity went astray, where virtue took a wrong turn. Marxism distorted the quest for equality and social justice into utopian dogmatism; the Enlightenment distorted the promise of science and the rejection of superstition into relativistic rationalism. And just as Kołakowski's positive political beliefs were hard to pin down (the closest he came was an essay called "How to Be a Conservative-Liberal Socialist"), so were his positive religious beliefs. For a long time he styled himself an "inconsistent atheist," but near the end of his life he resolved the inconsistency by returning to the Catholic Church.

Perhaps the philosophical equivalent of "conservative-liberal socialist" is "skeptical traditionalist." At any rate, that's a good description of Kołakowski's religious/philosophical stance until his (re-)conversion. He was not (at least in his writing) a God-haunted man so much as a scourge of secularism; not so much avid to penetrate the mysteries as keen to debunk their debunkers. He does not have much comfort for afflicted believers, but he rejoices in afflicting comfortable unbelievers.

One tradition of Christian apologetics, from Pascal to Benedict XVI, emphasized the social and psychological indispensability of belief. It is summed up in a sentence of Dostoevsky's: "If there is no God, everything is permitted." (Significantly, Kołakowski chose this sentence as the subtitle of his book *Religion*.) Unless God exists, there is no certainty of ultimate justice, no reliable criterion of good and evil, no firm ground of truth, no transcendent meaning of life.

This was Kołakowski's approach, more or less. He writes:

Human dignity is not to be validated within a naturalistic concept of man. The absence of God spells the ruin of man in the sense that it demolishes or robs of meaning everything we think of as the essence

of being human: the quest for truth, the distinction of good and evil,
the claim to dignity, the claim to creating something that withstands
the indifferent destructiveness of time.

But as Kołakowski recognizes, even if this is true, it *proves* nothing. Perhaps human dignity cannot be validated, only affirmed; and perhaps the essence of being human must be reconceived, or the notion of "essence" redefined. Kołakowski appeals to the "ontic condition of humanity" and the "moral constitution of Being" to vindicate natural law. Do these resonant phrases amount to anything more than "that's just the way things are"? I'm not sure they do.

Kołakowski was an admirable spokesman for the *philosophia perennis*, the common sense of (European) humankind since (roughly speaking) Homer. We *feel* free and responsible. Evil and conflict are in the nature of things, including ourselves. We sense mysteries in the deeps. Some of our intuitions are so strong that they *must* be eternal truths. He was baptized into an ideology that aggressively denied all these things. Skeptic that he was, he worked himself free of that ideology and also helped free a great many others. But as he continually reminded rationalists, the skeptical impulse can't be sustained indefinitely or directed toward everything simultaneously. We need traditions too. Kołakowski struck his own, distinctive balance, illuminating the ultimate questions even for those of us he could not persuade.

18

Yes to Sex

Ellen Willis

For thirty years, in a wide arc from the *Village Voice* and *Social Text* to the *New Yorker* and *Mirabella*, Ellen Willis has been the sixties' best exponent and a savvy interpreter of American politics and culture. Her output thus far is small—two sterling collections, *Beginning to See the Light* (1981) and *No More Nice Girls* (1992)—so one eagerly welcomes her new book, *Don't Think, Smile! Notes on a Decade of Denial* (notwithstanding the false note struck by its title, which insinuates cluelessness on the other side—always a mistake).

What do the sixties have to say to the nineties? In essays on crime, race, censorship, globalization, Bosnia, the Republican ascendancy, the culture of austerity, Zippergate, and right-wing libertarianism, Willis advocates left-wing libertarianism. The left should contend for the maximum of individual development and expression; and what it has to contend against are external constraints imposed by gross economic inequality and internal ones arising from the inculcation early in life of a rigid, self-denying morality. Among the tenets of left libertarianism:

that the point of life is to live and enjoy it fully; that genuine virtue is the overflow of happiness, not the bitter fruit of self-denial; that sexual freedom and pleasure are basic human rights; that endless work and subordination to bosses are offenses to the human spirit; that contempt for the black poor is the middle class's effort to deny that *we are next*; that Mom is not going back home again and so we need to rethink domestic life, child rearing, and the structures of work; that democracy is not about voting for nearly indistinguishable politicians but about having a voice in collective decision-making, not only in government but at home, school, and work. Naturally this vision should be accompanied by tough-minded analysis, in the first instance a thoroughgoing critique of the new economic order and its accelerating class war.

Attention to internal as well as external unfreedom yields much astute commentary. Willis's discussion of crime, "Beyond Good and Evil," takes note of its obvious roots in material deprivation but also links the "psychopolitics of crime" subtly and rigorously to the "dynamics of domination." "The Ordeal of Liberal Optimism" addresses the liberal critique of affirmative action, suggesting persuasively that it takes too little account of racial psychodynamics. Both essays are notable for lucidity, fairmindedness, and sureness in getting at the marrow of bitterly contested questions.

An essay on censorship and free speech starts out, like most feminist approaches to the pornography debate, by considering the "politics of sexual representation." But Willis moves quickly to "the politics of speech as such," where "the case against the censors is not so obvious after all." There turns out to be more substance to the critique of First Amendment absolutism than one might have supposed. Catharine MacKinnon and others

argue with some plausibility that the boundaries of speech protected by the First Amendment can only be specified by taking
no less seriously the Constitutional mandate of equality set out in
the Fourteenth Amendment. Speech undeniably has consequences, sometimes entirely predictable ones. "Distinguishing
talk about inferiority from verbal imposition of inferiority may
be complicated at the edges," MacKinnon writes, "but it is clear
enough at the center with sexual and racial harassment, pornography, and hate propaganda."

Willis avoids the untenable absolutist rejoinder: that the First
Amendment is unambiguous and that speech can infallibly be
distinguished from action. She acknowledges, as one must, that
speech is a particular kind of action; and of course she does not
deny that legally actionable harassment can sometimes be purely
verbal. But while MacKinnon's argument stops there, content
merely to demote speech from categorical uniqueness, Willis
goes on to root a defense of controversial speech in a theory of
freedom, which is in turn derived from a theory of moral psychology. It's not that speech is never wounding, she argues, but that
freedom is healing.

> Symbolic expression, however forceful, leaves a space between com-
> municator and recipient, a space for contesting, fighting back with
> one's own words and images, organizing to oppose whatever action
> the abhorred speech may incite. Though speech may, and often does,
> *support* the structure of domination, whether by lending aid and com-
> fort to the powerful or frightening and discouraging their targets, in
> leaving room for opposition it falls short of *enforcing* submission. For
> this reason the unrestrained clash of ideas, emotions, visions provides
> a relatively safe model—one workable even in a society marked by
> serious imbalances of power—of how to handle social conflict, with

its attendant fear, anger, and urges to repress: through argument, persuasion, and negotiation (or at worst grim forbearance) rather than coercion. In the annals of human history, even this modest exercise in freedom is a revolutionary development; for the radical democrat it prefigures the extension of freedom to other areas of social life.

I think this takes the debate a step beyond Stanley Fish's *There's No Such Thing as Free Speech*—no small achievement.

Throughout these essays it's a pleasure to watch the deployment of Willis's extraordinary dialectical skills. But not all her targets are equally deserving. A good deal of the book is devoted to rebuking the "economic" or "populist" or "majoritarian" left for insufficient attention to the psychocultural roots of inequality and domination. To those who suggest that perhaps a thoroughgoing demystification of truth, beauty, objectivity, morality, authority, law, and love can wait until the minimum wage goes up a dollar or two and not quite so many American households (currently one in three) are only a major illness away from bankruptcy, Willis replies that freedom and equality are indivisible. If Americans "do not feel entitled to demand freedom and equality in their personal and social relations," she insists, "they will not fight for freedom and equality in their economic relations." Furthermore, "people are not 'distracted' by the moral and cultural issues that affect their daily existence as much as the size of their paychecks; they care passionately about those issues."

Isn't there a non sequitur here? A popular majority might, after all, agree broadly with the left about freedom and equality in economic relations but disagree broadly about freedom and equality in personal relations. People no doubt care passionately about both economic issues and moral/cultural ones, but their views about the former may be much closer to those of economic leftists than their views about the latter are to those of cultural leftists. Actually, these are not merely logical possibilities. According to Alan Wolfe (in *One Nation, After All*) and other sociologists, they're the way things are.

And if this *is* the way things are, what follows? Would economic populists then be inclined to show cultural libertarians the door? I'm not nearly so sure as Willis. Which door, anyway? A little comradely recrimination may be good for the ideological blood pressure; but beyond that, I don't see what's at stake in this debate between partisans of class and of culture. There is no left-wing party or other organization awaiting its outcome, ready to carry the approved word far and wide. It won't and shouldn't lead anyone to drop one kind of political activity and take up another. Economic radicals and cultural radicals can pretty much count on each other's handful of votes, and neither has any resources or patrons to be raided by the other. The masses rarely peruse the *Nation* or *Jacobin*; they're busy or tired or glued to the screen, and we're not on the local newsstand.

In any case, economic democracy is surely the best thing that could happen to cultural radicalism. During his quixotic 1968 mayoral campaign, Norman Mailer won over an emphatically skeptical Bella Abzug by roaring back at her: "I can tell you that regardless of my views on women as *you* think you know them, women in any administration I could run would have more voice, more respect, more real opportunity for argument than any of the other candidates would offer you." Just so. A little (or better, a large) redistribution of wealth would put cultural radicals—most of whom, I suspect, inhabit the lower four-fifths of the income scale—in a much stronger position to ignore the rest of society, press their claims on it, or construct alternatives to it.

Willis's quarrel with the "culturally conservative" or "pro-family" left is more substantial. In recent years public discussion of abortion, divorce, welfare, and crime has been marked by near-universal deference for words like "virtue," "responsibility," "self-control," "discipline," "stability," "community," "family," and the like. Willis is deeply suspicious of this rhetorical tendency. It serves, she argues, to shore up a familiar system of domination and hierarchy based on self-denial and the subordination of women. The premise of traditional morality is some version of original sin; it "assumes the need to combat the human inclination toward evil by imposing coercive social controls as well as the internal controls of conscience and guilt." The agency of this repression is the family: "it is the parents' job to suppress their children's evil impulses and assure that they develop the requisite inner controls." These "evil impulses" are erotic: desires for bodily satisfaction and pleasure, which are imagined as potentially limitless and progressively consuming in later life if not firmly curbed in infancy and then, in childhood, channeled into forms of expression (i.e., maleness and femaleness) that allow for social order and continuity. The cost of these "inner controls" is a pervasive, largely unconscious unease: fear and submissiveness alternating with rage and resentment. "In demonizing children's desire, the family provokes the very destructive impulses it must then imperfectly repress."

The child's thwarted impulses persist in adulthood, this argument continues, where they are countered by an array of external controls—religious, legal, medical, economic, etc.—that teach and enforce one or another version of hierarchy. They are also countered by the need to repress the acutely painful memories of rage and humiliation that an open acknowledgment of long-unsatisfied desires would provoke. In addition, social, sexual, familial, economic, and other hierarchies are less oppressive for some (males, whites, parents, employers) than for others—an incentive for the more fortunate to make the best of a bad but apparently natural and inevitable situation.

Hence, according to Willis, our society's precarious equilibrium. "A moral system based on repression and coercion, on the stifling of desire, generates enormous stores of anger and frustration that can never be totally controlled. When those emotions find expression in destructive behavior, it is seized on as proof of intractable human evil and the need to maintain or increase repression. The result is a closed circle, a self-perpetuating, self-reinforcing system of tragic dimensions."

The way out of this circle, she argues, is the conquest of scarcity. As long as societal survival was not assured, hierarchical subordination and the disciplining of individual desire were self-evidently necessary. Over the last two centuries, however, it has become possible to see traditional morality as a strategy of social self-preservation, a strategy bound to be superseded and indeed already in retreat. When pleasure—or at least its material prerequisites—is more abundant, self-denial can cease to be the foundation of all collective life, and morality as a structure of internalized coercion, along with the patriarchal family that reproduces it, will wither away.

And what might come after? The only place Willis hints at an answer is a passage in her well-known 1979 essay "The Family: Love It or Leave It."

> The logical post-patriarchal unit is some version of the commune. Groups of people who agreed to take responsibility for each other, pool their economic resources, and share housework and child care would have a basis for stability independent of any one couple's

sexual bond; children would have the added security of close ties to adults other than their biological parents (and if the commune were large and flexible enough, parents who had stopped being lovers might choose to remain in it); communal child rearing, shared by both sexes, would remove the element of martyrdom from parenthood.

A little sketchy, this. But even those who are dubious about Willis's post-patriarchal alternative must acknowledge that her libertarian-socialist utopianism is based on something more than a sentimental attachment to sixties slogans. It is, on the contrary, a highly plausible deduction from the prevailing conception of modernity, which defines the good life in terms of leisure and abundance and envisions history as continuous moral and material progress, made possible by the spread of scientific and social rationality. Nearly all secular thinkers of both left and right subscribe to this conception, and in their case, Willis's exasperated exhortations to "think radically" are very much to the point.

At least one secular leftist, however, thought quite as radically about modernity as Willis and came to different conclusions. Christopher Lasch was not a believer in original sin but in what might be called original limits. These are limits imposed not by material scarcity or political inequality but by the process of individuation itself. Lasch's account of psychic development, like Willis's, focuses on the infant's response to frustration, but more convincingly. (Willis's fullest account is in "Toward a Feminist Sexual Revolution" in *No More Nice Girls*; I have outlined Lasch's ideas at considerable length in "A Whole World of Heroes," above.) Willis's "demonizing of desire" implies parental intent, a contingent matter. But as Lasch points out, some—in fact a great deal of—infantile frustration is inevitable, as are the outsized fantasies with which the infant typically responds. These fantasies, of omnipotence or terrified helplessness, of annihilating rage or undifferentiated union, of perfectly benevolent or implacably threatening parents, must gradually be mastered, reduced in scale, if the child is to assume the contours of a self.

Living down these otherwise disabling fantasies is the essence of psychological maturation. It requires the continual experience of love and discipline, gratification and frustration, from the same source. This can best—arguably can only—be done in the constant presence of the fantasied objects, i.e., the child's parents. Until the last two centuries, it usually was. But the displacement of household production by mass production drastically altered the child's relation to its father; and the centralized, interventionist state, overshadowing and sometimes replacing parental authority, complicated maturation still further. The result was frequently a weak self—which is the clinical meaning of "narcissism." (Narcissism has nothing to do with an excess of self-love, the popular meaning of the word.)

The essence of modernity is mobility and choice; the essence of premodernity was immobility and ascription. It *looks*, vexingly, as though successful individuation requires an irreducible minimum of the latter. Lasch, as the bearer of this bad news, was understandably greeted with something less than grateful enthusiasm by many of his leftist political comrades. But when he criticized modernity, Lasch had in mind mass production and the centralized state, not sexual equality. He believed that the family needed to be defended, not against feminism but against the effects of the separation of home and work. He was skeptical of "progress," not from a dislike of equality or pleasure but from a preference for the genuine rather than the ersatz articles. He maintained that freedom meant overcoming emotionally charged dependence on individual or local authorities, not taking for granted an abstract, universal dependence on distant, bureaucratic authorities.

Culture and psychology are central to politics; Willis is right about that. But cultural politics must reckon with our psychic ecology: the sum of our adaptations, over the course of two million years, to infantile dependence, territoriality, scarcity, mortality, and the other hitherto inescapable limits of human existence. We are organisms; we cannot flourish at just any tempo, pressure, or scale. Imagination itself is an evolutionary adaptation, whereby we master a threatening environment when young by binding or investing fantasy within nearby entities—parents, neighborhood, church, ethnic group. These intense primary identifications can and should be gradually left behind, but they cannot be skipped, on pain of shallowness, instability, and—paradoxically— an inability in later life to stand firm against authority.

Cultural politics should aim to reform rather than abolish marriage, the family, hierarchy, authority, morality, and law. These institutions and practices evolved to serve essential purposes. They are not purely, or even primarily, strategies of exploitation. To consider them prisons rather than temporary outposts is not radical but superficial, like considering religion and myth mere lies rather than inadequate attempts at explanation. Cultural radicals will sometimes, in fact, need to defend these institutions, i.e., insist that some way be found to achieve their formative or protective purposes. As the global economy and mass culture lay siege to inwardness, plow up our psychic root system, and alter the very grain and contour of our being, conservation increasingly becomes a radical imperative.

Foucault remarked sourly: "We must not think that by saying yes to sex, one says no to power." There are, of course, plenty of other good reasons for saying yes to sex and to pleasures of (nearly) every other kind, as well as for demanding a fairer distribution of pleasure's prerequisites: money and leisure. But the strength to persevere in such demands and also to pursue the sublimer, more strenuous pleasures—of craft, of thought, of devotion, of emulation—is not only, as Willis contends, "the overflow of happiness"; it is also the "bitter fruit" (tart, anyway) of self-discipline. Premodern cruelties and superstitions still bulk large; left-wing libertarianism is still the best answer to them. To recognize the subtler entrapments of modernity requires, however, another variety of radical imagination.

19

How (and How Not)
to Change the World

In late November the *New York Times* reported on a trending tweet. A law professor had posted three paragraphs from Richard Rorty's 1997 Massey Lectures at Harvard, published as *Achieving Our Country: Leftist Thought in Twentieth-Century America*, which seemed remarkably prescient:

> [M]embers of labor unions, and unorganized unskilled workers, will sooner or later realize that their government is not even trying to prevent wages from sinking or to prevent jobs from being exported. Around the same time, they will realize that suburban white-collar workers—themselves desperately afraid of being downsized—are not going to let themselves be taxed to provide social benefits for anyone else.
>
> At that point, something will crack. The non-suburban electorate will decide that the system has failed and start looking around for a strongman to vote for—someone willing to assure them that, once he is elected, the smug bureaucrats, tricky lawyers, overpaid bond salesmen, and postmodernist professors will no longer be calling the shots. . . .

One thing that is very likely to happen is that the gains made in the past 40 years by black and brown Americans, and by homo-sexuals, will be wiped out. Jocular contempt for women will come back into fashion. . . . All the resentment which badly educated Americans feel about having their manners dictated to them by col-lege graduates will find an outlet.

And where was the American left while these developments were brewing? Disenchanted by the Indochina war and labor's willing enlistment in the Cold War, leftists in the sixties, Rorty claimed, found new causes and new constituents: women, minorities, and homosexuals, all of them objects of regular hostility and sadism. Much was achieved: "the adoption of attitudes which the right sneers at as 'politically correct' has made America a far more civ-ilized society" than it was at mid-century. At the same time, much ground was lost: "Leftists in the academy have permitted cultural politics to supplant real politics and have collaborated with the Right in making cultural issues central to public debate. They are spending energy which should be directed at proposing new laws on discussing topics very remote from their country's needs." David Bromwich voiced similar concerns in *Politics by Other Means*, noting that while left-wing students in earlier dec-ades "would have seized any occasion to throw their weight on the liberal side of struggles in real communities, where people spend more than [a few] years, where they are compelled to live and to die," more recently "the activist tone in scholarship has been found compatible with a restriction of politics to the univer-sities themselves." In *The Trouble with Diversity*, Walter Benn Michaels expanded these insights into a pulverizing critique of identity politics (which however, like the villain in *Terminator 2*, has proved virtually indestructible, miraculously reconfiguring itself every time it is intellectually exploded). Focusing on culture rather than class, Michaels insisted, "gives us what we might call the fantasy rather than the reality of a left politics." Even Stanley Fish piled on in *Professional Correctness*: "If you want to do political work in the 'real world' sense, there are (or should be) better tools in your kit than readings of poems or cultural texts or even cultures."

Theoretically sophisticated readers will perhaps have cocked an eyebrow at so many invocations of the "real." Surely Rorty, Fish, Bromwich, and Michaels do not believe in . . . *objective reality*? It may be time to cash the word "real" with an example from life. Long before I encountered any of these books, I came across an account by Jonathan Kozol of a conversation with an inner-city Black parent. Kozol described to her some then-current controversy over community control of schools, and in particular over whether the principal of a majority-Black school should also be Black. She responded emphatically: "I don't give a damn whether my kids' school has a white principal or a black principal. I just want it to have textbooks and heat in the winter."

It is hard to imagine a person more worthy of the American left's sympathy and support than that poor Black woman. And indeed, over the last few decades the left has proven itself more than willing to show that woman respect, by celebrating her and her ancestors' culture and by insisting that a greater proportion of school principals as well as CEOs, political officeholders, and students at elite colleges share her ethnicity and culture. Respect is not, however, what that woman was after. She wanted material improvements in her children's daily life, improvements that would inevitably have meant taxing the members of the business, political, and professional elites rather than merely changing their ethnic and sexual composition. I suspect that woman—or by now, her daughter—is still waiting.

Am I suggesting that that woman's situation has not been affected by the successes, such as they are, of identity politics? No, I'm suggesting that they have probably made her situation worse. To begin with, if she lived in a school district without textbooks or heat, there's a fair chance she was poor enough to qualify for Aid to Families with Dependent Children. But Aid to Families with Dependent Children no longer exists. It was abolished by President Bill Clinton, with the support of First Lady Hillary Clinton, as a demonstration of the Democratic Party's recognition that "the era of Big Government is over." Needless to say, Clinton did not mean that the era of colossal defense budgets was over. Nor did he mean that the era of government-enforced race- and gender-based affirmative action was over. He meant that the era of government-administered redistribution of wealth was over. The government's job, according to the newly neoliberal, post–New Deal Democratic Party, was no longer to override the results of unrestricted competition by taxing and spending, but instead to make the competition fairer by opening it up to all, regardless of race, gender, or sexual orientation. Instead of presuming to correct gross market-generated inequalities, the Democratic Party humbly acknowledged the market's ineffable wisdom.

Identity politics are an essential component of neoliberalism, the extension of market relations across borders and into all spheres of life. If American capitalism is to be thus turbocharged, it must run on the highest-quality fuel. Discrimination is therefore irrational—a waste of talent our society cannot afford. When rewards are assigned efficiently in proportion to merit, then not only is total output maximized, but the winners need feel no qualms about the plight of the losers. That poor Black woman complaining about her local schools' lack of resources can be assured that it's nothing personal—why, the president is a Black man!—and encouraged, since schools are financed by property taxes, to move to an expensive suburb with high property taxes, where the schools are bound to be better. When she protests that she cannot afford to do that, she will be gently reminded that we all want things we cannot afford but that the market knows best.

Perhaps some intersectional leftists, having recently read Randall Robinson and Ta-Nehisi Coates, will plead eloquently with the state legislature that, slavery and subsequent discrimination having kept the means of moving to a richer school district out of this woman's reach, some extra money should be appropriated for her school district as a gesture of goodwill. Unfortunately, there is very little goodwill left. Somehow the majority of citizens have convinced themselves (with a great deal of help from the Republican Party and Fox News noise machines) that they have been all too generous to this woman and her like. "At the moment, we have identity politics for everyone except white men," wrote an alt-rightist recently. In *Strangers in Their Own Land*, a more serious observer, the sociologist Arlie Russell Hochschild, draws on her fieldwork among beleaguered working-class whites to formulate a parable or "deep story" with a powerful hold on them. They see themselves patiently waiting in line for jobs and educational opportunities, while government officials and diversity bureaucrats usher minorities and immigrants into line ahead of them. Americans born after 1950, she points out, are the first downwardly mobile generation in this country's history: the first to earn less at every stage of the life cycle than those born ten years earlier. "At some point," they tell Hochschild, "you have to close the borders to human sympathy"—especially if no one has shown much sympathy for you.

And so Black, inner-city kids still have substandard schools, perhaps now with heat and textbooks but also probably with armed guards and metal detectors; rural Louisiana whites (Hochschild's main interlocutors) have toxic fish gumbo and reduced unemployment benefits; and Rust Belt ex–factory workers currently stacking shelves at Walmart voted for Trump in sufficient numbers to elect (in combination with an archaic and undemocratic electoral system and unbridled gerrymandering by Republicans) a president who will at least treat them all equally, i.e., extremely badly.

How much blame, really, do identity politics and its most enthusiastic champion, the campus left, deserve for this debacle? It's tempting to imitate the spiteful liberals who blamed Al Gore's defeat in 2000 on Ralph Nader. But then as now, blame should fall primarily on the Republicans, whom minimal honesty would have impelled to campaign as the One Percent Party, and secondarily on the Democrats, who with steadfast pusillanimity have refrained from pointing that out. (In fact the Democrats, as Thomas Frank demonstrates in *Listen, Liberal*, ought to call themselves the Two Through Ten Percent Party, since they now cater chiefly to affluent though not super-rich professionals.) Far behind the Republicans and Democrats, in third and last place, slouches the academic left, increasingly impotent except to serve the demagogues of the right as examples of the present danger to the republic's civic and moral health.

Right-wing demagogues we will always have with us. But need we make it so easy for them? Every indigestible morsel of outlandish jargon, every Twitterstorm in a teacup over some unintentional and infinitesimal insensitivity, every reflexive exhortation to check one's privilege, is an own goal. Perhaps a bit of comradely advice from a sympathetic observer will help.

NO SLOGANS: As I sat outdoors with a friend in Harvard Square recently, a procession swung into view. A mixed group of students and dining hall workers, led by someone with a bullhorn, were chanting. I've forgotten the words, but the rhythm and meter were all too familiar: "Hey hey, ho ho; Something-something's got to go" and "Hey, Harvard, you can't hide; Something-something-something-ide." My friend and I winced at each other, as if to say: "Did *we* sound like that fifty years ago?" Indeed we did, and the local burghers looked equally unimpressed today. I wish the group had stopped at each street corner and stood with simple dignity while the speaker said: "Harvard's dining hall workers average $30,000 a year. University president Drew Faust makes $900,000, plus $300,000 for sitting on the board of Staples, a university supplier. And right there"—pointing to the gargantuan construction project that has inflicted nightmarish chaos on the square for two years— "the university is spending $100 million on a state-of-the-art student center for the benefit of undergraduates, three-quarters of whom come from households earning more than $100,000 a year." I suspect the university would have caved immediately.

NO EPITHETS: A great deal of shrewd strategic advice masquerades as homely counsels of virtue. Honesty generally *is* the best policy (though its efficacy is compromised when dealing with those who are cognitively disabled from recognizing truth, e.g., Republican politicians). Another pious maxim that actually works is "Love the sinner; hate the sin." The near-invariable effect of being called a racist or sexist or bigot is to make everything else the speaker says inaudible. Rigorous social-scientific research has shown that the probability of being conscience-stricken and experiencing a change of heart after being targeted with some such epithet is .0000001, or something equally infinitesimal. If you must use "racist," "homophobic," etc., apply them only to acts or opinions, not to people. And perhaps you don't, in fact, need to use them. What's bad about prejudice, after all, is that it's unfair and unkind. "Unfair" and "unkind" are words that actually resonate with Americans, even Trump voters. Give them a try, and give "racist," "sexist," "heteronormative," etc. a rest.

ASK, THEN LISTEN: Dale Carnegie had it right. People like more than anything else to talk about themselves; and they hold opinions they've talked themselves into much more firmly than opinions others have talked them into. As anyone from all those rural counties that voted for Trump would tell you, you can't just drop a seed any old place on the ground and expect it to grow. You've got to know your soil.

LOSE ARGUMENTS: It's a really efficient way to learn things. And it leads to a very useful habit: not caring who's right. There's nothing more persuasive in an argument than noticing that the other person doesn't care who's right, only what's right.

TAKE HALF A LOAF: The founder of quantum physics, Max Planck, remarked: "Science progresses one funeral at a time." So does liberation.

CHECK YOUR PRIVILEGE: Sorry, I couldn't resist. But I don't mean apologize for your whiteness, maleness, straightness, Europeanness, etc. I mean remember that if you're part of the campus left, you'll probably wind up in the top 10 or 20 percent of the national income distribution—comparatively rich, whether or not you feel like it. *Richesse oblige*—the greater the privilege, the greater the responsibility to the inhabitants of those "real communities" evoked by David Bromwich, "where people spend more than a few years, where they are compelled to live and to die."

PART III

The Role of the Critic

20

The Promise of an American Life

Randolph Bourne

The death of Randolph Bourne in 1918, at the age of thirty-two, was as great a loss as American intellectual life has ever sustained. "In no one," Alfred Kazin wrote, in an essay about Bourne's generation, "did 'the promise of American life' shine so radiantly." His career lasted seven years, during which he wrote more than 150 essays and reviews for the leading literary and political journals of his time. His book on the experimental public schools of Gary, Indiana, was an important event in the history of the progressive education movement. His essays on Dreiser largely rescued that novelist from critical neglect. His attacks on Puritanism and the genteel tradition helped found cultural radicalism in America. Above all, his lonely, bitter opposition to American participation in World War I was a brief but unforgettable demonstration of the dignity of the intellectual vocation. He was "the intellectual hero of World War I in this country," said Dwight Macdonald, who was the intellectual hero of World War II in this country.

Bourne was born in suburban New Jersey in 1886. The family doctor bungled the birth, and Bourne's face was badly deformed. At the age of four he suffered a severe case of spinal tuberculosis, which left him a hunchback and less than five feet tall throughout his life. His father, a business failure and an alcoholic, was banished by the stern maternal uncle who supported the family. When Randolph graduated high school, he was accepted by Princeton, but his uncle refused any further financial support. He tried to find a job in New York City, but his looks told against him. "Not once in two full years of applying," writes his latest biographer, Bruce Clayton, "did he ever get past the receptionist or initial interview." He gave up on the city and scrounged work in his hometown; he gave music lessons, punched out piano rolls in a local workshop, did factory work and odd jobs.

Somehow he kept his spirits up, and after six years, at the age of twenty-three, entered Columbia with a full tuition scholarship. It was like entering Paradise. The teachers were stimulating and accessible; his classmates were friendly; Bourne blossomed into a brilliant student and conversationalist. As a freshman he began contributing to the Columbia literary magazine. As a sophomore he began contributing to the *Atlantic Monthly*. His first essay for the *Atlantic*, "The Two Generations," was immensely popular; halfway through college he was a nationally known writer.

His early pieces for the *Atlantic* were a little callow, full of vague and occasionally vapid uplift, which presumably appealed to the attenuated Transcendentalism of that magazine's readership. "Youth" began: "How shall I describe Youth, the time of contradictions and anomalies? The fiercest radicalisms, the most dogged conservatisms, irrepressible gayety, bitter melancholy— all these moods are equally part of that great showery springtime of life." These essays probably owed their popularity to a kind of tame iconoclasm: for all that they twitted the older generation and lamented American provincialism and conformism, their upbeat, healthy-minded tone was also reassuring. The young Bourne preached "the experimental life," "vitality," "variousness," and openness to "American promise." Liberal, prosperous, prewar middle-class America read these sermons indulgently, rather proud of its youthful chastiser and confident that it could afford a certain quantity of self-improvement.

As graduation approached, he hoped for a teaching post at Columbia. But he had lampooned several professors and supported a strike of scrubwomen against the university. The English Department would as soon appoint him a professor, a friend told him, as "the Catholic Church would appoint Voltaire a bishop." He won a traveling fellowship and spent a year in Europe, meeting writers and radicals, observing architecture and town planning. While he was there, the flower of America's liberal intelligentsia came together to found the *New Republic*. Bourne was made a contributing editor.

After returning from Europe and joining the *New Republic* in the autumn of 1914, Bourne's radicalism became more forceful, but also more worldly and sardonic. He had been reading Nietzsche, Dostoyevsky, and the Fabian socialists, had watched Europe slide into war hysteria, and had begun to take stock of the American left—this last a sobering experience in any epoch. His wary editors asked him to concentrate on education and city planning, and his series on progressive education at Gary (soon afterward expanded into a book) was enormously influential. But his reports and reviews pushed on to larger themes, toward a criticism of American life as a whole.

Bourne's cultural criticism was partly an attempt to apply the pragmatic, instrumentalist philosophy of James and Dewey.

Today it may be hard to believe that pragmatism once seemed fresh, liberating, and subversive; but it did. Philosophical pragmatism was the last, best blossom of Victorian agnosticism, the modest, tentative Yea that followed the Everlasting No. It amounted to a cosmic wager on the adequacy of secular styles of thought and democratic forms of social life, a wager inspired and underwritten by the success of science. In the experimental, antidogmatic, and—not least important—communal character of scientific practice, pragmatists beheld the image of a possible future. Dewey had shown, Bourne wrote, that "scientific method is simply a sublimely well-ordered copy of our own best and most fruitful habits of thought." From this apparently innocuous formulation, Bourne drew a radical (though not fully worked out) conclusion: maximizing the national welfare was a technical problem, to be tackled with a resolute disregard of intellectual superstitions, traditional privileges, or special interests. Ingenuity, flexibility, goodwill, good nature—Americans' "best and most fruitful habits"—would, if imported into public life, gradually overcome America's class, ethnic, and generational conflicts.

Bourne would outgrow this cheerful meliorism, but it was a generous and plausible illusion. Faith in "the promise of American life" (the title of one of the most influential books of the era, by the first editor-in-chief of the *New Republic*) was not obviously misplaced in the years before World War I. Bourne took that promise more seriously than most. "Trans-National America," his finest *Atlantic* essay, asked "whether perhaps the time has come to assert a higher ideal than the 'melting pot.'" The assimilationist ideal was misguided, Bourne argued: "there is no distinctively American culture. It is apparently our lot rather to be a federation of cultures." This was an exceptional historical opportunity: "America is a unique sociological fabric, and it bespeaks poverty of imagination not to be thrilled at the incalculable potentialities of so novel a union of men." But "poverty of imagination" was precisely the characteristic failing of America's middle class. And so Bourne warned, in a prescient though fragmentary critique of mass culture, that dynamic capitalism and aggressive "Americanization" would produce not cosmopolitanism but deracination.

To read "Trans-National America" and other essays and reviews from Bourne's last three years is to ache with regret that his astonishing trajectory was cut so short. "The Price of Radicalism," a 1,000-word book review, is an even better manifesto for the New Left than the Port Huron Statement. "What is Exploitation?," a 1,500-word account of Bourne's correspondence with an unabashedly reactionary factory-owner, is a fine specimen of stylish, nondoctrinaire, unpatronizing socialist propaganda (not a thickly populated genre). And he was maturing rapidly. As late as 1917 there were still occasional touches of high-sounding vagueness, of undergraduate wistfulness, in his writing. But America's entry into World War I concentrated his mind wonderfully and provoked the series of furiously eloquent essays for which he is best known today.

"The war—or American promise," he pleaded; "one must choose." As censorship and irrationalism increased throughout the country, Bourne insisted, nearly alone, that cultural pluralism could not survive national mobilization. War enhances state power and undermines local, decentralized initiative; it makes passivity, apathy, conformism, and cynicism the normal relation between the citizen and the state; paradoxically, modern bureaucratized war makes public-spiritedness superfluous. In Bourne's memorable phrase: "War is the health of the State."

These arguments did not impress his fellow intellectuals, who lined up in support of American intervention. The *New Republic*'s editors and contributors, especially John Dewey, urged "realism" and a more indulgent view of the uses of force. They were confident that "intelligence" (i.e., they, the intelligentsia) could turn the forces let loose by the war to creative social purposes at home and abroad, could turn mechanized lunacy into a "democratic war." But to do this it was necessary to ally themselves with—actually, to subordinate themselves to—state power. They did so enthusiastically and thereafter devoted a good deal of polemical energy to jeering at radicals and pacifists, whose scruples, the "realists" claimed, could lead only to isolation and impotence.

All this outraged Bourne, who replied with a combination of penetrating analysis and coruscating sarcasm. In his colleagues' eagerness to subserve official policy he saw the corruption of pragmatism and, more generally, the proneness of intellectuals to a mystique of "action" and "commitment." They had supported intervention, he charged, from a "dread of intellectual suspense"—a readiness to minimize their own principled objections to the war for fear of ending up in a posture of futile opposition or of offering an appearance of sentimental idealism. They convinced themselves that power would allow itself to be guided by expertise—their expertise. Bourne exposed this illusion ruthlessly:

> But what then is there really to choose between the realist who
> accepts evil in order to manipulate it to a great end, but who somehow

unaccountably finds events turn sour on him, and the Utopian pacifist who cannot stomach the evil and will have none of it? Both are
helpless, both are coerced. The Utopian, however, knows that he is
ineffective and that he is coerced, while the realist, evading disillusionment, moves in a twilight zone of half-hearted criticism, and
hopes for the best, where he does not become a tacit fatalist. The
latter would be the manlier position, but then where would be his
realistic philosophy of intelligence and choice? . . . War determines
its own end—victory; and government crushes out automatically all
forces that deflect, or threaten to deflect, energy from the path of
organization to that end. All governments will act in this way, the
most democratic as well as the most autocratic. It is only "liberal"
naiveté that is shocked at arbitrary coercion and suppression. Willing war means willing all the evils that are organically bound up
with it. A good many people still seem to believe in a peculiar kind
of democratic and antiseptic war. The pacifists opposed the war
because they knew this was an illusion and because of the myriad
hurts they knew war would do to the promise of democracy at home.
For once the babes and sucklings seem to have been wiser than the
children of light.

Bourne's best antiwar writing forms part of a remarkable series
of essays by American literary and philosophical radicals: Thoreau's "Civil Disobedience"; Bourne's "War and the Intellectuals,"
"A War Diary," and "Twilight of Idols"; Dwight Macdonald's
"The Responsibility of Peoples"; and Noam Chomsky's "The
Responsibility of Intellectuals" and "Objectivity and Liberal
Scholarship." There are differences, of course, most notably
along a stylistic axis from the epigrammatic bravura of Thoreau
to the documentary doggedness of Chomsky. But the similarities

are striking: they were all outbursts of passionate moralism, occasioned by an imperialist war (in Macdonald's case, a morally dubious military strategy); they were aimed at the national chauvinism of the populace, the complacent pragmatism of the educated, and the routine mendacity of the state; and their authors were ignored, or derided as naïve and unserious, by the "realists" of their epoch. Perhaps more important, their authors were all amateurs; they asserted a kind of protestant principle of private judgment against the quasi-theological mystifications of the government and the policy intelligentsia. Taken together, they constitute something like a prophetic tradition within American radicalism, and the content of their prophecy is: "War is the health of the State."

As a prophet, Bourne met the usual fate. The *New Republic* politely declined to publish his antiwar essays, though it continued to accept book reviews from him. Bourne's antiwar writings appeared in *Seven Arts*, a new journal that featured several other young writers—Van Wyck Brooks, Paul Rosenfeld, Louis Untermeyer—and many established ones—Frost, Dreiser, O'Neill, Mencken, Sandburg, Max Eastman, Amy Lowell, Sherwood Anderson. Editorially, *Seven Arts* was a brilliant success; but its wealthy sponsor, aghast at Bourne's radicalism, withdrew her support, so it folded. Bourne began publishing more frequently in the *Dial*, but editorial control passed to a friend of John Dewey, and Bourne was frozen out. By the end of the war he was one of the most famous and least publishable writers in America.

Once again, he kept his spirits up. He began a novel and a philosophical study of the modern state. As the war wound down, he was poised to resume his place as one of the country's leading literary and social critics. And he found the "golden person" he had always yearned for, with an intensity heightened by his deformity: the talented, beautiful, aristocratic Esther Cornell. They became engaged a few weeks before Bourne's fatal influenza attack.

Bruce Clayton's *Forgotten Prophet: The Life of Randolph Bourne* (LSU Press, 1984) has not much of interest to say about Bourne's ideas, but it does manage to get inside his emotional life. There is something a little adolescent about the personality that emerges from Bourne's letters, which Clayton quotes extensively: the ardor, the high-mindedness, the wry self-mockery. Only a little, though; on the whole, Bourne's character was as admirable as his intelligence. He suffered a good deal from having to go about with one of the best minds of his time in a child's body. But he succeeded in growing up and in making himself loved as well as admired.

Clayton concludes by speculating that Bourne would have become a socialist Reinhold Niebuhr: skeptical, unaffiliated, anti-utopian, mindful of human limitations and the tragic dimension. Maybe so; he could not have remained indefinitely in the rarefied, supercharged atmosphere of the great antiwar essays. But he would doubtless have soared again, on occasion; and those later flights are much missed. As Sartre wrote after Camus's untimely death: "Rarely have the qualities of a work and the conditions of the historical moment so clearly required that a writer live."

Today, Bourne occupies an obscure place in the tiny pantheon of the American left. But he captured the imagination of his contemporaries, including John Dos Passos, who wrote in *U.S.A.*:

> If any man has a ghost
> Bourne has a ghost

a tiny twisted unscared ghost in a black cloak

hopping along the grimy old brick and brownstone streets

still left in downtown New York,

crying out in a shrill soundless giggle:

"War is the health of the State."

21

An Exemplary Amateur

Dwight Macdonald

In Saul Bellow's novel *Humboldt's Gift*, the narrator/protagonist returns to New York and meets an old friend, Orlando Huggins, who is clearly Dwight Macdonald:

> It came back to me that more than twenty years ago I had found myself at a beach party in Montauk, on Long Island, where Huggins, naked at one end of the log, discussed the Army McCarthy hearings with a lady sitting naked and astride opposite him. Huggins was speaking with a cigarette holder in his teeth, and his penis, which lay before him on the water-smooth wood, expressed all the fluctuations of his interest. And while he was puffing and giving his views in a neighing stammer, his genital went back and forth like the slide of a trombone. You could never feel unfriendly toward a man of whom you kept such a memory.

It seems to have been difficult for anyone in American intellectual life to feel unfriendly toward Dwight Macdonald. In the course of his long career as a political and cultural critic, he took issue with virtually everyone on the scene at one time or another, including (emphatically and often, whenever he had occasion to reconsider his own previous opinions) himself. Macdonald was a gadfly: a debunker of kitsch and propaganda, of radical, conservative, and mainstream sentimentality, vulgarity, and duplicity. Yet this inveterate argufier inspired nearly universal affection. What beguiled his readers (and listeners—as Bellow's anecdote suggests, he was an indefatigable talker) was less his arguments—though these were never negligible—than the distinctiveness of the voice in which they were delivered: "persnickety, contentious, vain, unafraid, passionate, garrulous, sometimes irritating, always honest," wrote one reviewer, who might have added "and often extremely droll." That admirable voice was stilled in December of 1982, but Da Capo Press has lately begun to reissue his books, starting with *On Movies*, a collection of film criticism, and *Against the American Grain: Essays on the Effects of Mass Culture*.

Macdonald's career traced an arc from literature to politics and partway back. He attended Phillips Exeter Academy and then Yale, and like a few other gifted adolescents amid the intellectual torpor of upper-class schools in the 1920s, he enlisted for life in the avant-garde. At Exeter he idolized Oscar Wilde, published a short-lived student magazine "of extreme preciosity," as he later described it, and joined an exclusive club (there were two other members) called the Hedonists, whose motto was "Cynicism, Estheticism, Criticism, Pessimism." At Yale he hectored the president, faculty, and student body about dress codes, compulsory chapel, and professorial dullness. Yet all of this flippancy was serious. His friends at Yale later became his colleagues at *Partisan Review*. And when an English teacher at Exeter put him in touch with James Agee, who arrived a few months after Macdonald left, they began an ardent lifelong correspondence about literature and film.

After graduating Yale in 1928, Dwight joined a management-training program at Macy's. "My plan was to make a lot of money very rapidly and retire to write literary criticism." He didn't last long. A Yale classmate got him a job on the staff of Henry Luce's new magazine, *Fortune*. There Macdonald learned the craft of journalism—the research and expository skills he picked up at *Fortune* were the foundation of his later, "higher" journalism—and acquired an intimate, enduring dislike of American business civilization. American business civilization, in the person of *Fortune*'s editors, did not exactly take a shine to Macdonald either, and after his series of articles excoriating the US Steel Corporation was bowdlerized, he quit.

In the late 1930s Macdonald's political education began in earnest. He read the Marxist classics plus an enormous quantity of economics and sociology, hung out with several Trotskyite groups, and became an editor of the newly revived *Partisan Review* (which had temporarily suspended publication because of the editors' disillusionment with Stalinism and socialist realism). In the intellectual hothouse of New York in those years, he evolved "with amazing speed," as he later commented wryly, from New Deal liberal to neophyte radical to Communist sympathizer to anti-Stalinist Trotskyite revolutionary to unaffiliated, unprogrammatic anarchist-pacifist. When World War II broke out, the other editors of *Partisan Review* supported American participation and tempered their radical opposition to capitalism and bourgeois society. But the logic of the lesser evil did not appeal to Macdonald. In 1943 he left the magazine, and the next year, with his wife, Nancy, he started his own magazine, *politics*.

Politics was a phenomenon. It was published from the Macdonalds' living room (Dwight was the entire editorial staff), and for the five years of its existence it was arguably the best political

journal ever published in the United States. Macdonald's own
varied and prolific commentary (collected in *Memoirs of a Revo-
lutionist*) was the magazine's staple, but some of the most
remarkable radicals of the time were also contributors: Albert
Camus, Simone Weil, Nicola Chiaromonte, Victor Serge, Paul
Goodman, George Woodcock, George Orwell. All of them, like
Macdonald, were morally fastidious, ideologically heterodox, and
fed up with brutality and propaganda, both official and opposi-
tional. They made a program and an ideology of honesty. It was
an impractical program and they accomplished nothing, but their
writing illuminated those dark times better than anyone else's.

Among many extraordinary articles in *politics*—including
Camus's "Neither Victims Nor Executioners," Weil's "The Iliad
or the Poem of Force," and Bruno Bettelheim's "Behavior in
Extreme Situations"—two by Macdonald stand out. "The
Responsibility of Peoples" (1945) asked why, if all Germans were
held responsible for Nazi atrocities, all Americans should not be
held responsible for Allied atrocities. The latter included the saturation bombing of German and Japanese cities (which took
more than a million civilian lives), widespread starvation in "liberated" Europe, bloody repression of the Greek Communist
resistance, refusal to allow more than a few European Jews to
immigrate to the United States, and the reckless initiation of
atomic warfare. In part the essay was an anarchist argument
against the "organic" corruption of the State, which underlay
notions of "collective responsibility" for war crimes. But equally
it was a challenge to national chauvinism, a rebuttal of the tacit
assumption that the other side's atrocities somehow extenuate
one's own. And since his audience consisted largely of leftists,
Macdonald felt obliged to address their own chauvinisms: much
of his most scathing wartime criticism, in "The Responsibility of

Peoples" and elsewhere, was directed at Soviet crimes and their American apologists. It required almost a heroic disinterestedness to say, or even perceive, such things in an atmosphere of inflamed patriotism and partisanship. That disinterestedness, his apparent lack of any temptation to equivocation or self-deception, was and is the basis of Macdonald's reputation.

"The Root Is Man" (1946) was more speculative. It was not only the war that had disillusioned Macdonald and his comrades, it was the whole sorry history of the organized left. How had the splendid ideals of the nineteenth-century socialists been perverted into Stalinist barbarism and Trotskyist scholasticism? Were there ethical values—socialist values—by which Marxism itself might be judged? "The Root Is Man" claimed to find in Marxism a contradiction between two legacies of the Enlightenment: individualism and humanism on the one hand, historical and scientific materialism on the other. Marx had shown that in every society, moral values and property relationships are connected. From this suggestive but ambiguous proposition, most of his followers concluded that morality was irrelevant to "real" politics, i.e., the class struggle, which progressed inexorably according to dialectical laws deducible from *Capital*. "Pragmatic" liberals drew analogous lessons from John Dewey's philosophy, and both Marxists and liberals tended in practice, as Macdonald demonstrated at length, to cynicism, opportunism, and state worship.

So Macdonald proceeded to reconsider the Enlightenment, modestly proposing to rethink "Determinism v. Free Will, Materialism v. Idealism, the concept of Progress, the basis for making value judgments, the precise usefulness of science to human ends, and the nature of man himself." He ended, predictably, perplexed. But he did succeed in arguing one crucial point against the

Marxist/pragmatists, or "Progressives," as he called them: "What can possibly be the content of this future *real* morality [*i.e.*, the one vaguely invoked in the *Communist Manifesto*] if it is not the persisting core of past morality stripped of all class-exploitative perversions?" It was in that "persisting core" of classical and modern humanism, rather than in an undefined (and, as he came to feel, largely mythical) Progress, that radical hope lay. As others were quick to point out, the explication and defense of "past morality" was what conservatives claimed to be up to. Was Macdonald a socialist, a conservative, both, or merely confused? Confused he was, yet "The Root Is Man" is at least as illuminating as anything else in the corpus of twentieth-century moral and political philosophy. But for Macdonald it was, politically, the end of the road.

Turgenev remarked about politics that "the honorable man will end by not knowing where to live." By 1950 Macdonald was politically homeless. "There is very little that we can honestly say in praise of the institutions and culture of Western capitalism," he wrote in 1949, "beyond the statement that, now that we have seen thirty years of Communist development, the comparison is greatly in favor of Capitalism." And the next year, in an even bleaker mood: "The scale of things is too big, the levers of power too far removed from people like us (perhaps from people like Stalin and Truman), the mood of the general population, after generations of Pavlovian conditioning by industrialism, world wars, and state bureaucracies, too demoralized and apathetic to respond to our appeals. Even if we could make them with the old fervor and rationality. Which we can't. For fervor we now have routine moralizing; for reason, the old stock of antiquated abstractions. . . . The pacifist and the socialist writings of today are to those of two generations ago as hay is to grass. Which is why I am no longer a pacifist, a socialist, or any kind of -ist."

Turgenev went into exile; Macdonald went to work for the *New Yorker*, writing what he called "social-cultural reportage and analysis." There were several reasons for this internal migration: ideological burnout; financial burnout—*politics* had lost a lot of money, and he had children to support; and a conviction—or at least a hope—that "the correction of taste" (T. S. Eliot's definition of the purpose of criticism) might be a form of political action. Mobilizing the masses was just not on the docket anymore, but perhaps one could begin to counteract, or anyway to document, that "Pavlovian conditioning."

Macdonald's essays, profiles, and reviews for the *New Yorker* (collected, along with occasional pieces from *Partisan Review* and other journals, in *Against the American Grain* and in *Discriminations*) ranged over the American scene, surveying how-to books, bestselling novels, the careers of Mark Twain and Ernest Hemingway, the state of literary journalism, the culture of poverty depicted in Michael Harrington's *The Other America* (which Macdonald's lengthy review rescued from obscurity), and much else. He punctured Marshall McLuhan, Tom Wolfe, Norman Cousins, and Mortimer J. Adler. He grumbled about the damage to language wrought by Webster's Third New International Dictionary, the Revised Standard Version of the Bible, and the theory of structural linguistics. He composed a perceptive, slightly querulous meditation on "The Triumph of Fact" before that theme became commonplace.

The point of all this witty, erudite grousing was to keep American culture honest. That tenuously persisting core of "past morality," of ethical and aesthetic values, seemed encrusted by commercialism and bureaucracy, in need of large doses of critical solvent. Macdonald's most influential effort of cultural hygiene was "Masscult and Midcult" (1960), an anatomy and theory of popular culture. Actually, Macdonald called his subject "mass culture," which highlights a fundamental distinction in his essay between "communities" and "masses." Communities (city states, craft guilds, artistic schools, political factions) have traditions, and their members have individual functions. But masses are "in historical time what a crowd is in space: . . . not related to *each other* at all but only to some impersonal, abstract, crystallizing factor. In the case of crowds, this can be a football game, a bargain sale, a lynching; in the case of the masses, it can be a political party, a television program, a system of industrial production." Art is individuality; so members of a community can produce genuine culture, either High or Folk. But masses are composed of "inchoate and uncreative" atoms capable only of an anonymous and homogenized nonculture, Masscult.

Macdonald (and plenty of others) had been making this argument for decades. But there was something new, he claimed, about post–World War II American culture: it was so abundant, various, and flexible as to induce acute anxiety. "The pattern of our cultural lives is 'open' to the point of being porous. For a lucky few, this openness of choice is stimulating. But for most, it is confusing and leads at best to that middlebrow compromise called Midcult." Midcult may be defined as the tribute mediocrity pays to excellence. It was a hybrid, combining the essential qualities of Masscult—"the formula, the built-in reaction, the lack of any standard except popularity"—with ersatz mimicry of High Culture, employing modern idiom and technique in the service of the banal. Midcult's intentions were good, but its effect was insidious: unlike Masscult, Midcult competed with serious new art for prestige and financial support.

Most of "Masscult and Midcult" was devoted to a review of typical Midcult phenomena: the Book of the Month Club, Norman Rockwell's *Saturday Evening Post* covers, Rodgers and Hammerstein musicals, Hemingway's *The Old Man and the Sea*, Thornton Wilder's *Our Town*, and so on. Macdonald's detailed criticism was scintillating and salutary, and his historical diagnosis was persuasive. But his prescription was bizarre: to re-create a cultural (though *not* a social, political, or economic) elite. "Let the masses have their Masscult, let the few who care about good writing, painting, music, architecture, philosophy, etc., have their High Culture, and don't fuzz up the distinction with Midcult." Macdonald admitted that this solution was both unattractive and impractical. Still, it seemed to him the only alternative to an even more farfetched (though much more desirable) solution: the creation of real, i.e., decentralized, communities within which lively popular cultures might flourish. Macdonald was a cultural elitist, but only by default. His democratic hopes were in abeyance, and he thought of High Culture, with its subversive playfulness and its fidelity to noncommercial, non-bureaucratic standards, worth defending against the encroachments of Midcult.

Like all doctrines, Macdonald's aristocratic moralism was both enabling and disabling. Fortunately, he was no doctrinaire. In 1966 Macdonald switched the subject of his monthly column at *Esquire* from movies to politics, in time to fulminate splendidly against the Vietnam War. Among his later essays were a startlingly detailed program for "Updating the Constitution" and a homage to Buster Keaton (October 1980; as far as I can tell, his last major piece). When he died in 1982 he was making dilatory efforts at writing his memoirs.

Did Macdonald matter? Some people (including Macdonald) have disparaged him affectionately (some not so affectionately) as a "dandy," charming and talented but fickle and, finally, light-weight. I think he mattered, in a general way and in a great many particular ways. For one: "The Responsibility of Peoples" found a surprisingly large and appreciative audience, considering its obscure venue. And it directly inspired one of the best and most influential essays of the next generation, Noam Chomsky's "The Responsibility of Intellectuals." (Macdonald and Chomsky were later co-founders of RESIST, one of the most successful New Left activities.) That alone is more than most of his contemporaries accomplished. For another, there was Macdonald's effect on the *New Yorker*. During the Vietnam War, the magazine's "Notes and Comment" section featured a good deal of surprisingly pungent criticism of American policy. An outsider can only guess, but I'd guess that Macdonald was partly, even if indirectly, responsible.

He mattered in a larger way, too, at least to those of us trying to be citizen-critics. He was an exemplary amateur. Like Chom-sky and Bourne, Macdonald was aroused by a calamitous war to a passionate moralism. Like them, he was dismissed or derided by "pragmatic" liberals as naïve and unserious. And in each case, while the "realists" were steeped in intellectual disgrace, the naïve moralists redeemed, in a small way, the humane promise of the intellectual vocation.

Macdonald despaired of politics—but only of "professional," organized politics and its ideological sideshows. He remained a political dilettante, in the pristine sense of that honorable old word: someone who prizes nobility or skill. In 1968 Nicola Chiaromonte, a frequent contributor to *politics*, responded to the French student uprising by admonishing the students to adopt "a non-rhetorical form of 'total rejection'": to approach politics with the integrity of artisans, to apply to social life "the standards of the craft itself, standards that in themselves are the simplest and strictest of moral principles and, by their very nature, cut out deception and prevarication, charlatanism, and the love of power and possession." That was also Macdonald's creed. He sought to apply to our politics and culture the strict critical standards of an honest intellectual craftsman—standards at once deeply conservative and deeply subversive.

Not his uncommon wit, but his common decency, was Macdonald's best legacy. Of Macdonald's friend George Orwell, Lionel Trilling observed that he was not a genius but was all the more useful for that. "We admire geniuses, we love them," Trilling wrote, "but they discourage us." To see Macdonald tilting year after year at the political and commercial barbarities of the age, armed with no system but only some peculiar moral and aesthetic intuitions, was—and still is—encouraging.

22

The Liberal Intelligence

Lionel Trilling

In 1975 Lionel Trilling died, at the height of his reputation and influence as America's foremost literary and cultural critic. Twenty years later, nearly all his books were out of print. Fortunately Trilling was survived by his remarkable wife Diana, who wrote a deeply affecting memoir of their marriage, *The Beginning of the Journey*, and who encouraged Leon Wieseltier, literary editor of the *New Republic*, to assemble a new collection of her husband's essays. *The Moral Obligation to Be Intelligent: Selected Essays* (Farrar, Straus and Giroux) is the result. It contains thirty of Trilling's finest essays, his famous prefaces to *The Liberal Imagination* and *Beyond Culture*, and a well-judged introduction by Wieseltier. It is exactly what anyone needs—urgently—who has no Trilling on his or her bookshelves.

Trilling was one of the "New York intellectuals," the brilliant writers and critics connected with *Partisan Review* who played a large part in American culture from the 1930s through the 1960s. In some ways he was central to this group, perhaps the one most respected internally and most visible externally. But in other ways he was untypical of them, notably in passing his career as a

professor (of English, at Columbia) rather than as an institution-
ally unaffiliated man of letters like, say, Edmund Wilson or Philip
Rahv. This made a difference to his writing, both in substance
and in style. For one thing, his writing was less topical than that
of most other New York intellectuals. Though nearly everything
Trilling wrote had an ultimate political relevance, almost nothing
he wrote had an immediate political reference. And then, though
he was not a scholar, he was surrounded by scholars. This
undoubtedly made him a little more circumspect, more respectful
of expertise, and more inclined to deal in depth with individual
works of literature and to reckon with their traditional interpretations than his almost defiantly non-professional fellow New
Yorkers were.

It also made him more inward. Academics work and socialize
at closer quarters than freelancers; and since an intellectual hatred
is the worst, or at least the most uncomfortable, kind, academics
place a high—sometimes excessive—value on courtesy. To reconcile this necessary academic civility with the boldness, even
aggressiveness, prized by his more freewheeling *Partisan Review*
colleagues required—what Trilling achieved—a style of incomparable tact and gracefulness. Some comments by Irving Howe
on the "characteristic style" of the New York intellectuals may
suggest how far Trilling was and wasn't a typical specimen. "The
kind of essay they wrote was likely to be wide-ranging in reference, melding notions about literature and politics, sometimes
announcing itself as a study of a writer or literary group but usually taut with a pressure to 'go beyond' its subject, toward some
encompassing moral or social observation." So far, pure Trilling.
But Howe went on: "It is a kind of writing highly self-conscious
in mode, with an unashamed vibration of bravura. Nervous,
strewn with knotty or flashy phrases, impatient with transitions

and other concessions to dullness, calling attention to itself as a form or at least an outcry, fond of rapid twists, taking pleasure in dispute, dialectic, dazzle . . ." Trilling's style was not nervous, knotty, flashy, impatient, or ostentatious; it was grave, smooth, deliberate, and restrained. But it had force as well as grace. As Wieseltier observes: "Trilling was not noisy in the New York manner. For that reason, he wrote the most lasting prose of any of the New Yorkers."

Every piece in *The Moral Obligation to Be Intelligent* is rewarding, but someone making a first acquaintance with Trilling's work might best begin with these acknowledged classics: "Keats in His Letters," "*Mansfield Park*," "*Huckleberry Finn*," "*The Princess Casamassima*," "George Orwell and the Politics of Truth." These essays, like his others, are full of illuminating juxtapositions, discriminations, and asides as well as subtle, shapely exposition. But the subjects of these essays evoke Trilling's keenest sympathies, and his affection kindles his usual intelligence to some unusually stirring formulations.

[*The Princess Casamassima*] is a novel which has at its very center the assumption that Europe has reached the full of its ripeness and is passing over into rottenness, that the peculiarly beautiful light it gives forth is in part the reflection of a glorious past and in part the phosphorescence of a present decay, that it may meet its end by violence and that this is not wholly unjust, although never before has the old sinful continent made so proud and pathetic an assault upon our affections.

[Keats] stands as the last image of health at the very moment when the sickness of Europe began to be apparent—he with his intense naturalism that took so passionate an account of the mystery of man's nature, reckoning as boldly with pleasure as with pain, giving so generous a credence to growth, development, and possibility; he with his pride that so modestly, so warmly and delightedly, responded to the idea of community.

> If we ask what it is [Orwell] stands for, what he is the figure of, the answer is: the virtue of not being a genius, of confronting the world with nothing more than one's simple, direct, undeceived intelligence, and a respect for the powers one does have and the work one undertakes to do. We admire geniuses, we love them, but they discourage us. . . . He is not a genius—what a relief! What an encouragement.

Trilling's enthusiasms were immensely attractive. But, some asked, were they specifically *literary* enthusiasms? In a generally admiring review of *The Opposing Self*, Denis Donoghue also entered a few shrewd reservations. Speaking for the New Criticism, he wondered whether Trilling's "central interest is not in literature at all but in ideas; which are not, need it be said, the same thing"; whether "in the last instance [Trilling] is not really interested in the fact that the words of an individual poem are *these* words and not some others, in *this* order and not another"; whether "he is happiest when roaming about the large triangle whose sides are Sociology, Politics, and Literature (in that order)." Wieseltier's introduction touches on this question, a bit defensively, conceding that Trilling was "a very un-literary literary critic," but countering immediately that "his conception of his critical duty was less professional and less playful—and bigger." Finally, Wieseltier concludes, "he was a historian of morality working with literary materials."

I don't know about "and bigger." I would also query Donoghue's "need it be said." It does need to be said, and patiently explained, at least to the likes of me. The relation of form and content in literature is a continually recurring question. The New Criticism was one very useful answer. But Trilling's dealings with literature were at least as fruitful.

It's true, though, that Trilling was best known for his exploration of (to use his celebrated phrase) "the dark and bloody crossroads where literature and politics meet." In the decades when he began to write, the 1930s and '40s, liberalism was, as he noted, America's "sole intellectual tradition." Like any one-party state, the state of American political culture had become, in certain ways, lazy and intolerant. It had become intolerant of complexity, of limits, of doubt—in short, of mind. Trilling thought he detected a "chronic American belief that there exists an opposition between reality and mind, and that one must enlist oneself in the party of reality." Which usually meant the revolutionary or, as we now more soberly say, the progressive party.

Trilling was quite willing to enlist in the progressive party, but only on one condition. Progressives must acknowledge that "to act against social injustice is right and noble but that to choose to act so does not settle all moral problems but on the contrary generates new ones of an especially difficult sort." There is, for example, the problem of elitism vs. mediocrity. "Civilization has a price, and a high one . . . all civilizations are alike in that they renounce something for something else. . . . To achieve the ideal of widespread security, popular revolutionary theory condemns the ideal of adventurous experience. All the instincts of radical democracy are against the superbness and arbitrariness which often mark great spirits." There is, for another example, the problem of individual liberty, of limiting collective power once we have "learned something of what may lie behind abstract ideals, the envy, the impulse to revenge and to dominance." These are not insoluble problems. But there are no final or perfect solutions, only imperfect, temporary, revisable ones.

Trilling called this attitude "moral realism" and defined it as "the free play of the moral imagination." The phrase recalls Matthew Arnold, and is meant to. Trilling began his career with a book on Arnold, and the resemblances between the two men—philosophical, political, and temperamental—go very deep. They both wrote a marvelously flexible, musical, allusive prose. They both suffered fools—i.e., intellectual antagonists—if not gladly then at least kindly and courteously. They both considered literature primarily in its moral aspect, as a criticism of social and political life. And they both saw their special contribution as helping to keep their fellow progressives (liberals, radicals, reformers) up to the mark, helping them to fail a little less often in detachment, discrimination, receptiveness, patience, magnanimity. Literature could teach this, perhaps because it has no political designs on us, or because stories get around psychological defenses that defeat arguments, or because rhythm, harmony, symmetry, and the other aesthetic qualities induce a deeper attentiveness. Whatever the reason, literature *can* teach us the moral virtues, at least the second-order, intellectual ones, as Trilling showed repeatedly in his discussions of Hawthorne, Twain, Howells, James, Kipling, Eliot, Dos Passos, Dreiser, Hemingway, Orwell, and others.

Yes, yes, impatient progressives will (and did) reply, the second-order virtues are fine, but what about the first-order ones: solidarity, compassion, a hunger and thirst for justice? Aren't these still in short supply? Characteristically, Trilling put this objection to his position better than anyone else has. "However important it may be for moral realism to raise questions in our minds about our motives, is it not at best a matter of secondary importance? Is it not of the first importance that we be given a direct and immediate report on the reality that is daily being brought to dreadful birth? . . . To speak of moral realism is all very well. But it is an elaborate, even fancy, phrase and it is to be suspected of having the intention of sophisticating the simple reality that is easily to be conceived. Life presses us so hard, time is so short, the suffering of the world is so huge, simple, unendurable—anything that complicates our moral fervor in dealing with reality as we immediately see it and wish to dive headlong upon it must be regarded with some impatience."

Trilling's answer is that the first-order moral virtues are dangerous without the second-order ones. "The moral passions are even more willful and imperious and impatient than the self-seeking passions. All history is at one in telling us that their tendency is to be not only liberating but also restrictive." Certainly the history of the Russian Revolution, which was present to the minds of all Trilling's readers, should have taught that. So should the histories of the Puritan Revolution, the French Revolution, the Chinese Revolution, the Cuban Revolution, and the Iranian Revolution.

But Trilling was not, as leftists have charged, a "quietist," any more than Arnold was. His position, like Arnold's, was in essence, "Yes, but . . ." Yes to greater equality, inclusiveness, cooperation, tolerance, social experimentation, individual freedom . . . but only after listening to everything that can be said against one's cherished projects, assuming equal intelligence and good faith on the part of one's opponents, and tempering one's zeal with the recognition that every new policy has unintended consequences, sometimes very bad ones. But after all that . . . yes. "It is not enough to want [change]," Trilling wrote, "not even enough to work for it—we must want it and work for it with intelligence."

Although neither the left nor the right appeared to notice, that "we" included Trilling.

In fact, both the left and the right simply heard "Yes, but . . ." as "No," which must have discouraged Trilling horribly. Both sides have assumed he was a proto-neoconservative, the left blaming him for it and the right blaming him for not owning up to it. But Trilling was not a neoconservative. He was, like Arnold, a friend of equality, of progress, of reform, of democratic collective action—a wistful, anxious, intelligent friend. He was, that is, a good—the very best kind of—liberal.

23

Just a Journalist

Edmund Wilson

It's said that Art Tatum's technique persuaded a great many young pianists to become insurance salesmen. Edmund Wilson's chops were equally phenomenal; not as sheerly, immediately dazzling as Tatum's, perhaps, but in range, erudition, penetration, clarity, and unfussy elegance, no less jaw-dropping. And just as Tatum's multi-volume *Complete Solo Masterpieces* (Pablo) is one of the summits of piano jazz, the Library of America's two-volume issue of Wilson's essays and reviews from the 1920s, '30s, and '40s (*Literary Essays and Reviews of the 1920s and 1930s: The Shores of Light, Axel's Castle, Uncollected Reviews*, and *Literary Essays and Reviews of the 1930s and 1940s: The Triple Thinkers, The Wound and the Bow, Classics and Commercials, Uncollected Reviews*, both edited by Lewis Dabney) is one of the summits of twentieth-century literary criticism.

Edmund Wilson's life story is well known from his many published journals (*The Twenties* through *The Sixties*), memoirs ("The Author at Sixty" and *Upstate*), and letters (a superb collection, *Letters on Literature and Politics*, edited by Elena Wilson, his fourth wife), other people's remembrances, and two good biographies by Jeffrey Meyers and Lewis Dabney. He was born in 1895—with difficulty, because he already had an unusually large head. His father was a reforming lawyer and attorney general of New Jersey but was disabled for much of his later life by hypochondria and depression. Young Edmund got an extraordinary education at the Hill School in Pennsylvania and a decent one at Princeton, especially after he encountered the literary scholar and peerless teacher Christian Gauss. At Princeton he also (like Dwight Macdonald at Yale) began several lifelong literary friendships, notably with F. Scott Fitzgerald and the poet John Peale Bishop.

During World War I, Wilson served as a hospital orderly in France. Afterward he freelanced for *Vanity Fair* and the *Dial*, and in 1925 he became literary editor of the *New Republic* until 1931, then traveled around Depression-era America as a correspondent. (His reporting is available in a marvelous collection, *The American Earthquake*.) In 1935 he spent some months in the Soviet Union, about which he was ambivalent. The second half of the decade he researched and wrote *To the Finland Station*, his brilliantly idiosyncratic history of revolutionary socialism. In 1940 he rejoined the *New Republic*, though not for long. Like Randolph Bourne before him and others more recently, Wilson fell afoul of that magazine's recurring enthusiasm for American military intervention.

In 1944 he began writing regularly for the *New Yorker*, where most of his subsequent work first appeared, except for *Memoirs of Hecate County*, a collection of stories and novellas, and *Patriotic Gore*, a study of American writing around the time of the Civil War. Besides literary criticism, Wilson produced a great deal of travel writing (much of it, as Lewis Dabney notes, "verging on cultural anthropology") about Europe, Russia, Israel, the

Caribbean, and the American Southwest, as well as a widely read and admired book about the discovery of the Dead Sea Scrolls. He was present at the creation of the *New York Review of Books* and first proposed the Library of America.

Wilson's love life was as busy as his writing life. He was married four times, most spectacularly to Mary McCarthy, and had (or attempted) romantic liaisons with Edna St. Vincent Millay, Louise Bogan, Anaïs Nin, Mamaine Koestler, and other celebrated women, most of whom remained good friends, as did Dawn Powell and Janet Flanner, who escaped his amorous attentions but keenly appreciated his encouragement and help with their careers.

T. S. Eliot wrote that in literary criticism, "the only method is to be very, very intelligent." This was Wilson's method. He made use of Marx and Freud, but pragmatically, as though their importance was not as system-builders or scientific innovators but as astute fellow-critics who had extended our limited perennial understanding of economic and psychological motives. These new approaches took their place in the critic's traditional repertoire alongside the biographical, formal, impressionistic, and others; and the choice of approach was dictated by the individual character of the work or author. The notion of literature as a body of evidence, a corpus over which to fit a conceptual grid, rather than a field for judgments about artistic merit, would have seemed to him perverse—a queer idea of theory.

His characteristic approach was biographical, comparative, historical. In "The Literary Worker's Polonius," a witty and trenchant "brief guide for authors and editors," he is apparently describing himself when he writes:

> a reviewer should be more or less familiar, or be ready to familiarize
> himself, with the past work of every important writer he deals with

and be able to write about an author's new book in the light of his general development and intention. He should also be able to see the author in relation to the national literature as a whole and the national literature in relation to other literatures.

"But this," he adds dryly, "means a great deal of work." Wilson was famously indefatigable, vacuuming up new authors and even languages at a rate apparently unimpaired by his sexual and alcoholic indulgences. Mary McCarthy related wonderingly to one of his biographers that "after drinking in his study late into the night, he emerged 'in his snowy-white BVDs in the morning,' freshly bathed and ready to go back to work."

Where energy and the large view were requisite, Wilson was unfailing. Correcting Irving Babbitt about Sophocles, estimating the relative merits of English comic writers from W. S. Gilbert to Kingsley Amis, paying a well-informed tribute to Houdini (Wilson was an amateur magician), comparing Poe's reception in Europe and America—each of these (and perhaps a hundred and fifty others from *The Shores of Light* and *Classics and Commercials*), compact but spacious, authoritative but not bullying, was a week's work (two at most) during the crowded decades these volumes cover.

Wilson was rarely starchy and sometimes quite funny, as in "The Delegate from Great Neck," an imaginary dialogue between Scott Fitzgerald and Van Wyck Brooks; "A Letter to Elinor Wylie," signed "Sam. Johnson" and perfectly pitched in the Doctor's epistolary style; and his dead-on parody in *Axel's Castle* of Eliot's hyper-magisterial critical prose:

"We find this quality occasionally in Wordsworth," Eliot will write, "but it is a quality which Wordsworth shares with Shenstone rather than with Collins and Gray. And for the right sort of enjoyment of Shenstone, we must read his prose as well as his verse. The 'Essays on Men and Manners' are in the tradition of the great French aphorists of the seventeenth century, and should be read with the full sense of their relation to Vauvenargues, La Rochefoucauld, and (with his wider range) La Bruyère. We shall do well to read enough of Theophrastus to understand the kind of effect at which La Bruyère aimed. (Professor Somebody-or-other's book on 'Theophrastus and the Peripatetics' gives us the clew to the intellectual atmosphere in which Theophrastus wrote and enables us to gauge the influences on his work—very different from each other—of Plato and Aristotle.)" At this rate . . . we should have to read the whole of literature to appreciate a single book, and Eliot fails to supply us with a reason why we should go to the trouble of doing so.

Of course Wilson revered Eliot, and in the same essay he praised Eliot's criticism, though in terms that throw light on their differences. Eliot "has undertaken a kind of scientific study of aesthetic values: . . . he compares works of literature coolly and tries to distinguish between different orders of artistic effects and the different degrees of satisfaction to be derived from them." Despite his "occasional dogmatism" and the "meagerness of his production," Eliot "has become for his generation a leader . . . because his career has been a progress, because he has evidently been on his way somewhere," unlike "many of his contemporaries, more prolific and equally gifted."

Unlike, for example, Wilson. "On his way somewhere" meant that Eliot had a critical program, a large view of how all of literature fit together, and that he aimed to work out and propagate a comprehensive philosophy of culture. Wilson's aims were nearly always more modest: to describe, to compare, to assess. It's not that he lacked philosophical interests; but he was satisfied with the Enlightenment, with science, with the main current of secular modernity, as Eliot was not. Wilson was a temperamental pragmatist and positivist, comfortable enough in his own philosophical skin to be able to muster at least an undoctrinaire sympathy, if not always much enthusiasm, for romantic and metaphysical heterodoxies.

Besides, he was, he insisted, just a journalist, whose beat was literature (with frequent excursions into politics, popular culture, and travel). He wrote to inform and edify contemporary readers and encourage (or, when necessary, discourage) contemporary writers, rather than, like Eliot, *sub specie aeternitatis*. The closest Wilson came to a critical manifesto was "The Historical Interpretation of Literature" in *The Triple Thinkers*. There he distances himself respectfully not only from Eliot's unhistorical aestheticism and from the impressionism of Edwardians like George Saintsbury ("his attitude toward literature was that of the connoisseur: he tastes the authors and tells you about the vintage; he distinguishes the qualities of the various wines") but also from the sociological, Marxist, and Freudian approaches ("The problems of comparative artistic value still remain after we have given attention to the Freudian psychological factor just as they do after we have given attention to the Marxist economic factor and to the racial and geographical factors").

Wilson was not one to shrink from confronting an implied question, however daunting. "And now how, in these matters of literary art, do we tell the good art from the bad?" Among the things named at one time or another as the defining characteristic of art are "unity, symmetry, universality, originality, vision, inspiration, strangeness, suggestiveness, improving morality, socialist realism." All plausible enough, as a first approximation;

but how is it possible to judge objectively of these qualities, and why are their effects so valuable?

Wilson answers these questions very much as William James would have. Art, like all other intellectual activity,

> is an attempt to give a meaning to our experience—that is, to make life more practicable . . . The writer who is to be anything more than an echo of his predecessors must always find expression for something which has never yet been expressed, must master a new set of phenomena which has never yet been mastered. With each such victory of the human intellect, whether in history, in philosophy, or in poetry, we experience a deep satisfaction: we have been cured of some ache of disorder, relieved of some oppressive burden of uncomprehended events. . . . This relief that brings the sense of power, and, with the sense of power, joy, is the positive emotion which tells us that we have encountered a first-rate piece of literature.

But this is a subjective reaction; what about objective judgment? Not everyone will feel the same "ache," the same "joy"; and "crude and limited people [will] feel some such emotion in connection with work that is limited and crude." True, but "the man who is more highly organized and has a wider intellectual range will feel it in connection with work that is wider and more complex." And if you ask,

> how can we identify this elite who know what they are talking about? Well, it can only be said of them that they are self-appointed and self-perpetuating, and that they will compel you to accept their authority. Impostors may try to put themselves over, but these quacks will not last. The implied position of the people who know about literature (as is also the case in every other art) is simply that they

know what they know, and that they are determined to impose their opinions by main force of eloquence and assertion on the people who do not know.

The pragmatist's answer is the same for art as for science and philosophy: truth is enduring consensus. That is all we know on earth, and all we need to know.

This conclusion—that all criticism is practical criticism—is persuasive, to me at least. And how good a critic, practically speaking, was Wilson? James Wood's brilliant essay on Wilson, tactful but unsparing, is the best assessment. With all respect for Wilson's "glinting, pugnacious clarity," his "comprehensive and solitary scholarship," and his "beautifully restrained and classically elegant expository prose," Wood nevertheless finds that he is "sometimes, in the major essays, disappointing as a literary critic." The meaning, background, and comparative worth of works and authors are reliably propounded, but "it is hard to find any sustained analysis of deep literary beauty"—the kind of analysis Wood excels at:

> Wilson's literary criticism, with its introductory relish, its recourse to biographical speculation, and its swerve away from aesthetic questions, now looks more journalistic than it once did. Pritchett seems to me to have had a more literary sensibility and a more natural understanding of how fiction works its effects; Empson explains poetry with a far richer respect for ambiguity; Trilling imbricates ideas and aesthetics with greater skill; and Jarrell accounts for beauty with more devoted vivacity.

It is a fair enough judgment, even if it only means that Wilson didn't do everything equally well.

One thing he did extremely well was make political judgments. This is not, however, the conventional view. His political
books are widely praised for their literary qualities. Everyone
acknowledges Wilson's superb Depression-era reporting in
The American Jitters, his incomparable dramatization of intellectual history in *To the Finland Station*, and his far-ranging
scholarship in *Patriotic Gore*. But everyone, it seems, has an
unkind word for his political views, or what they take to be his
views.

The principal charge is that Wilson idealized Lenin in *To the
Finland Station*. James Wood refers to Wilson's "willful roman-
ticizing of Lenin . . . who is seen as the gentlest and most selfless
of men." David Remnick too refers to Wilson's "romanticized
portrait of Lenin" and complains that "to turn Lenin into an
author, and to see him almost solely as an author or artist instead
of an architect of power, with incredible talent for grasping that
power, is a great problem and a self-deception." Paul Berman
finds an "enormous enthusiasm for Lenin" and claims that, in
Wilson's view, "the reason that Russia had indeed turned out
quite badly . . . was the mystical element in Marx. It was not
because of Lenin—Lenin was the good guy, Marx the bad guy."
Louis Menand concurs, seeing a "lack of enthusiasm for Marx"
and "enthusiasm for Lenin."

This consensus will probably endure, alas. But I found, along
with a vivid portrait of Lenin's many genuinely remarkable personal qualities (and flaws), plenty of lack of enthusiasm for Lenin
as a political leader in *To the Finland Station* and no failure to
notice Lenin's disastrous "grasping" for power. "Marxism at the
End of the Thirties," originally the last chapter of *Finland Station*
but later moved to *The Shores of Light*, contains these two forthright condemnations of Lenin's politics:

The takeover by the state of the means of production and the dictatorship in the interests of the proletariat can by themselves never guarantee the happiness of anybody but the dictators themselves. Marx and Engels, coming out of authoritarian Germany, tended to imagine socialism in authoritarian terms; and Lenin and Trotsky after them, forced as they were to make a beginning among a people who had known nothing but autocracy, also emphasized this side of socialism and founded a dictatorship which perpetuated itself as an autocracy.

And again:

Lenin's ultimate aims were of course humanitarian, democratic, and anti-bureaucratic; but the logic of the situation was too strong for Lenin's aims. His trained band of revolutionists, the Party, turned into a tyrannical machine which perpetuated, as heads of a government, the intolerance, the deviousness, the secrecy, the ruthlessness with political dissidents, which they had had to learn as hunted outlaws. Instead of getting a classless society out of the old illiterate feudal Russia, they encouraged the rise and the domination of a new controlling and privileged class, who were soon exploiting the workers almost as callously as the Tsarist industrialists had done, and subjecting them to an espionage that was probably worse than anything under the Tsar.

When Trotsky, jeering at Martov, coins the phrase "the dustbin of history," Wilson rejoins that Martov was right after all:

Today . . . his croakings over the course [the Bolsheviks] had adopted seem to us full of far-sighted intelligence. He pointed out that proclaiming a socialist regime in conditions different from those contemplated by Marx would not realize the results that Marx expected; that Marx and Engels had usually described the dictatorship of the proletariat as having the form, for the new dominant class, of a democratic republic, with universal suffrage and the popular recall of officials; that the slogan "All power to the Soviets" had never really meant what it said and that it had soon been exchanged by Lenin for "All power to the Bolshevik Party." There sometimes turn out to be valuable objects cast away in the dustbin of history.

And in the chapter on "Lenin at the Finland Station," Wilson gives the last word to the anti-Bolshevik revolutionary Bogdanov, who, revolted by Lenin's authoritarian declarations, "furiously scolded the audience: 'You ought to be ashamed to applaud this nonsense—you cover yourselves with shame! And you call yourselves Marxists!'"

It seems to me that, notwithstanding his later self-criticism about *To the Finland Station*, Wilson was as clear-sighted about the evils of Leninism as his critics.

The other usual occasion for condescending to Wilson is his introduction to *Patriotic Gore*, with its rejection of belligerent nationalism, which prompted Hilton Kramer to sniff that Wilson "was not really a political thinker" (unlike, say, Norman Podhoretz or Kramer himself). True, Wilson oversimplifies a little in the introduction:

In a recent Walt Disney film showing life at the bottom of the sea, a primitive organism called a sea slug is seen gobbling up smaller organisms through a large orifice at one end of its body; confronted with another sea slug of an only slightly lesser size, it ingurgitates that, too. Now, the wars fought by human beings are stimulated as a rule primarily by the same instincts as the voracity of the sea slug. . . . The difference in this respect between man and other forms of life is that man has succeeded in cultivating enough of what he calls "morality" and "reason" to justify what he is doing in terms of what he calls "virtue" and "civilization." Hence the self-assertive sounds he utters when he is fighting and swallowing others: the songs about glory and God, the speeches about national ideals, the demonstrations of logical ideologies. . . . This prevents us from recognizing today, in our relation to our cold-war opponent, that our panicky pugnacity as we challenge him is not virtue but at bottom the irrational instinct of an active power organism in the presence of another such organism, of a sea slug of vigorous voracity in the presence of another such sea slug.

This requires a slight qualification. The aim of American foreign policy is not to "ingurgitate" (i.e., conquer and occupy) other countries but to drain their vital fluids (i.e., to insure unrestricted inflow of American capital and outflow of profits). Once this small correction is made, Wilson's view is far superior to the views of his critics, who upbraid him for insufficient appreciation of American virtue or of Niebuhrian tragic irony.

(Arthur Schlesinger Jr., an admirer of Niebuhr, also opined that Wilson "wasn't really a man of politics." But Wilson's great, and still relevant, 1931 essay "An Appeal to Progressives"—included in *The Shores of Light*—was a more useful contribution to American politics than all of Schlesinger's loyal service in the corridors of the White House and at the dinner tables of Manhattan and Georgetown.)

Will there be another Wilson? Not for a while, certainly. There's too much to master and too many electronic distractions. Reading Greek and Latin for pleasure, as he did, is practically unheard of now. The very ideal of cultural authority is, rightly or wrongly—in my opinion, wrongly—suspect. Most important, the freelance life is less and less possible in an economically rationalized, hyper-managerial society. Investors want 20 percent returns; we know what that means for literary journalism. Tenure committees are not impressed by "comprehensive and solitary," idiosyncratic scholarship of Wilson's sort. And where can a freelancer live? Even Hackensack has been gentrified, or soon will be. On the Web? Yes, but one wants, if not to be at the center of things, at least to know where it is. Or *that* it is.

We can only hope that, even in a decentered world, Wilson's temperament and critical method—curious, energetic, humane, and, of course, very, very intelligent—will keep their appeal.

24

An Enemy of the State

I. F. Stone

Even before Barack Obama took the oath of office in January 2009, the ghost of I. F. Stone was weeping bitter tears. Asked on ABC News about the possible prosecution of Bush administration officials for violating domestic and international laws on the surveillance of citizens and the treatment of prisoners, the president-elect replied that "what we have to focus on is getting things right in the future as opposed to looking at what we got wrong in the past." Thus did our new conciliator-in-chief implicitly declare Stone's forty-five-year, 3.5-million-word effort to look at what our rulers got wrong irrelevant to forcing them to get things right. All that is "in the past."

Obama could not have been more wrong. In American politics, as elsewhere, the past is not dead; it's not even past. The greed and callousness Stone exposed week after week behind America's domestic and foreign policy throughout the last century had their source in institutions that remain in place today, and the difficulty of penetrating the screen of business and government propaganda is undiminished. If Obama cares to know what he is up against—he seems, most of the way through his first year in office, still largely clueless—a quick trip through *The I. F. Stone's Weekly Reader* (1971, edited by Neil Middleton), or better, a leisurely trip through Stone's invaluable six-volume collection, *A Nonconformist History of Our Time* (*The War Years: 1939–1945*; *The Hidden History of the Korean War: 1950–1951*; *The Truman Era: 1945–1952*; *The Haunted Fifties: 1953–1963*; *In a Time of Torment: 1961–1967*; and *Polemics and Prophecies: 1967–1970*; all published by Little, Brown), would help orient our personable president to America's deeper political realities.

The facts of Stone's life have been told well and often, most recently by D. D. Guttenplan in *American Radical: The Life and Times of I. F. Stone* (see also Robert Cottrell, *Izzy: A Biography of I. F. Stone*, and Myra MacPherson, *"All Governments Lie": The Life and Times of Rebel Journalist I. F. Stone*). He was born on Christmas Eve 1907, in Philadelphia, and christened Isadore Feinstein. His parents had a dry goods store, which prospered modestly during Izzy's boyhood and adolescence, and his cheerful, bustling mother doted on him. He was inordinately bookish, starting very young. (And continuing throughout life—he was, for what it's worth, far more literate, in his unostentatious way, than William F. Buckley Jr.) But he didn't care much for school or succeed at it very well. He was also moonlighting from schoolwork as a reporter for local newspapers, and after a year he left college to work full-time as a journalist. He never looked back, at least until retirement, when he learned Greek, investigated Socrates, and discovered that that universally revered martyr for free speech was actually a good deal more hostile to democratic freedoms in Athens than most of Senator McCarthy's victims were to democratic freedoms in America.

Neither Stone's inner nor his outer life seems to have been particularly complex or dramatic. He was a dutiful son: when his father's business suffered in the Depression and his mother inter-mittently became mentally ill, Izzy, who was well paid by then, helped. He met a lively, popular girl, not much given to reading but much taken with his ebullience; they stayed happily married for sixty years. He was an enthusiastic and good-humored but often distracted father. He had few but loyal friends, was close to his siblings and on good terms with his relatives and in-laws, and—especially during his years in Washington, DC—was not much of a partygoer. He led a full life, professionally and domes-tically, with few storms, and had a sunny and feisty personality, with few shadows or enigmas. The one moment of high drama was his decision in 1953, amid the ostracism that followed his fierce denunciations of the Smith Act and the publication of *The Hidden History of the Korean War*, to found *I. F. Stone's Weekly*. A lesser man would have folded his tent, or at least lowered his voice.

Stone was cursed all his life with interesting times, boiling over with war, depression, revolution, and totalitarianism. He covered these calamities not on the scene but behind the scenes, where policy was made. Some journalists could bring political action to life; Stone was one of the few who could bring polit-ical causation to life. He read official reports, studies, speeches, press conferences, congressional testimony, and budget docu-ments, voraciously, analytically, skeptically. He found the threads, connected the dots, and brought the substructure of real causes and motives to light.

An early example, which made Stone's reputation in Washing-ton, was his coverage of American unpreparedness for World War II. Long after it became obvious that US involvement in the war was likely, American industry simply would not stop doing business with fascist Germany and Japan, even in strategic commodities like oil, rubber, metals, minerals, chemicals, and machine parts. The trade was too profitable, and the ties between German cartels (by then an arm of the Nazi regime) and American banks, corporations, and law firms (including Sullivan & Cromwell, where John Foster Dulles represented a great many German clients) were too close. Stone tracked down the figures on industry after industry and hammered away at the story until even the Senate committee investigating war preparedness commended him. The additional German and Japanese war production enabled by the delivery of these materials may well have cost the lives of thousands of American and Allied soldiers—more damage, in all likelihood, than was caused by Communist infiltrators in the State Department.

Equally important were Stone's reports on how greed and incompetence retarded American industry's conversion to wartime production. General Motors could not be induced to stop making cars in record numbers even after its factories and workforce were needed for tank, truck, and aircraft production. Alcoa Aluminum would not increase supply of this vital component for fear that an early end to the war would result in a surplus, hence lower prices. Major oil companies would not open their pipelines to independents; and in general, dominant companies would not cooperate with smaller rivals. All this profitable foot-dragging was aided and abetted by the "dollar-a-year men," the business executives and corporate lawyers "loaned" to the federal government in order to keep an eye out for the interests of their employers and clients. These, of course, were precisely the "responsible" people, the men of substance—bankers, executives, and lawyers, along with professional diplomats and military officers—to whom Walter Lippmann proposed entrusting real power in a democracy, while the fickle public meekly registered its preferences every four years and hoped for the best.

Another high-profile demolition was Stone's reconstruction of the Gulf of Tonkin episode, which had prompted Congress to authorize the use of force against North Vietnam. Piecing together information from Senate and UN debates and from European and Vietnamese news reports, Stone showed that the official account was false. The US boats deliberately entered what they knew the North Vietnamese claimed as territorial waters; they were supporting, perhaps directing, a South Vietnamese military operation against the North; there was no second attack on the boats, as claimed; and the Pentagon had detailed plans already drawn up for the extensive bombing reprisals that followed the North Vietnamese "attack" (which in any case had caused no injuries or damage), suggesting that the US was hoping for, if not actually attempting to provoke, an incident.

As with the Korean War fourteen years earlier, Stone was virtually alone at the time in challenging a misleading official justification for an undeclared war. And once again, millions of lives were lost because Congress and the press were not as conscientious as he was.

Far more than a few million lives would have been lost in case of a nuclear war, and Stone was rightly obsessed with the arms race. It was plain to him that the US remained far ahead of the USSR through most of the nuclear era and could have had a far-reaching arms-control agreement at virtually any time. It was equally plain that the prospect of "limited nuclear war" adumbrated in Henry Kissinger's influential *Nuclear Weapons and Foreign Policy* was "poisonously delusive." And amid much high-minded hand-wringing about the malignant but mysteriously self-sustaining momentum of the arms race, Stone kept pointing out the extent to which it was not some "tragic" historical imperative but rather sheer, unstoppable bureaucratic self-aggrandizement by the armed services that drove the progress of weapons technology.

To expose corporate fraud, diplomatic obfuscation, budgetary sleight-of-hand, and wartime propaganda required the investigative enterprise for which Stone is renowned. To write about two of his other preoccupations, the internal security panic of the Truman era and the struggle for racial equality in the Eisenhower and Kennedy years, required only common decency—as uncommon in these cases as in most others. Stone harried—there is no other word for it—Senator McCarthy and J. Edgar Hoover. "Melodramatic bunk by a self-dramatizing dick" was his entirely typical comment on a speech by Hoover to the American Legion, and he was hardly less scathing about McCarthy. Stone had his reward: the FBI read his mail, searched his garbage, tapped his phone, and monitored his public appearances, while the State Department denied him a visa and tried to confiscate his passport—marks of distinction not granted to his more cautious colleagues. About race, Stone simply said the obvious—the now-obvious, that is—repeatedly and eloquently. His columns on the subject are still bracing.

Stone was an ardent Zionist in the 1940s and was the first American journalist to report on the Jewish exodus from Europe and the creation of the state of Israel. In 1944 he penned an open letter to American newsmen urging pressure on President Roosevelt to admit more displaced Jews into the United States, which would not only have saved many Jewish lives but might also have greatly reduced tensions in postwar Palestine. In 1945, when it was still feasible, he advocated a bi-national Arab-Jewish state. Beginning immediately after the 1948 war, he pleaded for the swift resettlement of Palestinian refugees. Immediately after the 1967 war, he warned Israel against occupying the West Bank and Gaza. Right from the start—and even before—he was right about Israel/Palestine.

Above all, he was right about the Cold War. He ridiculed the notion that the Soviet Union, bled dry by World War II, was poised to overrun Western Europe, or that it controlled every popular movement from Latin America to the Balkans to the Middle East to Southeast Asia. And he pointed out how much US-Soviet tension was the result of America's insistence on rearming West Germany and integrating it into a hostile European military alliance. The cornerstone of Cold War ideology— that US actions were primarily reactive and defensive, dictated by unrelenting Soviet aggressiveness—took no account of Stalin's fundamental conservatism or of American designs on Mideast oil and on Southeast Asian markets for its Japanese ward. Nor did it allow Americans to perceive how arrogant and threatening the rest of the world considered America's claim that Taiwan was our "first line of defense," a notion Stone sent up superbly in a satire, "The Chinese 7th Fleet in Long Island Sound." Finally, Stone recognized the role of defense spending in America's economic management, both as a subsidy for advanced technology and as a fiscal stimulus that entailed no government competition with private producers—what would later be called "military Keynesianism."

All governments lie, Stone reminded his readers, and none act morally except when forced to by an aroused public. This moral universalism is his most valuable legacy. It is true that Stone worked harder than most other journalists and hobnobbed less. But what set him apart was something else: that he applied to his own government the same moral standards we all unhesitatingly apply to others. No reporter would accept at face value a Communist or even non-Communist government's account of its own motives and intentions. Japan's insistence that it sought only to bring prosperity and order to the rest of East Asia in the 1930s, or the USSR's protestations that it invaded Czechoslovakia and Afghanistan at the request of their legitimate governments to save those countries from subversion by the international capitalist conspiracy, were met with ridicule or simply ignored in favor of explanations based on Japanese or Soviet self-interest, and in particular on the interests of their ruling elites. But very few journalists were equally skeptical (in public, that is) about the motives of American intervention in Indochina, Central America, or the Middle East. Those actions may have been deemed imprudent for one reason or another; criticism in this vein was "responsible." But to question America's good intentions—to assume that the US is as capable of aggression, brutality, and deceit as every other state, and that American policy, like that of every other state, serves the purposes of those with preponderant domestic power rather than a fictive "national interest," much less a singular idealism—was to place oneself beyond the pale. Then as now, such skepticism was the operative definition of "anti-Americanism." By that definition Stone was anti-American, and America badly needs more such enemies.

In recent years students of Soviet espionage in the United States have found what they judge to be evidence of Stone's collaboration with the KGB. Two leading scholars, summarizing this evidence in *Commentary* magazine, conclude that "in the light of these revelations, Stone's entire legacy will have to be reassessed." One can see why neoconservatives would welcome an opportunity to call Stone's "entire legacy" in question.

But—leaving aside for a moment the validity of the charges—is there any sense in this demand? Orwell's essays are no less admirable because on his deathbed he offered British intelligence some advice about the ideological soundness of some fellow writers; nor Silone's novels because he may have passed information about Communist activities to Fascist police. Günter Grass's, Milan Kundera's, and Peter Handke's writings are no less impressive because Grass remained silent for so long about his youthful service in an SS fighting unit, Kundera may have informed the Czech secret police about a political refugee, and Handke defended Slobodan Milošević. Our judgments of Heidegger's philosophy and Paul de Man's literary criticism are not (or should not be) affected by revelations about their varying degrees of sympathy with Nazism. Irving Kristol's critique of liberalism is no more or less valid because he concealed CIA sponsorship of *Encounter*. Arthur Schlesinger Jr.'s interpretations of Jacksonianism and the New Deal are no more or less valid because he lied to the press about the Bay of Pigs invasion. Noam Chomsky's views on American foreign policy would be no more or less valid if it were discovered that the Viet Cong or the Sandinistas had paid his children's college tuition. Even Henry Kissinger's scholarly history of diplomacy is no more or less valuable because its author is an authentic war criminal. If Stone, rather than Julius Rosenberg, had given American atomic secrets to the Soviets, he would still be the finest political journalist of the twentieth century; and if Rosenberg had actually written everything that appeared under Stone's byline, then Rosenberg would be the finest political journalist of the twentieth century. It is simply good intellectual hygiene to reject politically motivated demands to devalue art or arguments by citing the real or alleged failings of their author.

Nevertheless, whatever their significance may be, what are the charges against Stone, and how valid are they? Stone's harshest critics are Herbert Romerstein and Eric Breindel in *The Venona Secrets* and John Earl Haynes and Harvey Klehr in *Spies*.* Based on the FBI's Venona transcripts of intercepted Soviet cable traffic, on the notebooks of Alexander Vassiliev, who had research access for some years to KGB archives, and on speeches and interviews by former KGB general Oleg Kalugin, these critics infer that Stone was a "spy," a "fully active Soviet agent" who "worked closely with the KGB" for several years during the 1930s and '40s and remained an occasional contact and source until 1968; that he was paid for his work; and that he "really produced." What this production consisted of is not specified, with three exceptions: 1) "A group of journalists, including Stone, provided Pravdin [an undercover KGB officer] with information about the plans of the US General Staff to cope with the German counteroffensive in the Battle of the Bulge and resume the Allied offensive. Though the other journalists identified, Walter Lippmann [!] and Raymond Gram Swing, did not know that Pravdin was an intelligence officer rather than a fellow journalist, Stone knew full well." 2) Stone reported that William Randolph Hearst had friendly relations, and perhaps even business dealings, with Nazis. 3) Stone was asked to tell an American in Germany how to get in touch with a (presumably Communist) antifascist organization.

This seems like a very meager haul for decades of "close" and "active" collaboration with the KGB. There had better be a great

---

* *The Venona Secrets: Exposing Soviet Espionage and America's Traitors*, Regnery, 2000; *Spies: The Rise and Fall of the KGB in America*, Yale, 2009. For a lengthy and impartial examination of the Stone "case," see Max Holland, "I. F. Stone: Encounters with Soviet Intelligence," *Journal of Cold War Studies* 11:3 (2009). For a persuasive rebuttal of Haynes and Klehr, see D. D. Guttenplan's review of *Spies* in the *Nation*, May 25, 2009.

many more, and considerably more damning, revelations from the KGB archives, or else the charges against Stone will need to be taken down several pegs. In addition, some of his critics' descriptions of Stone's public career raise doubts about their own judgment and fairness. Stone was alleged to be an "openly pro-Communist journalist" in the 1940s; he was "an enthusiastic fan of Stalin" until the Soviet invasion of Hungary in 1956; and after a period of disillusionment, he fell back into his old ways until the 1968 invasion of Czechoslovakia "caused the KGB to lose Stone again." His "most outrageous" performance was *The Hidden History of the Korean War*, in which Stone "used bizarre reasoning" to prove "that the South Koreans attacked North Korea."

In fact, Stone was never a fan of Stalin or the Soviet Union. He sympathized with its effort at independent development and criticized its lack of political and intellectual freedom. After the Hitler-Stalin pact of 1939, he declared himself an ex–"fellow traveler," but I strongly doubt (his pre-1939 writings are unfortunately more difficult to access than his later ones) that he was ever an uncritical or dishonest one.

After 1939, in any case, he was sharply—though not, given the horrors already known, adequately—critical of the Soviet Union. He never referred to the USSR as anything but a "dictatorship." There is very little praise: Soviet communism is "the greatest social experiment of our time"—little more than boilerplate in 1937. Stalin, he wrote in an obituary, was a "giant figure"— though he seems to have meant this only in the sense that Napoleon and Bismarck and Churchill were giant figures and Harry Truman was not. In his collected writings at least, unfavorable references to the Soviet Union are very much more frequent than favorable ones. A sample:

- "The FBI is carrying out OGPU tactics." (1937)
- In "the Russia of 1937," there is "a hunt for and extermination of dissident elements that has left the outside world bewildered." (1937)
- Stalin has unleashed "an old-fashioned Russian orgy of suspicion of foreigners, intellectuals, and any kind of dissent." (1948)
- "No political dissident in the USSR could hope to get as much fair treatment as has been accorded the Communists even in the hysteria-haunted US of this date." (1949)
- "To picture Russia as a democratic utopia is only to store up explosively bitter disillusion." (1950)
- "I [have been] represented as saying there was more freedom in the Soviet Union than in the United States. I consider a statement of that kind wholly untrue and politically idiotic." (1951)
- "What was wrong with Stalin's regime that such miscarriages of justice could occur under it? And how many unjustly accused or framed political prisoners may there be in the penal labor camps of the USSR?" (1953)
- "[Many observers], friendly to socialism, with a great respect for the Russian people, have been shamed and antagonized by much that has occurred since the Revolution. Amid the gigantic achievements . . . there has also been an indifference to mass suffering and individual injustice, a sycophancy and an iron-clad conformity, that has disgraced the socialist ideal." (1953)
- "[By World War II], communism in practice had become not a brotherly society working for the common good, but an authoritarian hierarchical system run by a bureaucratic caste, on the basis of unquestioning obedience by subordinates." (1957)
- "The snoopery that goes on in our own country is still a long way from the perpetual surveillance to which the Russian people are subjected by their own political police." (1958)

- "I well remember thirty years ago how the Communists boasted that freedom of the press in Russia under the Constitution promulgated by Stalin was broader than in the United States. . . . Thirty years later this is still a bitter hoax." (1967)
- "Fifty years after the Revolution, there is still neither free discussion nor free press in the Soviet Union. It has become a gigantic caricature of what socialism was meant to be." (1967)

Then again, all this criticism may have been merely an elaborate cover, so that Stone could serve the KGB more effectively.

As for the Korean War, six weeks after it began, Stone told a left-wing audience:

> You won't like what I have to say, so better prepare your tomatoes. I'm sorry to report to you that I couldn't find any proof to justify the Communists' claim that South Korea started this war. . . . North Korea started the war, and North Korea was well prepared for such a war. . . . Where did a little power like North Korea get such a strong war machine? The Soviet Union equipped the North Korean Communist forces, and the Soviet Union is behind the North Koreans in this war.

Nowhere in *The Hidden History of the Korean War* does Stone claim to "prove that the South Koreans attacked North Korea," only to show that the provocations preceding the war were mutual. His final judgment on the war's origins is spelled out plainly in the book's preface: "I believe that in Korea the big powers were the victims . . . of headstrong satellites itching for a showdown, which Washington, Moscow, and Peking had long anticipated, but were alike anxious to avoid." What was "hidden," and what he claimed to have brought to light, was not a South

Korean attack but rather "the operations of MacArthur and Dulles, the weaknesses of Truman and Acheson, the way the Chinese were provoked to intervene, and the way the truce talks were dragged out and the issues muddied by American military men hostile from the first to negotiations." He might have added that the book, published in 1952, was one of the first to call attention to the barbaric American bombing campaign, which foreshadowed the holocaust in Indochina.

The book's deeper purpose was to serve as "a study in war propaganda, in how to read newspapers and official documents in wartime. Emphasis, omission, and distortion rather than outright lying are the tools of the war propagandists, and this book may help the reader learn how to examine their output—and sift out the facts—for himself." Which was, *mutatis mutandis*, Stone's purpose in everything he wrote.

The case against Stone reduces to: he did not see, or at any rate acknowledge, the full horror of Soviet totalitarianism in the 1930s. Robert Cottrell summarizes admirably:

> [Stone] did not view the Soviet Union uncritically, acknowledged that there was a stench behind the judicial proceedings in place there, had little liking for the American Communist Party, was no celebrant of any brand of totalitarianism, and certainly did not genuflect toward Moscow. Nevertheless, there was something disingenuous in his unwillingness to criticize still more forcefully the terror that was being played out in Soviet Russia. . . . Stone, like many of his political and intellectual counterparts, continued to afford Russia and even Stalinist communism something of a double standard, fearing that to do otherwise would endanger the Popular Front and the very possibility of socialism.

Stone's stance toward the Soviet Union in the 1930s rested on three premises. First, that the dictatorship had achieved remarkable economic growth and greatly improved the country's standard of living, including consumption, health, and literacy. Second, that, given Hitler's apparent determination to crush Bolshevism, the USSR would be a reliable and powerful ally in case of a European war. Third, that the United States and Britain would be secretly (in fact, it was no secret) pleased if Germany and Russia went to war and destroyed, or at least exhausted, each other.

These premises were largely true and together justified Stone's criticism of American hostility toward Russia in the 1930s. Unquestionably, he should have been more forthcoming about Soviet crimes. He seems to have feared that, given the rancor and dishonesty of his ideological opponents, such candor would unduly complicate his arguments against American policy; and moreover, that the situation was desperate. Plausible fears, but still he was wrong. It would have been more effective as well as more honest to have said, perhaps at the beginning of every column on the subject: "The Soviet Union is indeed a bloody tyranny. Of course, that is not at all why our rulers are hostile to it. American policy is often friendly toward bloody tyrannies. But a country that tries to withdraw from the global economy, which we dominate, and develop under its own auspices, restricting the scope of American business, is a threat. And a country that seems to be making a success of it and may thereby arouse that dangerous and perverse inclination in other countries, is an intolerable threat."

Stone did say this, in effect, but far too implicitly. His anxieties about authoritarianism at home and anti-Semitism in Nazi

Germany got the better of him, along with an undiscriminating sympathy for what he—and many others who should have known better— called "socialism." Like his ideological opponents, both Communist and capitalist, Stone seems to have identified socialism with state control of the economy. Hence his frequent insistence that "socialism" and "democracy" were *both* indispensable. But socialism—an ideal long predating the Russian Revolution—simply means popular, democratic control of social life, including economic life. The Bolsheviks were no socialists: immediately on taking power they destroyed all independent factory councils, local councils ("soviets"), and popular assemblies and remained as hostile to them as any plutocrat or archbishop. The Communist Party owned the economy; socialism was outlawed and persecuted even more fiercely in the Soviet Union than in the United States. Impressing this distinction on conservatives (and liberals) was no easier in the 1930s than it is today. But Stone, who was by instinct a genuine and not (like Lenin and Trotsky) a pseudo-socialist, should have been more careful with the word.

Although not much of the right-wing attack on Stone stands up, it has succeeded nonetheless. Every word spent defending Stone against attacks on his character is one not spent drawing renewed attention to his powerful criticisms of American political economy, foreign policy, and civic culture. These criticisms are Stone's real legacy, which his attackers are understandably far from eager to confront.

Above all, right-wing hostility to Stone betrays a shallow understanding of republican virtue and the nature of freedom. More than anything else, what makes totalitarianism possible is a people's submissiveness to authority: its slowness to perceive and unwillingness to resist injustices committed not by distant villains and official enemies but at home, by those with the power to make resistance dangerous. Lippmann, Reinhold Niebuhr, Arthur Schlesinger Jr., Sidney Hook, and Cold War liberals generally, whatever their other merits, did little to discourage such submissiveness in the American public. They were, instead, fierce in urging resistance to evils to which their readers would never have either occasion or inclination to submit, such as the advent of Communist rule in the United States or the conquest of the rest of the world by the Soviet Union. To warn the populace against remote and implausible threats, toward which incessant government and business propaganda had in any case already rendered them implacably hostile, was not much of a contribution to preserving the spirit of freedom. Stone, in contrast, by regularly exposing the mendacity, greed, callousness, and incompetence of their rulers, did more to unfit the American people for totalitarianism than all the Cold War liberals combined. Of non-liberals—*National Review, Human Events, Reader's Digest*, the Luce publications, and their conservative and neoconservative descendants—it is unnecessary to speak.

"I know," Stone joked, "that if the Communists come to power I'd soon find myself eating cold *kasha* in a concentration camp in Kansas *gubernya*." Actually, it is possible to imagine a Soviet America with a Soviet Reinhold Niebuhr as the regime's favorite moralist, a Soviet Sidney Hook as chief ideological arbiter, a Soviet Arthur Schlesinger Jr. as court historian, and a Soviet Walter Lippmann as high pundit and counselor. But it is impossible to imagine an unfree society of any political hue that would not send an I. F. Stone to prison and keep him there.

25

People Who Influence Influential People Are the Most Influential People in the World

New Republic

"Twentieth-century liberalism has won." So ran the first sentence of the *New Republic*'s eightieth anniversary anthology in 1994. Liberalism "inspired democratic revolutions from the Soviet Union to South Africa," according to the anthology's editor, Dorothy Wickenden, and finally "disabused this country of its prolonged infatuation with conservatism." Occupying the White House were two men with "intellectual edge and moral intuition," the magazine's editors enthused, who offer "the best chance in a generation to bring reform and renewal to a country that desperately needs both."

How accurate you think this judgment is depends on what you understand by that perennially disputed word, "liberalism." Originally it meant the opposite of mercantilism, the close government regulation of commercial policy to benefit domestic merchants by means of tariffs and restrictions on the movement of capital and technology. Mercantilism, protectionism, and industrial policy all name various aspects of the impulse to favor the economic home team and limit competition from abroad. Most rich countries, including the US, Britain, France, Germany, China, Japan, and South Korea, became rich thanks to state-directed economic policies; and still, in most of them, the state is far less subservient to business than in the anglophone world. As Britain and the United States became the world's leading economic powers in the nineteenth and twentieth centuries respectively, each decided that other countries' efforts to favor the home team were no longer cricket and that unregulated (i.e., "free") competition—which, by the merest coincidence, they were most likely to win—was in everyone's best interest. "Liberalism," from the Latin word for "free," is the name of this ideology. Even now, European political parties that call themselves "liberal" mean by it "pro-business." The leading voice of nineteenth-century liberalism was the *Economist*, which famously criticized famine aid for Ireland as an interference with the necessarily benign workings of the free market.

In the United States, the word "liberalism" has had a different, more complicated history. In English (as in Latin), "free" has more than one meaning. Besides "unconstrained," it also means "generous," as in "Give freely to those in need" or "Though a Nobel Prize winner, she's pretty free with her time when students ask." So "liberal" also came to denote redistributive, welfare-state policies that aimed to guarantee the non-affluent equality of opportunity, civil rights, and a modicum of economic security. This sense of "liberalism," the bête noire of the right from Nixon to the Tea Party, might seem to have swept the field terminologically, but the bipartisan consensus since the Clinton administration on free trade, privatization, financial deregulation, and all other dictates of the sovereign Market also goes by the name of "neoliberalism." No wonder books with titles like *What Is Liberalism?* appear regularly.

Whatever liberalism is, the *New Republic* is generally considered its American avatar. The magazine was founded in 1914 by Herbert Croly, a sometime architecture critic who had written a book five years earlier, *The Promise of American Life*, that had greatly impressed a wealthy philanthropic couple. Croly's book argued that Hamilton's federalism had been right against Jefferson's localism, and that America's destiny was to be a national, indeed global, commercial power, its activist executive branch coordinating policy with business, financial, and cultural elites. "The whole point," Croly wrote to Willard Straight, the magazine's first owner, "is that we are trying to impose views on blind or reluctant people." This self-conscious elitism, a conviction that an inert, ignorant populace needed to be mobilized from above by executive power, public and private, which in turn required the guidance of enlightened, responsible intellectuals, has remained the core of the journal's self-conception throughout its variegated history. Populism, class conflict, radical democracy, mass movements—all these were for outsiders. The *New Republic*, from the beginning, was for insiders.

Croly himself, though well-off and well-connected, was not exactly an insider, but his fellow *TNR* editor Walter Lippmann certainly was. Like generations of his successors at the magazine, Lippmann was a very bright young Harvard graduate who quickly plugged himself into political Washington and literary New York. Soon he and Croly were dining regularly with President Wilson's senior adviser, urging him to "let us know whether or not we are misinterpreting what the president is trying to do," lest the magazine unintentionally "conflict with the purposes of the government." Intelligence at the elbow of power—this has always been the *New Republic*'s ideal. *Respectful Suggestions of the Mind* would have been, on the whole, a more accurate title for this anthology.

The "marriage of welfare-statism and civil liberties," Franklin Foer writes in his introduction to *Insurrections of the Mind: 100 Years of Politics and Culture in America*, "is essentially the definition of American liberalism." The marriage came under strain in the 1980s and '90s. The New Right's largely bogus critique of big government conquered official Washington and the mass media. Faced with a choice of righteous irrelevance or glamorous relevance, the *New Republic* chose relevance. They supported cuts in taxes and social spending, criticized affirmative action, published a notorious cover article opposing Hillarycare, and hired a slew of conservative editors and writers. Official Washington and the media loved it—the Reagan White House even sent a courier over every week for twenty copies. But though this rightward shift was opportunistic, it wasn't unprincipled opportunism. Opportunism, after all, *was* the *New Republic*'s bedrock principle. Not the uncomplicated, self-serving kind, but the well-meaning, deluded kind that believes above all in maintaining credibility with the powerful, since how else can anything be accomplished except by whispering in their ear?

Not all the results were bad: Mickey Kaus's "civic liberalism," in particular, was an honest if eccentric effort to craft a humane alternative to the welfare state. But mostly the magazine spent these two decades distancing itself from grassroots liberalism, following Clinton, Gore, Schumer, and other centrist Democrats in embracing the business-friendly neoliberalism of the Democratic Leadership Council, and supporting such ultimately disastrous initiatives as NAFTA, financial deregulation, and welfare reform, which helped kill the New Deal. Al Gore's candidacy was the magazine's last gasp. Since 2000, they have seemed demoralized, rousing themselves only for occasional spiteful attacks on the left (Nader, Occupy, Snowden), fervent warnings about the dangers of Islamic radicalism, and frequent exhortations to presidents to use American military power wherever possible.

Foer's definition of American liberalism was incomplete: the "marriage" has actually been a love triangle. From the outset, American liberalism's preference for government activism at home has been matched by its internationalism: advocacy of a unilateral, interventionist foreign policy. Here is where liberalism—and *TNR*—have gone most egregiously and damagingly wrong. "Liberalism cherishes skepticism more than any [other] ideology," Foer writes in *Insurrections*, with a touch of self-congratulation—and self-deception. On the contrary, it is the *New Republic*'s credulousness, its uncritical acceptance of the premises of official policy, that is most apparent when the use of force is in question.

The magazine supported America's entry into World War I, accepting Wilson's argument that only American participation would give us the moral authority to ensure a fair and democratic peace settlement. The actual peace settlement was nothing of the sort, and the *New Republic*, having trusted Wilson's assurances, looked foolish. *TNR* enthusiastically embraced the Truman Doctrine and blamed the Soviet Union for the ensuing Cold War, which actually resulted in good part from the United States' insistence on rearming Germany, maintaining nuclear superiority, and keeping even democratic leftists out of power everywhere in the postwar world. The Indochina war was a "colossal blunder," which should lead us, the editors admonished, to reflect on "the contrast between our idealism and our crimes." That it was blundering "idealism" rather than a strategy of global economic integration, requiring the suppression of independent nationalism, that led to America's intervention in Vietnam and dozens of other places in the twentieth century—this "American exceptionalism" has always been an article of faith. The same "fighting faith"—the title of a 2004 manifesto by editor Peter Beinart, included in *Insurrections*—led *TNR* to welcome the invasions of Iraq and Afghanistan. The war against Islamic totalitarianism is, like the former war on Communism, "the defining moral challenge of our time," Beinart wrote, the "arena in which [liberal] values find their deepest expression." Those who urged skepticism about government claims or proposed abiding by international law were "softs."

Credulousness toward another favored state—Israel—has led the *New Republic* into supporting still other futile and bloody military interventions. The magazine has continually harangued its anxiously pro-Israel readership about the existential dangers the plucky little nuclear-armed, American-backed regional superpower faces from the revanchism and irredentism of the prostrate Palestinians; implied that Palestinian rather than Israeli intransigence is primarily responsible for the failure of peace negotiations; and scolded the left for maliciously exaggerating Israel's faults and irresponsibly indulging Palestinian terrorism. But although thousands of Palestinian noncombatants have been killed by Israeli forces in Lebanon, Gaza, and the West Bank—roughly a hundred times more Palestinian civilians than Israeli civilian victims of Palestinian violence—no one at the *New Republic* has entertained, even to reject, the idea that these old-fashioned war crimes and law-enforcement excesses also deserve to be called "terrorism." Notwithstanding Israel's frequent assurances that it was eager to trade land for peace, by now it is clear that no Israeli government, Labor or Likud, has been willing since 1967 to halt the gradual annexation of the West Bank and its resources. Occasional meekly expressed misgivings from the magazine's doves— Irving Howe, Michael Walzer, and, occasionally, Leon Wieseltier—have always been drowned out by an unceasing barrage of pro-Israel apologetics from Peretz, Charles Krauthammer, Michael Oren, and the magazine's other resident *hasbarists*.

Why has the liberal "intelligence" the magazine boasts of lined up so often in support of brute force? Part of the answer, at least for the last few decades, was supplied by Christopher Hitchens, who knew what to think of contrarianism before he himself succumbed to it:

> In the charmed circle of neoliberal and neoconservative journalism, "unpredictability" is the special emblem and certificate of self-congratulation. To be able to bray that "as a liberal, I say bomb the shit out of them" is to have achieved that eye-catching, versatile marketability that is so beloved of editors and talk-show hosts.

It must have given Michael Kinsley, for example, a considerable frisson to coolly admonish his more squeamish fellow liberals that although the Reagan administration's goals in Central America "may be impossible to attain without vast civilian suffering," they shouldn't get too worked up about that. It might still be a "sensible policy" if it "meets the test of cost-benefit analysis": i.e., a comparison of "the amount of blood and misery that will be poured in, and the likelihood that democracy will emerge at the other end." This bracing tough-mindedness certainly got Kinsley on the talk shows, along with the even bloodier-minded Krauthammer.

But the more serious intellectuals who founded the *New Republic* were no less eager to rationalize state violence than their lightweight present-day successors, and with similar motives. In a masterly essay on "The *New Republic* and the War" (i.e., World War I), Christopher Lasch retraced the tortuous arguments by which Lippmann, Dewey, and the rest of the original cohort convinced themselves to follow Wilson to war, and concluded:

> Logic may have dictated non-intervention, but something deeper than logic dictated war. The thirst for action, the craving for involvement, the longing to commit themselves to the ongoing march of events—these things dictated war. The realists feared isolation not only for America but for themselves. Accordingly, they went to war and invented the reasons for it afterward.

Skepticism? Not when the war drums are beating.

(A minor continuity: the old *New Republic* and the new were about equally ungracious to those who got it right, from forcing Randolph Bourne off the magazine in 1917 because of his searing critiques of their arguments for intervention to setting up an "Idiocy Watch" in 2004 to ridicule those who doubted the wisdom of invading Iraq.)

What the *New Republic*'s long history teaches above all is that power goes its own way. Political leaders don't care about good new ideas; they have their own ideas, which in any case don't matter any more than intellectuals' ideas do. What matters is a society's balance of institutional power. The control of investment and employment, of opinion-formation and electoral finance, confer the power to set the state's priorities and constrain its initiatives. Intellectuals can help those in power to market their strategies, or to refine them. But they can't change them. "You've convinced me," FDR is said to have told a group of left-leaning visitors. "Now go out and force me." But that—mobilizing popular pressure to counterbalance the power of business—is just what the *New Republic* has never shown any interest in doing, or even advocating. At its most daring, the magazine has fancied itself speaking truth to power, and sometimes it has. But the real responsibility of intellectuals is to speak truth, patiently and perseveringly, *about* power to the powerless. About this, the *New Republic* has never had a clue.

The cover or masthead of the *New Republic* has, for most of its life, sported the subtitle: "A Journal of Politics and the Arts." If it had only been a journal of politics, there would be very little reason to regret its recent frontal lobotomy at the hands of its new owner. Like liberalism itself, the magazine had already definitively surrendered to technocratic managerialism. But there was always the back of the book. The *New Republic* has been lucky in its literary editors: Edmund Wilson, Malcolm Cowley, Doris Grumbach, Jack Beatty, and Leon Wieseltier. Peretz and Wieseltier each spent around three decades at the magazine, and each launched quite a few young writers. But while Peretz's recruits are a very mixed legacy, Wieseltier's—James Wood, Sven Birkerts, Ann Hulbert, Ruth Franklin, Jed Perl, William Deresiewicz, Adam Kirsch, and, when *compos mentis*, Lee Siegel—are a gift to criticism. So were Wieseltier's own, all-too-infrequent reviews. (His all-too-frequent "Washington Diarist" entries, on the other hand, were a calamity. Rarely has so much verbal ingenuity been expended to so little point, except perhaps in fulfillment of some imagined moral obligation to sound intelligent. And they bear a heavy responsibility for the plague of pseudo-clever putdowns that eventually infested the magazine—and lately the internet— like kudzu.)

The richness of the magazine's arts coverage was bound to be underrepresented in any anthology, but even so, there is far too little of it in *Insurrections of the Mind*. There are a few distinguished pieces of criticism, above all W. H. Auden's "Freud" and Irving Howe's "The Value of the Canon." But not nearly enough. Even Wieseltier's finest essay, "Matthew Arnold and the Cold War," is left out. If Wieseltier would employ his forced retirement in compiling a selection of *TNR*'s best criticism, it would (besides keeping him out of political mischief) be a real service to the culture.

The last item in *Insurrections* is a short afterword by Chris Hughes, the Facebook billionaire who rode to the magazine's rescue two years ago. Apart from a passing phrase or two promising "adaptation"—a cloud no bigger than a man's hand—it is largely boilerplate, offering no hint of the "vertically integrated digital media" clusterfuck just around the corner. Mostly, it makes the right noises, genuflecting toward "quality writing" and "putting politics, culture, and ideas side by side and on an equal plane." Hughes even gets what's wrong about the magazine right, albeit inadvertently: "[our mission] is to offer deep, thought-provoking analysis that encourages critical dialogue between [*sic*] influential people in our country and world." Too true. As though "influential people" weren't the problem rather than the solution. But of course, anyone who understood that would have come to bury the *New Republic*, not to save it.

26

Living by Ideas

Hilton Kramer and Roger Kimball

"'Lord, enlighten thou our enemies,' should be the prayer of every true reformer," wrote Mill in his essay on Coleridge. "Sharpen their wits, give acuteness to their perceptions, and consecutiveness and clearness to their reasoning powers. We are in danger from their folly, not from their wisdom: their weakness is what fills us with apprehension, not their strength." Over the last three decades, those of us who share these sentiments have had our prayers answered in the shape of the *Public Interest*, the *National Interest*, *Commentary*, and the *New Criterion*. True, neoconservatism may have sometimes seemed to consist mainly of superficially plausible arguments for profoundly pernicious policies—a blessing we would perhaps rather do without. But for such ingratitude Mill had an answer:

Even if a Conservative philosophy were an absurdity, it is well calculated to drive out a hundred absurdities worse than itself. Let no one think that it is nothing to accustom people to give a reason for their opinion, be the opinion ever so untenable, the reason ever so insufficient. A person accustomed to submit his fundamental tenets to the test of reason will be more open to the dictates of reason on every other point. Not from him shall we have to apprehend the owl-like dread of light, the drudge-like aversion to change, which were the characteristics of the old unreasoning race of bigots.

And anyway, not all their opinions are untenable. In its crusade against the politicization of contemporary culture, the *New Criterion* is—on the whole, in the main, and not to put too fine a point on it—right. Notwithstanding the importance of legal and social equality for women, homosexuals, and members of racial minorities, most of the cultural strategies employed in the service of these ends have been—again, on the whole, and with many exceptions not always duly acknowledged by conservative critics—misguided and counterproductive. Multiculturalist pedagogy; the promotion of "cultural diversity" through arts administration, philanthropy, and public policy; academic departments of Women's Studies and Afro-American Studies; the project of "critical theory"; and in general, the greatly increased weight—in teaching and research, hiring, programming and grant-making—given to explicitly political considerations: altogether these things have done more harm than good. They have undoubtedly made possible some valuable work and attracted some people to culture who would otherwise have been lost to it. But they have also generated a staggering amount of mediocre and tendentious work. And not only do these ideological priorities make for less accomplished artists and scholars; they also make for less effective citizens. Gratuitously politicizing one's professional or artistic activity can distract from—can even serve to rationalize the avoidance of—everyday democratic activity, with all its tedium and frustration. As Richard Rorty has pointed out: "One of the contributions of the newer [that is, the radical-academic] left has been to enable professors, whose mild guilt about the comfort and security of their own lives once led them into extra-academic political activity, to say, 'Sorry, I gave at the office.'"*

This, at any rate, is my interpretation of (admittedly a very small sample of) the vast literature on the contemporary culture wars. It is a view formed in not insignificant measure by reading the *New Criterion*. Along with books and essays by Richard Bernstein, Russell Jacoby, Christopher Lasch, Diane Ravitch, Robert Hughes, David Lehman, Frederick Crews, Harold Bloom, Helen Vendler, Camille Paglia, Irving Howe, Katha Pollitt, Harold Fromm, Robert Brustein, and others, the *New Criterion*'s steady documentation of absurdity and outrage, its chronicling of intellectual sins both grave and venial, has worn down and finally worn away my initial sympathy with the cultural program of my political comrades. Of course, excruciating firsthand experience with the writings of Houston Baker, bell hooks, Donna Haraway, and other leading cultural radicals has also done its part.

Against the Grain: The New Criterion *on Art and Intellect at the End of the Twentieth Century* (Ivan R. Dee), forty-five selections edited by Hilton Kramer and Roger Kimball from the *New Criterion*'s first thirteen years, is a less polemical volume than one might expect—that is, it is less than wholly polemical. Much of it is simply very good critical writing: John Simon on Nabokov, Joseph Epstein on Cavafy, Guy Davenport on Gertrude Stein, Brooke Allen on Shaw, Brad Leithauser on Housman, John Gross on Beerbohm, Samuel Lipman on Walter Gieseking, James Tuttleton on Frederick Douglass. In one of the book's more programmatic pieces, Kramer calls for a return to connoisseurship—that is, "the close,

---

* Richard Rorty, "Intellectuals in Politics" (*Dissent*, Spring 1992).

comparative study of art objects [and literary texts] with a view to determining their relative levels of aesthetic quality." It is a cogent formulation, which the above-mentioned essays and others in *Against the Grain* well exemplify.

The more contentious selections are less consistently satisfying. Plenty of points are scored, but the point is sometimes missed. According to Roger Kimball, for example, Foucault was nothing more than a con man. Certainly he was a con man, but nothing more? A short chapter in Michael Walzer's *The Company of Critics* carefully, dispassionately analyzes Foucault's theory of politics, past its occasionally brilliant insights down to its fundamental incoherence. The result is no less devastating than Kimball's skillful hatchet job but vastly more illuminating. Similarly, Gerald Graff's suggestion that radicals and conservatives argue out their differences before students becomes, in James Tuttleton's account, a devious stratagem preparing the way for academic totalitarianism. The golden rule of polemics is: state your antagonist's view as persuasively as possible. This rule is frequently broken in *Against the Grain* (as well as in every issue of the *New Criterion*). Still, some pieces in this vein are undeniably fine, like Kramer's fierce, gloomy, eloquent, and heartfelt vindication of traditional high culture as the proper content of undergraduate education; and a characteristically witty and penetrating address by Christopher Ricks, "What Is at Stake in the 'Battle of the Books'?"

There is an essay by Immanuel Kant (not found in *Against the Grain*) titled "On the Old Saw: That May Be True in Theory, but It Doesn't Hold in Practice." Contrariwise, I find the *New Criterion* generally right in practice—in its judgments about "relative levels of aesthetic quality" and intellectual merit—but mistaken on what it identifies as the crucial theoretical issue in the culture wars: that is, relativism. The politicization of culture, Kramer and Kimball write, "rests on the contention that nothing is meaningful or valuable *in itself*: that everything, from literary texts and paintings to personal relations, must be understood as an interchangeable token for the exercise or expression of power." They cite as the purest statement of this execrable doctrine a sentence by Stanley Fish: "There is no such thing as intrinsic merit." This, they thunder, is "a version of nihilism and a license for sophistry."

> For if there is no such thing as intrinsic merit, then no judgment of quality can be anything more than a veiled political commendation or a statement of personal partisanship. Without the idea of intrinsic moral, intellectual, and artistic value, criticism and scholarship degenerate into a species of propaganda, and morality becomes little more than a cynical calculus aimed at increasing personal advantage. The *New Criterion* takes categorical exception to such beliefs. We proceed on the conviction that there *is* such a thing as intrinsic merit, that it can be discerned and rationally argued for, and that its rejection is a prescription for moral and cultural catastrophe.

Well then, what is intrinsic merit? "Intrinsic" can't mean "universally agreed upon," since no aesthetic criteria are. It can't mean "independent of inherited, unconscious, or other local determination," since no beliefs are. It can't, in short, mean supra-historical and non-contingent, since nothing whatever is. What Fish, Rorty, and other pragmatists contend is that all criteria start out equal and must be justified to those who would be affected by their adoption—that democracy, in other words, is prior to philosophy. Beyond this, as Fish never tires of pointing out, antifoundationalism has no consequences. In any case, if Kramer and Kimball believe there are objective, irrefragable, rationally demonstrable aesthetic and moral criteria, they ought by now to have offered the rest of us a fairly precise idea of what they are, or in whose writings they can be found.

They haven't, and they can't. But then, they needn't. They need only muddle along, employing and occasionally articulating the criteria that have emerged from our culture's conversation since the Greeks, showing that what used to and still usually does underwrite our judgments about beauty and truth is inconsistent with giving Robert Mapplethorpe a one-man show, or Karen Finley a National Endowment for the Arts grant. More than that, no one can do.

The patron saint of the *New Criterion* is Matthew Arnold; and rightly, for no one has written better about the proper relation between culture and politics. Arnold's notions of "disinterestedness" and "the free play of mind" are an excellent corrective for contemporary left-wing cultural practice. All values may be political in an ultimate, metaphysical (or rather, antimetaphysical) sense. But that—as Fish would be the first to acknowledge—is a null, an empty sense. In the ordinary, everyday, practical sense, there are indeed nonmoral and nonpolitical values. The hunger for beauty, for perfection of form, is as organic as the hunger for justice. To subordinate one to the other, or ignore one for the sake of the other, is, as Kramer and Kimball rightly warn, a prescription for universal mediocrity.

Quite possibly, however, if the shade of Matthew Arnold returned to preside over the contemporary cultural-political debate, he would have a word or two to say to his disciples at the *New Criterion* as well. For one thing, Arnold's polemical manners were impeccable, while Kramer's and Kimball's are atrocious. Arnold never wrote a rancorous word, and they never wrote a gracious one. "Sourness and light" is their critical formula, *toujours attaquer* their polemical maxim. "We have discovered," they assert, "that a more delicate phraseology is not so much con- ciliatory as feckless: an invitation to discount the seriousness of the issue." One can imagine Arnold's (or, for that matter, Lionel Trilling's) astonishment and disgust at this pronouncement.

For another thing, the *New Criterion*–ists sometimes boast that they and not the multiculturalists are the true democrats, apply- ing to themselves Arnold's words in *Culture and Anarchy*: "The men of culture are the true apostles of equality. [They] are those who have a passion for diffusing, for making prevail, for carrying from one end of the society to the other, the best ideas of their time." But in their case, it is a hollow boast. Arnold freely acknowledged, as Kramer and Kimball do not, the dependence of spiritual equality on at least an approximate material equality. Here are a few words on that subject from *Culture and Anarchy*:

> Culture, or the study of perfection, leads us to conceive of no perfec- tion as being real which is not a *general* perfection, embracing all our fellow-men with whom we have to do. . . . Individual perfection is impossible so long as the rest of mankind are not perfected along with us. . . . So all our fellow-men, in the East of London [today we might say, "the South Bronx"] and elsewhere, we must take along with us in our progress towards perfection, if we ourselves really, as we pro- fess, want to be perfect; and we must not let the worship of any fetish, any machinery, such as manufactures or population [today, "eco- nomic growth" or "national security"]—which are not, like perfection, absolute goods in themselves, though we think them so—create for us such a multitude of miserable, sunken, and igno- rant human being, that to carry them all along with us is impossible, and perforce they must for the most part be left by us in their degra- dation and wretchedness. But evidently the conception of free-trade

[now "freedom from government interference"], on which our Liberal [i.e., Republican] friends vaunt themselves and in which they think they have found the secret of national prosperity—evidently, I say, the mere unfettered pursuit of production of wealth, and the mere mechanical multiplying, for this end, of manufactures and populations threatens to create for us, if it has not created already, those vast, miserable masses of sunken people [the "underclass"]—one pauper, at the present moment, for every nineteen of us [much higher today]—to the existence of which we are, as we have seen, absolutely forbidden to reconcile ourselves, in spite of all that the philosophy of *The Times* [*Wall Street Journal*] . . . may say to persuade us.

In *Culture and Anarchy*, in "Democracy," where he argued against the antigovernment party that "the action of a diligent, an impartial, and a national government . . . can really do much, by institution and regulation, to better the condition of the middle and lower classes"; and in "Equality," with its affirmation that "certainly equality will never of itself alone give us a perfect civilization. But with such inequality as ours, a perfect civilization is impossible"—in these and other passages, Arnold demonstrated his humane moral imagination and democratic good faith. Kramer and Kimball have yet to demonstrate theirs.

Finally, there is the complicated matter of disinterestedness, or intellectual conscience. That both Kramer and Kimball would sooner die than fake a fact or twist a quote, I do not doubt. But disinterestedness is something larger, finer, rarer than that. To perceive as readily and pursue as energetically the difficulties of one's own position as those of one's opponents; to take pains to discover, and present fully, the genuine problems that one's opponent is, however futilely, addressing—this is disinterestedness as Arnold understood it.

Arnold thought he had found a splendid example of it in Burke, who, at the close of his last attack on the French Revolution, nevertheless conceded some doubts about the wisdom of opposing to the bitter end the new spirit of the age. In "The Function of Criticism," Arnold cited this passage and commented:

> That return of Burke upon himself has always seemed to me one of the finest things in English literature, or indeed any literature. That is what I call living by ideas: when one side of a question has long had your earnest support, when all your feelings are engaged, when you hear all round you no language but one, when your party talks this language like a steam-engine and can imagine no other—still to be able to think, still to be irresistibly carried, if so it be, by the current of thought to the opposite side of the question, and, like Balaam, to be unable to speak anything "but what the Lord has put in your mouth." I know nothing more striking, and I must add that I know nothing more un-English.

I wish I could imagine someday praising Kramer and Kimball in such terms. But alas, I know nothing more un—*New Criterion*—ish.

27

Fearless

Pier Paolo Pasolini

The afterlife of Italian poet, novelist, critic, and filmmaker Pier Paolo Pasolini brings to mind some familiar lines from Auden's "In Memory of W. B. Yeats":

> Time that is intolerant
> Of the brave and innocent . . .
> Worships language and forgives
> Everyone by whom it lives . . .

Time has doted on Pasolini's friends, countrymen, and sometime antagonists Eugenio Montale and Italo Calvino but has neglected the once equally celebrated Pier Paolo. His films have never gone into full eclipse, but his poems, fiction, screenplays, literary criticism, and political commentary, which engaged all literate Europe during his lifetime, have seldom traveled across the Atlantic. "Mad Ireland hurt you into poetry," Auden continued, addressing Yeats. Though the young Pasolini worshipped language, mad and ineffably wicked Italy eventually hurt him into idiosyncratic politics and extravagant rhetoric. He adopted one medium after another, fascinated at first by new formal possibilities and soon distracted into perfervid polemic. His preaching was sometimes inspired; it was also, inevitably, time-bound. He was braver and more innocent than Montale, Calvino, or virtually anyone else among his contemporaries. But political passion overwhelmed aesthetic concentration, and so, outside Italy at any rate, he has forfeited literary immortality.

Pasolini was born in 1922 in Bologna. The family spent summers with relatives at Casarsa, in Italy's northeastern corner. The local peasantry spoke an ancient dialect, Friulian, in which Pasolini wrote his first poems and plays. Interest in dialects was reviving in mid-twentieth-century Italy, and Pasolini became one of the foremost practitioners and critics of Italian dialect poetry.

After the Second World War, with a degree from the University of Bologna, the beginnings of a literary reputation, and a secure job teaching secondary school, Pasolini was happy with provincial life. But for the first of many times, his uncontainable sexuality landed him *al brodo*—in the soup. Accused of paying for sex with teenage boys—his lifelong, unashamed practice—he was expelled from the Communist Party and forced to resign from public school teaching.

Self-exiled to the anonymity of Rome, he spent the first months of the 1950s as a walker in the city, discovering the slum districts and absorbing Romanesco, the Roman dialect. Though his work—teaching private school and freelance writing—was poorly paid and exhausting, his passion for the life and above all the *ragazzi* of the Roman streets was inexhaustible. By the end of the decade, his novels (*The Ragazzi* and *A Violent Life*) and his first film (*Accattone*), full of vivid sex, colorful and often incomprehensible slang, and a murderous poverty that belied postwar Italy's "economic miracle," exploded him into national prominence, while *The Ashes of Gramsci* (1957), an anguished meditation in verse on the condition of Italy, was hailed by Calvino as "one of the most important facts of Italian postwar literature and certainly the most important in the field of poetry."

His career thereafter was a dazzle of publicity and controversy. Anna Magnani and Maria Callas both emerged from legendary seclusion to make films with him. (Callas was also to fall in love with him, only to suffer bitterly when he could not reciprocate.) *The Gospel According to Matthew*, the first (perhaps the only) great religious film by a homosexual Marxist atheist, nonplussed both the Church and the left. Alternating with the harsh realism and surrealistic symbolism of his contemporary subjects, he made film versions of the Oedipus story, *Medea*, an African *Oresteia*, the *Decameron*, the *Canterbury Tales*, and the *Arabian Nights*. He was arraigned for immorality thirty-three times, usually in connection with the banning of one or another of his films, an ordeal that provoked parliamentary protest and contributed to the liberalization of Italy's postwar constitution. He was regularly invited to speak or write in various Communist forums and regularly denounced in others. The *Corriere della Sera*, Italy's *New York Times*, offered him an unprecedented front-page column. In 1975, at the zenith of his fame and talent—his last year's columns set all of newspaper-reading Italy on its ear and drew responses from Calvino, Alberto Moravia, the Italian prime minister, and thousands of others—he was murdered by a teenage boy he had picked up.

His life was a maelstrom of contradictions: the anarchical Communist; the anticlerical Christian; the sexual revolutionary with grave reservations about legalizing divorce and abortion; the scholar of antique poetic forms who became an avant-garde cineaste; the cordial hater of the bourgeoisie and its minions, who nevertheless scoffed at the student revolt of 1968 and instead defended the police; the notorious transgressor, almost the living negation, of traditional values, who nevertheless inveighed incessantly against "false modernity," called for the abolition of television, compulsory education, and long hair, and told an interviewer that "the people I respect most are those who haven't gone beyond the fourth grade."

What explains Pasolini's chaotic sensibility, if anything does, is (in his own words) "a violent load of vitality." His molten temperament made aesthetic reserve, rhetorical restraint, or analytical detachment impossible. And besides, so much seemed to him at stake: not merely institutional change but the extinction of a form of life, the paganism of rural Southern Italy and of the "paleo-industrial" Roman *borgate*, where adolescents had "barely even heard of the Madonna" but at least lived and judged from first-hand rather than predigested experience.

"I have become convinced," he wrote near the end of his life, "that poverty and backwardness are not by any means the worst of ills." Has the (partial) conquest of premodern poverty and servitude been worth the price in psychic stability and in physical rootedness, spontaneity, and grace? In one form or another, this question has troubled a great many modern intellectuals. Along with its blessings, modernity has entailed, or at least been accompanied by, a vast blight of uniformity and superficiality. The disappearance of the dialects, with their unique rhythms and nuances, destroyed by "the horrendous language of television news, advertising, official statements," was Pasolini's first clue, which he followed up brilliantly, even if sometimes eccentrically (as in his pronouncement that the sex organs of the Roman underclass had decayed from one generation to the next). Consumerism, he warned, is "a genuine anthropological cataclysm," threatening to eclipse "the grace of obscure centuries, the scandalous revolutionary force of the past."

He raged against television, not only for homogenizing language and deadening imagination but also for fostering a meaningless, weightless sexual permissiveness. "It is television," he charged, "which has brought to a close the age of *pietà* and begun the age of *hedone*." Many people were astonished by this, coming from the avatar of cinematic sensuality. What he meant, as biographer Barth David Schwartz put it (in his splendid *Pasolini Requiem*), is that "the demystification of sex has passed directly into its predictable and obligatory merchandising," leaving most people—or so he judged—neither freer nor wiser nor happier.

It was not always clear—in fact, it was scarcely ever clear—exactly what Pasolini opposed to the depredations of "progress." (Calvino once wrote that debating him was "like hailing a racing car driver circling the track, to ask for a ride.") He admitted freely that he was often too impatient and too exasperated to make sense, that he only had time and strength to articulate "the full force of cold rejection, of desperate useless denunciation." Here is a typically maddening and illuminating specimen of Pasolini's sublime, crackpot antimodernism:

> Young males are traumatized nowadays by the duty permissiveness imposes on them—the duty always uninhibitedly to have sex. At the same time, they are traumatized by the disappointment which their "scepter" has produced in women, who formerly either were ignorant of it or made it the subject of myths while accepting it supinely. Besides, the education for and initiation into society which formerly took place in a platonically homosexual ambiance is now, because of

premature couplings, heterosexual from the onset of puberty. Yet the woman is still not in a position—given the legacy of thousands of years—to make a free pedagogic contribution: she still tends to favor definite rules, a code. And this today can only be a codification more conformist than ever, as is desired by bourgeois power; whereas the old self-education, between men and men or between women and women, obeyed popular rules (whose noble archetype remains Athenian democracy). Consumerism has therefore ended by humiliating the woman, creating for her another intimidating myth. The young males who walk along the street, their hand on the woman's shoulder with a protective air, or romantically clasping her hand, either make one laugh or cause a pang. Nothing is more insincere than the relationship to which that consumerist couple gives concrete, unwitting expression.

Daft, of course. Still, I'm not sure that Michel Foucault, who spent the last decade of his life assembling immense, arid tomes about sexuality, produced in them a more suggestive paragraph.

In his last column, published two days before his murder, Pasolini complained poignantly: "I am, finally, angry at the silence that has always surrounded me. . . . No one has intervened to help me forward, to develop more thoroughly my attempts at an explanation." Nor has anyone since. Instead, what Norman Mailer had written a few years earlier about D. H. Lawrence in *The Prisoner of Sex* now seems true of Pasolini, too: "The world has been technologized and technologized twice again in the forty years since his death, the citizens are technologized as well. . . . What he was asking for had been too hard for him, it is more than hard for us; his life was, yes, a torture, and we draw back in fear, for we would not know how to try to burn by such a light."

~

Stories from the City of God: Sketches and Chronicles of Rome, 1950–1966 is a small garland of narratives and essays that chronicles Pasolini's ambivalent relationship with Rome. In the stories, most of the protagonists are young boys from the slums. The youngest of them, an urchin whom Pasolini befriends at a public beach, is innocent, generous, trusting. All the rest are hustlers. ("Hustlers" is actually the meaning of *ragazzi di vita*, which is the Italian title of Pasolini's first novel, *The Ragazzi*.) Some are amusing, like Romoletto, who steals a big fish at the fish market, finds that it's rotten, and figures out how to sell it anyway. For the most part, though, they're not particularly clever or vital. What interests Pasolini, more than their beauty or wit, is their pathos. Their bodies have not yet thickened, their intelligence narrowed, or their sympathies withered, but they are afflicted nonetheless by a dim sense that all this is inevitable. The book opens with a lovely sketch of a nameless Trastevere boy, a chestnut vendor. ("Trastevere" means "across the Tiber," where the slums are.) "I would like to understand," Pasolini writes, "the mechanics by which the Trastevere—pounding, shapeless, idle—lives inside of him." "Trastevere Boy" was written in 1950; by the end of the decade Pasolini had fulfilled his ambition.

The best of the stories here is the longest, "Terracina." Luciano and Marcello steal a couple of bicycles and ride out to the fishing village of the title, where Marcello has relatives. Uncle Zocculitte takes them on as assistants. The age-old routines of Mediterranean fishermen are briefly but vividly described against the charmed background of sea and bay, which are separated by the stony promontory of Circeo, where Circe bewitched Ulysses. Luciano is also bewitched, but unlike Ulysses he doesn't escape. He takes the boat out alone one Sunday and foolishly, longing for a first taste of freedom, passes beyond the promontory into the open sea, where a gale blows the boat over. Terracina is an idyll, but Trastevere is a fate.

"Women of Rome," seven short vignettes written in 1960 to accompany a book of photographs, is more trenchant and melancholy, less tentative and wistful, than the sketches of ten years before. There is a brief portrait of Anna Magnani at a party, as elemental and magnetic as onscreen. There is another couple walking down the street, this one pre-consumerist, their handclasp signifying a "right of ownership," in which she is "silently, sadly complicitous." There are open-air fruit sellers, "strong as mules, hard as stone, ill-humored." And with good reason: "Their lives are limited to two or three things: a small, dark house, old as the Colosseum, in a dark alley behind the Campo dei Fiori . . . two, three or four children, half boys and half girls, half toddlers and half adolescents, perhaps one of them in the army; and a husband with a beat-up car, who speaks as if he had a boiling hot battery in his throat, red in the face and pasty-skinned, with a face so wide you can fit a whole village in it." It was by no means only Rome's *ragazzi* that Pasolini knew, cared about, and despaired over.

The essays or "chronicles" in this collection are slight but marvelous. They are mostly short reports for newspapers or magazines: some humorous, like "The Disappearing Wild Game of the Roman Countryside," about the travails of hunters at the hands of the Italian bureaucracy, and "The Corpse'll Stink All Week Long!", about styles of soccer fandom; others on slang, the postwar *literati*, urban renewal, and (naturally) the psychology of the *ragazzi di vita*. There is a powerful trio of pieces on new and old Roman shantytowns (written for the Communist journal *Vie Nuove*, where PCI leader Togliatti had once tried unsuccessfully to bar him from appearing because "such a man is unfit for family readers"); an uncharacteristically solemn but moving report on the funeral of a well-known labor leader, tens of thousands of workers silently raising and lowering their fists as the coffin plods down the Corso d'Italia behind a band; and a witty throwaway "day in the life" piece about being cheated by film producers and party-hopping with his friend Alberto Moravia. In Marina Harss's lively translation, these "chronicles" are more concrete and colorful than the furious polemics of Pasolini's last years (only a few of which are available in English, as *Lutheran Letters*), to which they make an excellent prelude.

The Sicilian writer Leonardo Sciascia—wry, skeptical, reserved—could not have been more different from Pasolini. One might have expected antipathy. And in fact, they often disagreed. But they understood each other. After one or another of Pasolini's provocations, an editor asked Sciascia for a reaction. Pasolini "may be wrong," Sciascia replied, he "may contradict himself," but he knows "how to think with a freedom which very few people today even aspire to." Exactly. Like Lawrence, Pasolini had no truck with common sense or conventional wisdom, and he paid the price. The deepest fear of any intellectual is making a fool of himself. Pasolini was fearless.

28

The Price of Selfhood

Vivian Gornick

Literature has always been about love; the modern novel has been about love as a problem. More precisely, about love as one instance of the fundamental modern problem: autonomy, individuality, selfhood. Enacting one's identity, living up to one's inherited role, offered premoderns plenty of scope for literary heroism; but devising one's identity, choosing one's role, is a peculiarly modern difficulty. It has been the burden above all of modern women, the response to which has included several waves of feminism and a line of great novels: *Wuthering Heights*, *Daniel Deronda*, *The Portrait of a Lady*, *The House of Mirth*, *Tess of the d'Urbervilles*, *Women in Love*, *To the Lighthouse*, *The Golden Notebook*, *Wide Sargasso Sea*, and others by Meredith, Gissing, Forster, Cather, and more.

These novels show women—and men—struggling for self-knowledge, self-reliance, or self-definition against the weight of traditional expectations and dependencies. The terrain of this struggle is love-and-marriage, which is where—at least in the world in which those novels take place—most people have their deepest experiences and meet their most significant fates. The essays in Vivian Gornick's *The End of the Novel of Love* canvass this seemingly familiar territory with urgent intelligence.

Gornick's three slender essay collections and short, lambent memoir *Fierce Attachments* (1987) contain some of the best feminist writing in recent decades. In spare, penetrating prose that leaves out little of the essential and all of the inessential, she has returned passionately, relentlessly, to a single cluster of insights: Romantic love can be—as often as not has been—a salvation myth. We are all—for historical reasons, women especially—desperately eager to be saved from the excruciating daily effort of emotional independence. What "visionary feminists have seen for two hundred years" is that power over one's own life comes not from complementary union, from two-in-oneness, but from "the steady command of one's own thought"; that "only one's own working mind breaks the solitude of the self"; that "to live consciously is the real business of our lives," and if this means living alone, hardening our hearts, refusing to melt or merge, then so be it.

The End of the Novel of Love locates these insights at both the center and the periphery of modern fiction. Meredith's neglected masterpiece *Diana of the Crossways*, for example, shows one of the most appealing heroines in literature hardening her heart at "the exact moment" when heroines traditionally "melt into romantic longing and the deeper need for union." So, in similar circumstances, do Gwendolen Harleth in *Daniel Deronda*, Lily Bart in *The House of Mirth*, and Clarissa Dalloway in *Mrs. Dalloway*. Why? Because "[each] woman has taken a long look down the road of her future. What she sees repels. She cannot 'imagine' herself in what lies ahead. Unable to imagine herself, she now thinks she cannot act the part. She will no longer be able to make the motions. The marriage will be a charade. In that moment of clear sight sentimental love, for her, becomes a thing of the past."

Each of these characters ends badly, but the spectacle of their bravery and clearsightedness arouses pity and terror. So do the real women whose lives Gornick contemplates: Clover Adams, Kate Chopin, Jean Rhys, Willa Cather, Christina Stead, Hannah Arendt. All of them tried, with varying success, to escape the undertow of convention and compromise—meaning, for most of them, a life centered on relationship and intimacy rather than on work. All of them arrived at an "awful, implicit knowledge": that the effort of soul-making "is a solitary one, more akin to the act of making art than of making family. It acknowledges, even courts, loneliness. Love, on the other hand, fears loneliness, turns sharply away from it."

This shift in our spiritual center of gravity—primarily women's, but not exclusively—leaves everything changed, including the premises of fiction. In two superb essays Gornick takes the measure of this change. "Tenderhearted Men" groups Raymond Carver, Richard Ford, and Andre Dubus as contemporary exponents of male loneliness, desolation, inarticulate suffering: a sensibility formerly (as in Hemingway) hardboiled, now tenderhearted. For all these writers' honesty and skill, Gornick finds, they have not faced up to why things are not, and cannot be, as they used to be between men and women. They do not, as Hemingway did, blame women; they like and admire women. But they yearn for what is no longer attainable and no longer even desirable: to find in romance "comfort against the overwhelming force of life."

The title essay puts the case against romantic love even more fully. Not, of course, against love as a precious experience; but against love as the meaning of life, the royal road to self-knowledge, the way down toward the deepest possibilities of thought and feeling—love, that is, as it has functioned in the modern novel: in "*Anna Karenina* and *Madame Bovary* and *The Age of Innocence* . . . as well as the ten thousand middlebrow versions of these books, and the dime-store novels too." This is no longer a plausible expectation, Gornick contends. It used to be, when marriage was sacred, sex outside marriage was sinful, pregnancy outside marriage was catastrophic, and much of the psyche was terra incognita. But love as mystery and revelation could not survive the democratization of experience and the commodification of sex. The ignorance, the suffering, the risk associated with illicit love have shrunk drastically; and so, proportionately, have the courage required and the enlightenment gained.

This is not a cause for regret. Bourgeois respectability cannot be resurrected and does not deserve to be. But it can no longer serve, either, as the main arena of self-creation for real or fictional characters. The "long line of slowly clarifying thought" that ultimately constitutes a self will have to find a new starting point; we now know too much about love. A century of feminism (with a little help from technology) has done its work; the novel of the future will have to be about something else.

The End of the Novel of Love is small in bulk but large in implication. Gornick's language and literary acumen are beyond cavil; the book is a pleasure and a stimulus: persuasive, finely wrought, quivering with intelligence. It is also disturbing, as it's meant to be. Here and in her other writing, Gornick is almost lyrical on the grim subject of loneliness. Not loneliness as deprivation but loneliness as integrity: the possible price—sometimes it sounds as though she means the necessary price—of uncompromised, fully conscious individuality. About this ideal of untrammeled selfhood there is much to be said (and much is currently being said) pro and con. Gornick's advocacy is effective, even inspiring. But modern individualism is not, it seems to me, the last word.

In recent decades we have begun to reckon the moral and psychological consequences of our almost incomprehensibly slow and complex biological evolution: how it enables and constrains us; how it reveals each of us to be a kind of organic iceberg with a tremendous hidden mass, inertial but alive and delicately engineered. The genus *Homo* is around 2.5 million years, or 125,000 generations, old. Romantic love is, for all but a minuscule elite, no more than twenty generations old; reliable contraceptive technology, perhaps three. We do not yet know how much of our sexuality and psychology is hard-wired, but probably a lot. In which case, we will need a better wiring diagram before we can wisely adopt any ideal of selfhood.

Notoriously, the theory of evolution cut no ice with D. H. Lawrence; he didn't, he scoffed, "feel it in my solar plexus." Nevertheless, his misgivings about modern individualism—the weightiest that have yet been expressed, in my opinion—rested on kindred intimations of animality. "To live consciously is the real business of our lives," Gornick writes, out of a feminist and rationalist tradition that Lawrence encountered in the shapes of Bloomsbury and Bertrand Russell, two of its finer manifestations. Lawrence would have demurred; he thought that instinct, impulse, and reflex, physical grace, emotional vividness, and ritual unison were no less important than critical judgment and self-conscious individuality. Consciousness, he believed, is accessory, epiphenomenal, "the glitter of the sun on the surface of the waters," as he wrote on one occasion; and on another: "I conceive that a man's body is like a flame, and the intellect is just the light that is shed on the things around."

Lawrence, too, wrote in a tradition: the Romantic critique of the Enlightenment. It has had its incautious, even unsavory exponents; and Lawrence too, as everyone knows, lurched down many a rhetorical blind alley. It's hard, after all, to be explicit about primal realities. But it's essential to try. Somewhere between, or beyond, these two great traditions, with their complementary imperatives—intellect and imagination, analysis and instinct, freedom and rootedness, individuality and communion—is the best way we can live now.

Acknowledgments

Thanks to some of the editors who sped me on my way: M. Mark, Kit Rachlis, Brian Morton, Elizabeth Pochoda, John Palatella, Dave Denison, John Summers, Jackson Lears, Laura Marsh, Matt Boudway, Chris Lehmann, Sven Birkerts, Askold Melnyczuk.

Thanks also for inspiration to Barbara Ehrenreich, Steve Fraser, Russell Jacoby, Jim Sleeper, James Wood, Norman Rush, Katherine Powers, Vivian Gornick, Ellen Willis, Alexander Cockburn, Christopher Hitchens, Scott McLemee, and right up there with my dedicatees: Richard Rorty, Christopher Lasch, and I. F. Stone.

Publication History

The following pieces were published in the following places:

Boston Phoenix: "Shipwrecked" (May 13, 1986); "South of Eden" (January 13, 1987); "An Exemplary Amateur" (May 8, 1984)

Boston Review: "The Liberal Intelligence" (December 1, 2000); "The Wages of Original Sin" (July 1, 2007); "The Price of

Selfhood" (December 1, 1997); "Preserving the Self" (June 22, 2015)

Commonweal: "Are We All Liberals Now?" (March 31, 2014); "Last Men and Women" (April 1, 2021); "The Common Fate" (September 4, 2012); "A Conservative-Liberal Socialist" (August 5, 2013)

Dissent: "Agonizing" (Fall 1991); "A Whole World of Heroes" (Summer 1995); "Living by Ideas" (Fall 1995); "Yes to Sex" (Fall 1999)

LA Weekly: "A Critical Life" (February 18, 1991)

Raritan: "Still Enlightening after All These Years" (Summer 2017); "An Enemy of the State" (Fall 2010)

Salmagundi: "Progress and Prejudice" (Fall 2012); "How (and How Not) to Change the World" (Winter–Spring 2018)

The American Conservative: "The Radicalism of Tradition" (11/15/10); "The Workingman's Friend" (July 17, 2015)

Baffler: "Against Everything" (March 2017); "Back to the Land?" (January 2020); "People Who Influence Influential People Are the Most Influential People in the World" (March 2015)

Nation: "Just a Journalist" (January 16, 2008); "Fearless" (February 9, 2004)

Village Voice: "The Promise of an American Life" (February 1, 1985)